The Story Is True

The story of our life is not our life; it is our story.

—John Barth, *On With the Story*

Words have their own reality

—Robert Creeley

The Story Is True

The Art and Meaning of Telling Stories

Bruce Jackson

TEMPLE UNIVERSITY PRESS
Philadelphia

Bruce Jackson is SUNY Distinguished Professor and Samuel P. Capen Professor of American Culture, University at Buffalo. He is the author of more than 20 other books as well as a documentary filmmaker and photographer. The French government named him Chevalier in L'Ordre des Arts et des Lettres, France's highest honor in the arts and humanities.

TEMPLE UNIVERSITY PRESS
1601 North Broad Street
Philadelphia PA 19122
www.temple.edu/tempress

♾ The paper used in this publication meets the requirements of the American National Standard for Information Sciences— Permanence of Paper for Printed Library Materials, ANSI Z39.48-1992

Library of Congress Cataloging-in-Publication Data

Jackson, Bruce, 1936–
  The story is true : the art and meaning of telling stories / Bruce Jackson.
      p. cm.
  Includes bibliographical references and index.
  ISBN-13: 978-1-59213-606-3 (hardcover: alk. paper)
  ISBN-10: 1-59213-606-0 (hardcover: alk. paper)

1. Narration (Rhetoric)   2. Storytelling.   3. Tales—United States.
I. Title.   PN212.J33 2007
  808—dc22

                                    2006035598

2   4   6   8   9   7   5   3   1

Contents

Contents

Acknowledgements

The *Story Is True* would not have been possible had it not
been for all the people who told or wrote or filmed or
otherwise transmitted the stories I tell you or tell you about in these
pages. Most of them are named throughout the book so I won't
anticipate the roll here. Honor and eternal peace to those who have
departed this mortal coil, and an endless supply of fine listeners to
them, and to those still among us.

Earlier versions of some of these chapters were presented at
various universities and conferences, and others grew out of discussions in my graduate seminars at University at Buffalo. My
thanks to the students, colleagues, and friends who discussed these
matters with me along the way. Especially important were conversations about these and associated matters with Howie Becker,
Warren Bennis, George Beto, Ben Botkin, Jim Card, Bill Chris-
tenberry, John Coetzee, Bob Creeley, Leslie Fiedler, Lydia Fish,
Michel Foucault, Bud Johns, Bill Kunstler, Gershon Legman, and
Jean Malaurie, as well as fellow folklorists and ethnographers
during the decade I was editor of *Journal of American Folklore* and
then a trustee of the American Folklife Center in the Library of
Congress. Marianne Fulton explained to me what was really going

on in the 2000 Elian Gonzalez story. Loretta Condin-Grupp, a member of my spring 2006 Oral Narrative seminar, reminded me of the importance of listeners to the several storytellers who tell us nearly everything we know or think we know about Thomas Sutpen in Faulkner's *Absalom, Absalom!* I especially want to thank my University at Buffalo colleague Michael Frisch for his help at the final stage of this project.

My thanks to Penelope Highton Creeley for her friendship these past thirty years, and for permission to include the text of Robert Creeley's "Bresson's Movies," from which this book takes its title.

I especially thank Robert Fogarty, the editor of *Antioch Review*, for permission to publish, in revised form, five articles that originally appeared in the *Review:* "The Stories People Tell" (55:3, 1997), "The Deceptive Anarchy of Let Us Now Praise Famous Men" (57:1, 1999), "The Fate of Stories" (60:1, 2002), "The Real O. J. Story" (62:2, 2004), and "Silver Bullets" (64:1, 2006). Earlier versions of "The Storyteller I Looked for Every Time I Looked for Storytellers" appeared (with the title "The Perfect Informant") in *Journal of American Folklore* 103 (1990) and in Bruce Jackson and Edward D. Ives, editors, *The World Observed: Reflections on the Fieldwork Process* (Urbana: University of Illinois Press, 1996). The first version of "Bob Dylan and the Legend of Newport '65" appeared in the August 2002 print edition of *Counterpunch.*

Much of the material in this book came out of projects funded or contexts provided over the years by generous grants from the Harvard Society of Fellows, National Endowment for the Humanities, National Endowment for the Arts, John Simon Guggenheim Foundation, American Philosophical Society, Institute of the American West, American Council of Learned Societies, and State University of New York at Buffalo. Thanks to them all.

Anyone who has gotten many grants knows it is relatively easy to get money for the clear winners, the projects that just can't miss. What's really difficult is getting support when you are trying to figure things out, before you know if the road goes anywhere at all. In that regard, I especially want to thank the three chairmen of the Harvard Society of Fellows during my four years as a Junior Fellow—Crane Brinton, Harry Levin, and Wassily Leontief. The Society gave me time early in my career to putter around and try things that might have gone nowhere. And likewise I want to thank former University at Buffalo President William R. Greiner and Provost Thomas Headrick for appointing me Samuel P. Capen Professor of American Culture. That endowed chair gave and continues to give me the flexibility late in my career to try new things.

I don't have words to thank Diane Christian, my friend, lover, editor, translator, careful reader, provider of ordinary and arcane information and grand ideas informing this entire book, and more things than would be seemly to note here. Let *The Story Is True* itself be thank you to Diane, who was so much a part of it, and part of so many of the events that led up to it.

Finally, my mother, Julia Blanche Pinsky Jackson, to whom I owe it all. Julia never rested with a fact when a story would do and never let reality get in the way of the way she thought the story ought to go. She taught me to read early, and her whole life let me know that writing books was the best thing of all, even better than being a doctor or lawyer or dentist—which, considering, was a big thing. Although she could not permit a fact to exist without embellishment, she gave them what honor she thought they deserved. From the time I left home at seventeen until her death, she regularly mailed me newspaper and magazine clippings of things she thought I ought to know, a practice I continue now with the web items I email to my children and grandchildren. It was a horror when, as a child, I realized I could trust almost nothing Julia said, and a shock when, as an adult, I understood she'd been getting it right all along anyway. She taught me something so basic and simple I never quite understood until my friend Robert Creeley told it to me straight out not long before she died: "Words have their own reality." That, at heart, is what this book is all about, and if by the final page Bob's line makes sense to you, it's because Julia taught me to test the stories people tell, taught me to hear the things the stories were trying to say, and taught me to tell my own.

Introduction

The Plot

Without an informing idea, the details of real life are clutter, noise, chaos. We need an idea given form for things to make sense. And that's what stories are: ideas given form, ideas given breath.

The Story is True is about making and experiencing stories as something people do, as one of our basic social acts. It is about how stories work, how we use them, how they move about, how they change, how they change us. It is about stories we tell friends, family and strangers, and it is about stories made for us at a distance, such as movies, television programs, newspapers and books. It is about when it is appropriate to tell what kinds of stories, and when it is permissible to tell stories that don't make sense, stories that are crazy or incoherent or disconnected. It consists of three interrelated sections:

Part I, "Personal Stories," is primarily about stories we tell one another, stories told in the human voice. Many of the stories and storytelling events in this section are out of my own experience, ranging from conversations I had with the poet Steven Spender in

1962 and a dying lifer in a Texas prison hospital two years later, to a May 2006 speech at a university commencement by Senator Charles Schumer and a birthday party dinner-table conversation a week later with family and friends about where we were when the towers went down.

My friends and family turn up frequently in these pages. If I were writing about Shakespeare, the plays of Shakespeare would turn up a frequently, but I'm writing about the way stories work in ordinary life and it seemed reasonable to work as much as possible with the life to which I had the best access. We could do the same things with your stories, your life.

Most of Part I is about oral narrative, but it is bracketed by an opening chapter that touches on aspects of all kinds of storytelling that will be explored in the rest of the book and ends with an examination of ways four masters of print fiction—Homer, Mary Shelley, William Faulkner and Dashiell Hammett—incorporated, utilized or explored the kinds of personal storytelling techniques I discuss in the preceding chapters. (Yes, I know Homer is presumed to be an oral poet, but no one in well over two thousand years has experienced Odyssey or Iliad as an authentic oral poem: our experience of them is every bit as literary as our experience of *Gone With the Wind* or *Harry Potter and the Half-Blood Prince*.)

Part II, "Public Stories," is about the character and career of several key stories that took life in the public sphere, but which continued in the interpersonal. I begin with a look at a few situations in which stories are exempt from the rule of reason and common sense, and then examine the O.J. Simpson story in fact, conversation, imagination and media; what really happened when (and after) Bob Dylan went electric at the 1965 Newport Folk Festival; the Western in American popular media and its larger contexts; the problem of narrative voice and representation in James Agee's and Walker Evans's multi-media Depression-era documentary masterpiece, *Let Us Now Praise Famous Men*; and, in "Words to Kill By," how stories and diction are instrumental in the individual and official administration of death—murder, Nazi extermination camps, execution of criminals, and rationalizations of war.

Part III, "The Story is True" (which takes its title from the final line of Robert Creeley's poem, "Bresson's Movies") consists of one long chapter ("The Storyteller I Looked for Every Time I Looked for Storytellers") and one short chapter ("Farinata's Silence"). Both deal with the incorporation of stories into our lives. The first is about lies that became something resembling truth. The second is about the place of stories, whether true or not, in the lives of every one of us.

I Personal Stories

ANECDOTE OF THE JAR

I placed a jar in Tennessee,
And round it was, upon a hill.
It made the slovenly wilderness
Surround that hill.

The wilderness rose up to it,
And sprawled around, no longer wild.
The jar was round upon the ground
And tall and of a port in air.

It took dominion every where.
The jar was gray and bare.
It did not give of bird or bush,
Like nothing else in Tennessee.

—WALLACE STEVENS

1 Telling Stories

John Coetzee's Question

It seems to me now that *The Story Is True* has its genesis in a question John Coetzee asked one evening after dinner about twenty-five years ago. The three of us had spent much of the evening catching up and talking about politics (John and Diane had shared an office in the University at Buffalo English Department for a year in the early 1970s, when she first came to Buffalo and just before he returned to South Africa).

It was well after midnight and we'd moved on to talking about writing. John's third novel, *Waiting for the Barbarians*, had been published a few years earlier, in 1980, about the same time as *Death Row*, a book and documentary film Diane and I had done based on conversations we'd had with condemned men in Texas in 1979.

A production company had optioned my first novel, *The Programmer*, and one had optioned John's second, *In the Heart of the Country*, both of which had been published in 1977. We talked about how many books are optioned and how few get made into films, and how it would be fairly easy to film *The Programmer* but extremely difficult to film *In the Heart of the Country*. (*The*

Programmer never did make it to film; *In the Heart of the Country* did, in 1985 as Marion Hänsel's *Dust*, which was not well reviewed and quickly disappeared.)

We talked about the difference in writing a novel, where the characters—however much they take on their own personality—are at least initially determined by the author, and writing a book based on taped interviews or conversations, where the structure— though not the primary words—is the author's. In fiction, the characters can usually be counted upon to say what they ought to say at that point; real-life speakers are often less accommodating. It was, in other words, the kind of conversation that writers have all the time.

Then John said: "Those men you and Diane interviewed and filmed on death row, how can you know when they were being self-serving and how can you know what truth is in what they say?"

I don't know if I'd ever consciously thought about that until that moment, but it must have been something I'd been thinking about at some level and dealing with for years. "I never know whether they're telling the truth," I said. "But I do know that at that moment, in that place, that is what they said. There is the truth of utterance."

As there is for all stories. All stories—whether a statement by one lover to another or a prisoner to a guard the other side of the bars or a politician talking to a crowd at a university commencement pretending he is there to celebrate education rather than court voters in the next election—have at the very minimum that perfect truth of utterance: that story was told at that time in that place by that person.

The stories people tell about themselves and their lives always occur after the fact. Life itself has no narrative. It is serial and multiple: a million things happening at once, and then another million things happening at once, forever and ever. Narrative is one of the ways we apply order to that unimaginable overabundance of information.

The process begins with exclusion of almost everything. In that regard, stories are like photographs. A decision about what a photograph will be is simultaneously a decision about what a photograph will not be; stories, which tell about and describe a finite number of things, simultaneously do not tell or describe everything else.

Every story implies a theory about what—in the infinitude of detail that comprises any moment in time or is available to an artist imagining one—matters and what does not, what was going on and what wasn't going on.

Keeping Time

Did you ever wake in a strange room and find yourself briefly unable to know where you were? Do you remember that sense of not disorder, but no order at all, of chaos? Then you remembered: "It's not home, it's the hotel in St. Louis (or Paris or Beijing or Brooklyn or wherever you, in fact, were), and the reason I am here is. . . ." In seconds—once you knew the place and the reason—everything else coalesced into order and coherence: the things you did to get there, where you were immediately before, why you were in that place at that time. A piece of paper with the coordinates in space and a clock with the correct time would have given you the exact facts of your location in the world, but they would have told you nothing you needed to know. You needed the story.

Or perhaps you remember coming out of anesthesia in the recovery room or coming to after a knock on the head. The world doesn't look as it should, hence the question: "Where am I?" That interrogation of location requires for response more than naming the place. "You're in the hospital" doesn't suffice; it is too spare. You need more: "You had surgery, you're in the hospital, and everything went fine," or "You were crossing the street, and you slipped on the ice and rapped your head on the curbstone. Don't try to get up yet. You'll be okay."

To know where you are, you need an explanation of how you got there. An explanation provided by your own memory retracing the steps or someone else doing it for you. That . . . then this. You need a story.

Stories orient us in time. Stories take the form: this, then this, then this, then this. Sometimes they include the reasons for things; sometimes they just name them. Change the order of events in a story and you have another story. Faulkner's *The Sound and the Fury* told in chronological order, Jean-Paul Sartre insisted, wouldn't be a clearer way of telling that complex story; it would be a different story entirely. The events as narrated may not be in chronological order, but the usual experience of the narrative itself proceeds from first word or scene to last word or scene. You can run a film backwards or read a book beginning with the final word and ending with the first, but not if you want to experience the film the director actually made or the story the author actually wrote.

A story is a group of details arranged in a structure, one component of which is time. That's what we mean when we say stories have a beginning, middle, and end. All stories have these three parts, but not necessarily in that order. You violate that order, and the violation becomes part of the story. Makers of stories can put events in any order they think fits the story they are trying to tell. In the first part of Faulkner's *The Sound and the Fury,* the free-associating mind of the idiot Benjy leaves one moment, goes to another, leaves again, either to return to the first moment or, more often, to go to yet another. Benjy's scrambled present is part of his story, not something imposed on it. Harold Pinter's play *The Betrayal* might have been just one more nicely-written account of friendship destroyed by an adulterous affair, but for one thing: Pinter's narrative begins after the affair is over, and then, in successive acts, carries us to a time just before the fatal process begins.[1] Instead of a set of conditions leading to a denouement that only in retrospect seems inevitable—the condition of most good linear narratives—Pinter works toward a moment of perfect innocence, a moment before the elements necessary for the affair were in place. We do not understand the end of *Betrayal* until we reach the beginning of the affair; we cannot understand its now until we reach its before. Pinter's narrative doesn't develop so much as it unwinds. It is difficult to tell that old story of friendship and love and lust and decay freshly, but Pinter manages it by reversing the arrow of time.

Pinter was perhaps mapping his narrative on a plot device used at least as early as 1934 by George S. Kaufmann and Moss Hart in their play *Merrily We Roll Along*, which was about a young idealist who becomes a middle-aged cynic; the action runs backwards, so the play begins in cynicism but ends in the promise of youthful idealism. Director Christopher Nolan, building on Pinter's idea, made scenic memory running in reverse the core of his revenge drama, *Memento* (2000). Two years later, Gaspar Noé lifted Pinter's entire *Betrayal* structure for his rape/botched-revenge film *Irréversible* (2002).

The apparent details of reality can be fitted into a wide variety of apparently coherent structures. Details of political events are re-evaluated and reorganized by historians as new ideas come along; new ideas about political events develop as facts are discovered or linked. Do you think that you've seen the end of books about the war in Vietnam or the War to End All Wars or the War Between the States or the Trojan War or The Bush Family and the Middle East?

In the light of a new theory about the physical world, what scientists once considered clutter is now data, and what was once considered data is now irrelevant. The global positioning devices that seafarers, drivers of luxury vehicles, and soldiers in the field now use to know exactly where they are and how to get to the next place utilize relativity-based technology. Program such devices on the basis of Newtonian physics, and they're useless. Charles Darwin, biologist Ernst Mayr pointed out in his 1999 Crawfoord Prize speech in Stockholm, didn't just give us a new theory; he gave us a new narrative. If you want to talk about species and speciation now, you must do it in terms of Darwin's narrative. Even if you're a Christian fundamentalist who doesn't buy any aspect of evolution, you've got to tell your tale in reaction to Darwin's narrative, otherwise people say, "Yeah, but what about . . . ?" It's there: you can disagree with Darwin, but you cannot ignore him. Darwin introduced time into the biological conversation, and there was no going back from that without rejecting the entire idea of scientific cause and effect, action and reaction, event and consequence. This, then this, then this, then this, a totally different narrative than "Let there be . . ."

Stories as Theory

Historians and scientists are constantly engaged in the creation of narratives, of stories that purport to tell us how this or that came about. Physicians do it as a matter of course: the patient reports pain, the physician asks questions about the nature and possible cause of the pain, then arrives at a probable diagnosis, a structure in which some apparent facts matter and others do not. The physician says: "This is what happened, this is where we are now, and if we treat you, one thing will probably happen. If we don't treat you another thing will probably happen." They try it. If things work out as predicted, the narrative is completed, and everyone goes on to something else; if things do not work out as predicted, they go back to the parts of the story they are sure about and try coming forward differently. Eventually, they get it or they don't. Medical diagnosis and treatment are a process of working out a believable story with alterative endings, then separating by trial and error what matters from what does not.

"All theories tell a story," wrote Roald Hoffman in a 2005 *American Scientist* article on Einstein's initial presentation of his theory of relativity as a narrative.[2] What historians and scientists and physicians do professionally, the rest of us do all the time. We organize the events of our lives in the form of narratives. Our stories are not just file cabinets or movies of ordinary life; they are also the devices with which we explain and justify ourselves to ourselves and to others. Through story we make the facts of our lives accessible and bearable. Every story we tell, specifically or by implication, includes a theory about what happened and what matters. Whether or not we ever articulate that theory, without it we would know neither what to exclude nor where to begin and when to stop.

As our needs or situations or audiences change, so do our stories. As our perceptions about the world change, so do our understandings of the stories we've told or have heard others tell. Our stories are doubly protean: we tell them differently and we understand them differently, depending on everything else.

That's why a story isn't just the specific details linked together in this specific way; it is also *every aspect of physical performance in that specific situation*. The story doesn't exist in words only; it is also in intonation, velocity, context, and language. The language of print is not the same as the language of film or the language of oral performance. The same plot told in these three narrative realms isn't three ways of telling the same story; it's three different stories sharing the same plot.

If I were to say, "This is a story about a man named Fred who took a wrong turn on a country road and found true love," I wouldn't be telling a story; I'd be talking about one. Stories exist in performance, whether it's one we read or hear, or one we experience in a movie, an opera, a novel, or the morning paper.[3]

The only absolute thing about the story is the story itself. The story told or heard or read or seen isn't the real or imagined event depicted in that story; it's the story about that event. "The story of our life," as novelist John Barth put it, "isn't our life; it's our story."[4]

Performing narratives—telling stories—is the primary way we tell what we know and express who we are. Or who we think we are. Or who we would like to think we are. Or who we would like our listeners to think we are.

Which is to say: storytelling is active, organic, responsive, reactive; it is here and now.

Frames

When does the experience of a story, told or read or heard or seen, begin and end? Does the experience of a film start with fade-in and end with fade-out? What about the transition from ordinary to narrative space involved in seeing a film in a theater? You move from street to outer lobby, acquire a ticket, move to the inner lobby. There the light is not like the light of an office or a department store or a café or the daytime or nighttime street. From there you move into the auditorium. If it's a modern multiplex, between the inner lobby and the auditorium is a corridor, usually darker than the lobby, with entrances to the several auditoriums. Somewhere between ticket booth and auditorium, someone takes the ticket, tears it, and returns part of it to you. You enter the auditorium, then choose a seat and, if you haven't arrived at the last minute, talk in a muted voice to your companion or wait (in a room usually too dim for reading) while other people find their seats. The room darkens, trailers roll, and then the film begins. Older films had credits at the beginning. On the last shot of the film, almost always the words "The End" were either superimposed on the film's final scene or against a black background immediately after it. Modern films have the credits at the end, and these sometimes go on for a considerable time. They are part of the film but of another order of information since they report the names and functions of the individuals and organizations responsible for what you just saw and heard. They are, therefore, a step away from the imaginative world of the film itself back toward the world of the ordinary. With all films, when the last frame passes through the projector and the auditorium lights come back up, the entire immersion process is reversed: corridor, inner lobby, outer lobby, and finally the street.

You no more step from the ordinary world to the world of filmic narrative than you step from the ordinary world into the heart of a Catholic mass in a church or from the street into an appellate court. These places you must get inside of before you can experience what happens. The layers of transition are part of the event.

And likewise most other forms of art, most other venues of performance, follow this same transition. To get to a painting or photograph or group of paintings or photographs in a museum you go through many of the same displacements from the ordinary: lobby, corridor, and gallery, each with its specific lighting. The painting or photograph is separated from the plane of the wall by mat and frame and, if there is no mat or frame, by the edge of the image, which is always discontinuous with whatever is surrounding it. Whether a play in a theater, jazz in a club, or music in a concert hall, things have edges, boundaries, rules, gates, and gatekeepers.

And likewise books. The most famous opening sentence of any novel in British and American literature is the one that begins Charles Dickens's *A Tale of Two Cities*. Say the first phrase aloud—"It was the best of times"—and even people who have no idea of the source will often say the second phrase—"and it was the worst of times"—for or with you.

However, the experience of the novel does not begin with that sentence. The experience of the printed novel begins with the physical experience of picking up and opening a book. Books have covers. End papers. Half-title pages. Main title pages. Copyright pages. Dedication pages. Contents pages. Books have all those pages before the fiction or poems begin—more fore and aft if the book is nonfiction: acknowledgments, foreword, introduction, notes, bibliography, and index.

And so also the stories we tell. Perhaps only small children, psychotics, and people rehearsing shift from ordinary speech into recitation when no one is listening—and the first two may very well posit a listener the rest of us do not see. For the rest of us, the stories we tell are always social, always embedded in human context, immediate and specific. The dreamiest story about long ago occurs in the unique now of this moment, this group of people, this space. Stories aren't just told; they're caused. They only work if they're told at the right time, in the right place, and to the right people.

Joseph Conrad's *Heart of Darkness* draws its immense power not just from Marlow's narration of his travels and his encounters with Kurtz and his fiancée but also from the story's opening and closing scenes aboard the cruising yawl *Nellie* on the Thames estuary, a physical, temporal, and social contextualization that licenses and frames the narrative that follows for both Marlow's four fictive listeners within the story and for you and me outside of it.

Storytellers, as Conrad knew perfectly well, don't create by themselves. They are only half of the event. Storytellers need listeners, writers need readers, filmmakers need film watchers. The people occupying roles in the narrative moment are not passive no matter how transfixed they may seem. "In fact," writes Primo Levi in *The Monkey's Wrench,*

> just as there is an art of story-telling, strictly codified through a thousand trials and errors, so there is also an art of listening, equally ancient and noble, but as far as I know it has never been given any norm. And yet every narrator is aware from experience that to every narration the listening makes a decisive contribution: a distracted or hostile audience can unnerve any teacher or lecturer; a friendly public sustains. But the individual listener also shares responsibility for that work of art that every narration is: you realize this when you tell something over the telephone, and you freeze, because you miss the visible reactions of the listeners, who in this case can only express his interest through an occasional monosyllable or grunt. This is also the chief reason why writers, those who must narrate to a disembodied public, are few.[5]

Blake put it more succinctly in *For the Sexes: The Gates of Paradise:* "The Sun's Light when he unfolds it/Depends on the Organ that beholds it."[6]

Stories That Hold Their Shape

Some of our stories are fixed, always out there and available for our attention. To access them, all we need do is pick up the book or turn on the projector or run the DVD. There are many well-known literary anecdotes of the great work never published in the author's lifetime, or published but long ignored and then discovered or rediscovered and, soon thereafter, enshrined in the literary canon—the poems of Emily Dickinson, for example, or Melville's *Moby-Dick,* or all of William Faulkner's novels, except *Sanctuary,* which were out-of-print the year before he won the Nobel Prize.

Although some texts are constant, always the same, no narrative experience is fully replicable. The things you've learned and experienced between the hearings, readings, or screenings—including your having heard, read, or seen it before—alter how and to what you respond. Absent amnesia, you cannot step into the same narrative stream twice.

In the first two or three years after I came to Buffalo as an assistant professor in 1967, I taught a seminar dealing with the work of William Faulkner, who had died in 1962. I didn't teach Faulkner again for maybe twenty years, until a delegation of graduate students came to my office, pointing out that nobody was teaching Faulkner in our department. Would I do it? In preparation, I reread all of Faulkner's novels. I was astonished at how much Faulkner had learned in those two decades we'd been out of touch, how much wiser some of his older characters, how much more naive some of his younger characters were, and how resonant had become the literary character of those parts of his novels written in his own voice.

In addition to the alterations in oneself, there are variations in where, when, and how we encounter these works of somebody else's imagination. You've perhaps had the experience of trying to read a novel but not being able to get into it. The characters don't catch your interest or there is too much noise from the street or you have a persistent itch in a place you can't reach. So you are reading words and sentences rather than experiencing the action, and sometimes you read the same sentence or paragraph two or three times and still it doesn't register. Another time, you engage the same book, perhaps in the same room and chair, and you are so immersed in the narrative you don't hear the phone when it rings or notice evening has fallen, and you now can barely see the words on the page.

Or perhaps you see an excellent print of a film, well projected in a theater with good seats and a fine sound system. At some other time, you see the same film, but the print is scratched and spliced, the seats are lousy and so are the loudspeakers, the guy behind you keeps bumping the back of your chair every time he sneezes, and someone nearby seems to have been dipped into the cologne you loathe more than any other. During the good screening, you're not aware of anything but the action of the film; during the bad one you're aware of nothing but the environment in which the film is projected.

For the past seven years, Diane Christian and I have run a film series that meets once a week at a theater in downtown Buffalo.[7] The screenings are built around a University at Buffalo English department class limited to forty-five students, but anyone who buys a regular movie ticket can come to the screening and join the discussion. We're familiar with almost all the films we show—some more than others—but as part of our preparation, the two of us watch a tape or DVD of each film once or twice a few days before the screenings. The difference in the two modes of watching—two of us at home and two of us as part of 250 to 350 people in a theater—is astonishing and instructive. We, of course, see details on the big screen that we missed on the small screen. The theater is dark, so our eye is not distracted by peripheral goings-on. The narrative is uninterrupted by phone calls or dogs wanting to go out. All of that, of course, is important.

More important, parts of the narratives and aspects of the characters that seemed to be one thing at home often seem to be something quite different in the company of all those other people. What was merely interesting at home may be deeply moving in the theater; what was mildly amusing at home may be uproariously funny in the larger company. The reactions of those other people—loud and noticeable like laughter, or soft and barely perceivable like changes in breathing as tension builds and ebbs—influence our own responses, mostly at a level far below consciousness. Simply knowing that the film in a theater will not be stopped and backed up to recover ground we missed while our attention wandered keeps our attention from wandering, keeps us focused, keeps us inside the projected narrative.

Your own emotional state matters at least as much as the ambiance. Romantic movies or novels are very different if you are in or out of love when you see or read them. A theme song you hadn't noticed when you first saw a film may evoke very different emotional responses if, between your first and second viewing, that song had played when your true love promised to be yours until the end of time or, contrarily, said you were not the one and never would be, ever. War movies or novels that were very realistic when you were innocent of war may not be so realistic after you have been shot at a few times in firefights. Realism that was once merely entertaining may, after the experience of real combat, be terrifying because of the specific memories it evokes.

Our relationship to the kinds of stories I have just mentioned may change in time, in place, and with mood, but their beginnings, middles, and ends do not. The physical things of this world are there whether we encounter them or not; they have, in James Agee's words, their own "great weight."

You and I might have hugely different reactions to looking down into the Grand Canyon because one of us is acrophobic and the other is not. That makes not an iota of difference to the Grand Canyon, which remains exactly the same, whatever our level of tranquility or perturbation. And the Canyon is there for experiencing by someone else, whatever the quality or fact of our experience. Likewise, the first folio of *Hamlet* existed before you and me, and it will be there long after we are gone. No matter whether the reader is a new critic, a reader respondent, deconstructionist, Freudian, Jungian, or Lacanian, *Hamlet* will continue to end with Fortinbras ordering four captains to "Bear Hamlet, like a soldier, to the stage" with other appropriate pomp, and *Moby-Dick* will always end with the *Rachel* finding not the crewmen she sought but Ishmael, the sailor the *Rachel*'s master had not even known was the lone survivor of the lost *Pequod.*

2 The Fate of Stories

The Other Kind of Story

What I said at the end of the previous chapter has to do with stories that are fixed in form, that are always there in all essential regards whenever you want to encounter them. There is, however, another kind of story in which nothing is necessarily fixed. These are stories that themselves change with those very factors I just said change our reactions to fixed stories: the moment, the company, the condition, and the mood. They're the stories we tell one another; they're our personal stories.

Stories that we tell one another vary in detail and emotional rendering, and sometimes even in basic structure, depending on the context. In oral storytelling, different listeners elicit different performances, and the same listener will, at different times, elicit different versions of narratives and different sets of narratives.

When I began noticing personal narratives, I was young; now I'm old. I don't get the same kinds of stories from people, and they don't tell them to me in the same way. Not only are my responses different because of the years of experience or because I select different people to whom I listen, but I also have different subjects that interest me. Also a person talks differently to someone who is of the age of a son, father, younger brother, older brother, student, or teacher. When I was young, older people seemed to feel they had to explain a lot of things to me. Now that I'm old, people assume I know more than I, in fact, sometimes do.

Psychotics and drunks may tell stories to no one in particular; for the rest of us, the listener modulates what stories we tell and how we tell them. I noted earlier Primo Levi's observation that "Just as there is an art of story-telling, strictly codified through a thousand trials and errors, so there is also an art of listening, equally ancient and noble, but as far as I know it has never been given any norm. And yet every narrator is aware from experience that to every narration the listening makes a decisive contribution. . . ."[1]

Similarly, but more poetically, at the end of Italo Calvino's *Invisible Cities*, Kublai Khan asks the young Marco Polo, "When you return to the West, will you tell your people the same tales you tell me?"

"It is not the voice that commands the story," Marco Polo replies, "it is the ear."[2]

Which is to say, these life stories that we tell one another are protean, one thing one time, another thing another time. The shape they take at any moment is a function of who is calling them forth, and why, and under what conditions. That word—"protean"— comes to us from book 4 of *The Odyssey*, a long poem filled with storytellers. Menelaus of Sparta is telling his visitor, Odysseus's twenty-year-old son Telemachus, of his encounter years earlier with Proteus, "the Old Man of the Sea who never lies." Proteus had the answers to Menelaus's questions about the past, present, and future, but Menelaus wouldn't get to hear them unless he could grab Proteus and not let go until Proteus wearied of trying to escape. Menelaus held on as Proteus transformed himself into a lion, serpent, panther, wild boar, raging water, tall tree, and, finally, once again himself. Then, and only then, did Menelaus have access to Proteus's truth.

I said earlier that our experience of fixed narrative—such as novels and films—is contextual. With oral narratives—the kind you and I tell and hear all the time—both the experience and the narrative performance are contextual. They are uttered in a certain way because certain factors are present, because certain conditions obtain.

We do not think about this experience any more than we think what to do with the fork once we've speared a piece of food with it. Unless we're interrupted, neither the eater nor the storyteller has to check in with the conscious part of the brain for the mouth to do its job.

Rachel's Crab

This discussion is perhaps getting too abstract, so before I say more about the process, let me give you an example of the kind of story I'm talking about. I heard it in my kitchen. It has to do with a crab named "Hermie."

My son Michael, a musician who was then thirty-eight, had just returned from a concert trip around the world, five days of which he spent on the small Indian Ocean island of Diego Garcia, in the Chagos Archipelago. It lies south of India and between Africa and Indonesia—about as far as you can get from Buffalo, New York, where we live. The sparse family of wildlife on the island, Michael said, includes wild chickens, wild mules, rats, and coconut crabs.

"They're nocturnal," he said.

"The rats?" I said.

"No, the crabs. The rats you see all the time."

He told us of waking late one night to a peculiar sound coming from the jungle not far from his cabin. The next day, someone told him he had heard a coconut crab having a meal. They climb the palm trees, Michael was told, clip off a coconut, carry it down the tree, and crack it open. Michael said they aren't bothersome if you stay out of their way, but they are powerful. He described them snapping in half a two-inch-thick stick of wood waved in front of them, and imitated the action by making a pincer of the thumb and forefinger of his right hand and a circle with the thumb and forefinger of his left hand. Then he spread his arms to show us how big the coconut crabs were with their claws extended.

Rachel, his thirty-one-year-old sister, had been listening with great interest. She made several brief comments, the kind of comment that keeps the narrator talking, the things engaged listeners do as a matter of course: "Really?" "Wow!" "Sounds fantastic!" "When did you sleep?" "Who paid?" "Weren't you scared?" "You were awake HOW long?" She didn't really interrupt him until he told about the huge nocturnal coconut crabs on Diego Garcia.

"I had a crab once," she said. The flat way she said it and the way she paused after the fifth word let us know that more was coming, but we had to shift our attention from Michael's story to hers if we wanted to hear it. Michael, Diane, and I turned toward her and waited for her to continue.

She told of a pet hermit crab when she was eight years old. Its name, reasonably enough, was "Hermie." She'd come home from school, go to her room, take him from his tank (the gender was assumed rather than determined), let him scuttle up and down her arm and across her hands, put him back in his tank, and then feed him. As she described her experience with Hermie, she traced the motions with her hands.

She paused for a moment, and then said that one day her mother had taken her to a pet store. She saw a tank with several crabs in it, and over the tank was a sign that said, "Do not touch the crabs."

"I knew they wouldn't pinch me," she said. "I had Hermie at home and he crawled up and down my arm and across my hand and he never bit me. So I put my hand in the tank. And one of the crabs pinched me. It grabbed my hand, and it was horrible. It really hurt! I couldn't get it off. I screamed. The lady who owned the shop came over with a screwdriver and whacked it really hard, and it went flying and it hit the wall."

She sat there in our kitchen, her eyes welling with tears.

"So you feel terrible because you got that poor crab killed," I said.

"No," she said, and then fell silent. We waited but she did not say anything.

"So what do you feel terrible about?" Michael asked.

She was silent for another moment and then said, "I never fed my crab again."

"*Never?*"

"No." Her voice was really small.

"You let it die?" one of us said.

"You were mad at all crabs because one crab bit you?" someone else said.

"You really starved your crab to *death*?" someone else said.

"Yes." More tears. After a while she said, "When we moved from that house three years later, mom found it in the cellar. I put it down there right after that other crab bit me."

I suppose all of us have things we've done or not done which, if they're in the forefront of consciousness, might bring tears to our eyes—but we do not usually bring them to the forefront of consciousness. We don't even know they're lying in wait for us. And if they do come forward, they rarely come with the emotional weight they bore all those years ago. Rather, they come very close to being about another person, a person we used to know very well but now know only slightly, a person who shares our name and parents.

Lots of kids have fish or crabs or turtles or birds they don't take care of well enough, or get bored with, or decide to experiment with. As a result the fish or crabs or turtles or birds die. But do they cry about them twenty-three years later? Will you cry about your dead fish or crab or turtle or bird now that I've reminded you of it?

A few observations: Rachel didn't just come out and tell us about her long-ago neglected crab. She said "I had a crab once" in reaction to her brother's graphic description of the faraway Indian Ocean coconut crabs. She paused. We shifted to the attitude of people about to hear a story. But she didn't just recite the whole story of her crab, Hermie. Most of it was elicited by our responses, our questions, our teasing. Clearly, she wasn't just telling it; she was also actively remembering it, and we had to be part of it. What started as a simple statement became, in a very few minutes, a huge rush of emotion. Her voice and body movements changed as she got closer and closer to the end. Initially, she was telling us a story; by the end she was—as the folklorists say—"performing it." What was interesting or a curiosity or amusing for us was something far more complex for her.

That is something central to our personal stories: they are always instrumental. They're not just there (like a story in a book); they're at once reactive and active. They're doing something. Furthermore, what they're doing this time is not necessarily what they'll be doing next time.

What was Rachel doing with that story? Or what was reconstituting that story doing to or for her? I can only speculate, which is all any of us can ever do about another person's motives. Anyhow, such speculation is peripheral to my subject in this chapter, which is about how our stories change rather than what they mean. Even so, I will tell you what I think was going on, but first I have to say more about my primary subject, the protean character of the stories you and I tell.

Tuning

Ordinary storytellers, people like you and me, consciously and unconsciously tune and revise all the time. Change is as much a condition of our stories as are beginnings, middles, and ends. Our narratives change for a host of reasons: because we decide to alter them, because we forget, because it is okay to use certain words in some company but not in other company, because we just feel they work better one way than they do another, because the responses of our listeners encourage us to emphasize and expand some aspects and downplay and contract others, because we're interrupted before we're done, or because when we're done someone says, "And what happened then?"

When I say we unconsciously tune and revise, I refer to the same order of act as when we taste food at dinner and decide the dish needs more salt. We don't, and perhaps can't, articulate our sense of the particular balance of flavors that at that moment require adjustment. We just know the balance isn't right, and we're pretty sure that it will take two (and not one or three) shakes of the salt shaker to get it the way we prefer. We refine that even further: when we see how much salt comes out with the first shake, we decide if another shake is really needed and how vigorous that shake should be. (It's similar to what engineers call a "servomechanism.") What is a proper amount of salt one time may not be a proper amount another time; it depends on what else is being served and on how we feel at that specific moment. How we change the taste of that particular dish is not merely the work of a moment; rather it is grounded in a lifetime of eating, tasting, and putting on salt—sometimes too little, sometimes too much—until we know how to get it the way we want it without giving it a conscious thought.

Ownership

We tell stories about what happened to us, like Rachel and her crab, and we tell other people's stories, like my telling you about Rachel and her crab. I suspect most of us give little conscious thought to the way we make other people's stories our own. These may be personal stories, but just like a good winter coat, they may fit and serve people other than their original owner. But, unlike a good winter coat taken over by someone else, the fact that someone adapts and incorporates someone else's story into his or her own repertoire doesn't diminish the original teller's store. Your story, my version of your story, and someone else's version of my version of your story can coexist with no diminishment, however long the cycle of adoption, adaptation, and incorporation goes on.

An example. I gave the keynote address at a session on gunfighter westerns at the 1976 Sun Valley Institute on Arts and Humanities conference celebrating seventy-five years of western films. The session was chaired by the actor Peter Fonda. When I was done with my presentation, Peter told a story about his father that I often tell when I'm trying to describe the way artists relate to their work. It is probably my favorite representative anecdote about artistic sensibility.

A transcript of the way I told the story at a recent lecture, which happened to be tape-recorded, follows:

> Peter Fonda said that his father was once outside by the pool practicing a fast draw for a scene that was to be filmed the following day. For a long time Henry was out there by himself, whipping the pistol out of the holster, putting it back in, whipping the pistol out, and putting it back in again.
>
> There was a guest at the house and they were calling Henry to come in for dinner. He said he needed just a few more minutes. The guest, who was also in the movie business, asked what was going on. Henry said that his character had to have a very fast draw so he was trying to get his speed up. The guest said, "So let them undercrank."
>
> That means you slow down the film going through the camera so when it is run through the projector at normal speed, things seem faster than they really were. That's why people in some old silents seem to be running everywhere, because film meant to be projected at silent speed of 18 frames per second is being projected at sound speed of 24 frames per second.
>
> "We can't do that," Fonda said. "The character is wearing a Phi Beta Kappa key on his watch fob. It will swing too fast."
>
> "The audience will never notice that," the guest said.
>
> "No," Fonda said, "but they'll feel it."

That's what the artistic sensibility is all about, right? The artist doing things at a level the consumer of the art will never consciously notice but will feel at the level and in the place where the work really matters. "The audience will never notice that." "No, but they'll feel it." I just love it. Every time I've told the story, people have nodded their heads in agreement, getting the point immediately.

A few years ago, after I had begun working on this book, I listened to a tape of that 1976 symposium to make sure I had Peter Fonda's story right, something I never felt the need to do previously. There hadn't been any need for me to check the tape in those intervening years; I remembered the story perfectly and other than the obvious changes, the *mutatis mutandis* stuff, of Peter saying "my father" and me saying "Peter's father" or "Henry," I'd changed nothing of moment.

Sure.

This is what Peter Fonda actually said in Sun Valley in 1976:

> I watched my father prepare for a movie called *Warlock*, which I heard you mention. And, my father really liked the movie a lot and he really liked the book and he tried to buy it and found that Fox had bought it from the galleys, which means from the publisher. And, he practiced drawing. He's right-handed and I'm left-handed and he would draw day after day and I asked him why he was practicing so much because they could just— you know, undercrank the camera and it would look really fast. He said, "No, no, no. He's got this watch fob, you see, and it hangs here and there's a little key-like thing, like a Phi Beta Kappa or something." He says, "If they speed up the film they'll see the thing go like that [Peter made a rapid back-and-forth motion with his index finger about where a PBK key would hang], and they'll know they sped up the film." So he learned how to draw fast enough that it looked like he could shoot the target as best as any of the quick draws. And, I admired that; I felt that was part of the perfection of the gunfighter and that's why I threw that into this conversation.

A lot of differences. I introduced a major character, the dinner guest. I also introduced a good deal of dialogue. I changed the temporal structure. Peter's story was vague about time: his father was out there "day after day," and the conversation took place on one of those days; in my narrative, it all happens in a single afternoon. Peter mentioned—and I omitted entirely—that his father is right-handed and he's left-handed, and that Henry got so good at the "perfection of the gunfighter" that "he could shoot the target as best as any of the quick draws."

And the "ands": Many of Peter's sentences begin with "and"; none of mine do. In ordinary speech, "and" at the beginning of a sentence often functions as punctuation rather than as a conjunction; it's a way of saying, "I'm starting a new sentence now." The several "ands" in his statement and absence of them in mine would tell an experienced analyst of oral narrative something important: Peter was recalling an event, but he probably wasn't telling a story he had told very many times; I was telling a story I had honed or polished enough so I didn't need those oral punctuation marks.

That's style. What about substance? Did I change the substance of Peter's story? Oh, did I ever! I did what oral storytellers and novelists do all the time. I populated an event I knew a little about with sufficient detail to make it more effective and dramatic so it would do what I wanted or needed it to do.

For me, that story is about two things. First, details matter, whether or not anybody other than the artist notices them. Second, Henry Fonda was revealing to his son his aesthetic principle that if the audience becomes conscious of the actor or the mechanics of filmmaking, even if only at an unconsciously emotional level, then they're out of the experience of the film, and part of the artist's job is to be aware of the nuances that keep them inside the dramatic experience. I like the story because it is a perfect illustration of my aesthetic about dramatic film or fiction: if we're consciously noticing what was just done (what a great shot, how well the actor—as opposed to the character—uttered that line, how that phrase alliterates), as opposed to experiencing what just happened, we're out of the action; we're engaging in aesthetic criticism.

Some writers and filmmakers want you to do that. When you're watching their work, it's fine for you to have moments when you are outside the narrated experience: for example, when you come upon the obvious anachronisms in John Fowles's *The French Lieutenant's Woman*, or almost anywhere in Ross McElwee's 1986 documentary *Sherman's March*, which is about Ross McElwee making *Sherman's March*. Henry Fonda, on the other hand, was working on getting a story told, not with showing people how the story was made. He wanted the narrative building blocks to be invisible. It is the difference between saying, "What a wonderful job you did putting on your makeup" and "How lovely you look tonight." For that reason, I liked the story, and I tuned it the way I did to enhance that very point.

But that wasn't Peter's point. I never knew I had tuned his story at all until I listened to the 1976 tape. I tuned his story without deliberation, intent, or plan.

When I tell the story, it is an illustrative anecdote about the relation of artist to craft. In my telling, Henry is the central character; Peter figures only as the source of it. For Peter, the story is far less about Henry Fonda's aesthetic than it is about the very difficult relationship between Henry Fonda and Peter Fonda, father and son.

When Peter told it, he was a grown man reflecting on a moment when his famous, obsessive father put the family on hold (surely not the first time) because work was more important or interesting. Peter told it at a time in his life when he had been working with middling success for many years in the trade for which his father had become famous and successful. Peter told an anecdote about Henry, and central to it was the relationship between father and son, one of them right-handed, the other left-handed. That different handedness meant something to Peter, which is why he put it in. It was useless to me, which is why I cut it out. I doubt that Peter gave any conscious thought to the possible import of their different handedness when he told the story in Sun Valley, and I am even more certain that I never consciously decided to delete it when I told it later.

So when I say, "I'm going to tell you a story Peter Fonda told," and I tell the story, am I telling you a story Peter Fonda told? Yes and no. I'm telling you a story Peter Fonda made possible for me to tell. It is a story that did one thing for Peter Fonda and something quite different for me, a story Peter told one way and I told another.

Things We Remember Well

We ordinarily think of memory as a condition rather than a process: "It's in memory"; "I got it from my memory"; "As I recall"; "I've got a good memory."

That kind of memory may be fine for computers, but human memory isn't nearly so passive. Human memory is active, busy, and meddlesome. Without corroborating evidence, a good story from human memory is never more than a good story. You don't have to lie to get history wrong, all you have to do (as Leonard Shelby, the protagonist of Christopher Nolan's film *Memento* demonstrated—and promptly forgot) is put total confidence in the innocence and infallibility of memory.

David Tereshchuk, a documentary filmmaker for the United Nations Educational, Scientific, and Cultural Organization (UNESCO), wrote about being a young reporter in Northern Ireland covering a protest march in Derry in 1972. Suddenly, British paratroopers began firing. Tereschuck's primary memory of the event was of "a soldier in a red beret, down on one knee, leveling his self-loading rifle toward me and shooting."

Fourteen people were shot to death that day. At the official inquiry, Tereshchuk testified about what he had seen. The inquiry exonerated the British army of wrongdoing. Anger over the verdict never went away, so in 1998 British Prime Minister Tony Blair ordered a new inquiry. An investigator taking a deposition asked Tereschuck a question he had never been asked before,

about my most vivid memory, the soldier firing toward me. "What was on his head?" Without a moment's pause, I recalled his red beret. But as all the photographs clearly demonstrate, he was wearing a helmet. After checking more pictures and news film, I have come to see that—however certain my recollection—I was simply wrong.

I may have fused two memories into one, or given the soldier some features of a nearby senior officer who was wearing a beret. For us in the crowd that day, realizing that the paratroops of the Parachute Regiment with their distinctive red berets had crashed onto the scene was crucial. Amid the panic, or afterward as I struggled to make sense of everything, that detail stuck with me. At least that is how I can best explain it. . . .

Today, I'm older, possibly wiser, but so much less certain—not only about the precise details of what I saw but also about how I have observed the world for more than 30 years. As a reporter, I have always insisted that facts are facts and supposition is something else. My own involuntary fudging of the narrative has harshly mocked that ingrained belief. I winced when the new inquiry's chairman announced, "Reporters often make excellent witnesses."

For all I have recently admitted about the malleability of memory, I still have no doubt that 29 years ago British soldiers opened fire, unprovoked, on innocent British citizens. But unlike the hordes of conspiracy theorists that Bloody Sunday has attracted, I still have no idea why. My life's effort to extract hard truth from its messy surroundings has been severely humbled by the essential messiness of my brain. And yet, even with an indisputable set of photographs in front of me, I close my eyes and still see a red beret.[3]

This is the problem with the things you remember well: the fact that you remember them well doesn't mean that they happened. It means only that you remember them. Memory melds things, tunes things up, rounds the edges, and provides connections. Memory is an artist, not a computer.

The process begins immediately; it's not merely a function of the mind getting busy or working busily or badly over time. When the National Transportation Safety Board studied 349 eyewitness accounts of the crash of American Airlines Flight 587 in Queens, New York, on November 12, 2001, they found that more than half of the witnesses said they saw a fire while the plane was in flight, 22 percent saw the fire in the fuselage; others put it in the left engine, right engine, left wing, right wing, or someplace they couldn't remember. But there had not been any fire or explosion. The plane, which had been airborne only ninety-three seconds, crashed because a portion of the tail broke off.

"None of this is surprising," said Dr. Charles R. Honts, a professor of psychology at Boise State University and the editor of the *Journal of Credibility Assessment and Witness Psychology*. "Eyewitness memory is reconstructive," said Dr. Honts, who is not associated with the safety board. "The biggest mistake you can make is to think about a memory like it's a videotape; there's not a permanent record there."

"The problem," he said, "is that witnesses instinctively try to match events with their past experiences: How many plane crashes have you witnessed in real life? Probably none. But in the movies? A lot. In the movies, there's always smoke and there's always fire."

Benjamin A. Berman, a former chief of major aviation investigations at the safety board, said pilots actually make the worst witnesses, because their technical knowledge can lead them too quickly to identify a mechanical problem that may not have occurred. "Children make among the best witnesses," he added, "because they don't tend to place an interpretation on what they've seen."[4]

Economy

Memory doesn't like clutter. It economizes, a process I first understood during a dinner with my old friend Warren Bennis and his new wife, Grace Gabe, in Santa Monica in 1994.

I met Warren in May 1967, when I was living in Cambridge and in the final months of my four years as a junior fellow in the Harvard Society of Fellows. He called and introduced himself as a professor at MIT. He was going to Buffalo in the fall as the new provost of social sciences. Norman Zinberg, a psychiatrist at Harvard Medical School with whom I'd taught a seminar at Harvard the previous fall, had told him that I was going to Buffalo as an assistant professor.[5] He invited me to a Sunday morning brunch at his house in Boston.

I've been in Buffalo ever since, but Warren left Buffalo after three years to become president of the University of Cincinnati, after which he joined the faculty of University of Southern California. We fell out of touch for more than twenty years.

Then in 1994 we had occasion to exchange some letters, and shortly afterwards, I was in Los Angeles consulting for a film company. Warren and I had breakfast in Venice and talked for hours about what we were doing now. He invited me to dinner that night so we could continue the conversation, and so I could meet Grace.

That evening, we immediately got into telling Buffalo stories. Ostensibly, we were telling the stories to Grace, but we were really doing what people do who have shared an experience and are re-establishing contact: moving the past into the present by reciting it. Where, after all, does the past exist but in narrative. "Yes, yes," each says and responds with his story, or amends the one just told: "Yes, and then he . . . ." Curiously, we hadn't shared memories at all in the morning: in our morning conversation we'd talked about recent and present matters only. As is typical of such narrative exchanges, we needed Grace as audience to catalyze the reconstruction work; we needed to perform the stories for her, even though we were primarily telling them to each other.

One story Warren told was about the brunch at his Beacon Hill house in May 1967. Martin Meyerson, president of University of Buffalo, was there recruiting Warren for the Buffalo social sciences job. Warren said that Martin was very impressed with the house, which had been designed by Charles Bullfinch. Martin was an urban planner and was interested in such matters. During the brunch a Buffalo professor named Aaron Rosen called to tell Martin that Leslie Fiedler, perhaps then the best-known literary critic in America and a member of the Buffalo English Department, had been arrested on a drug charge.

When Warren finished I said, "Martin wasn't there for that call. I was there. And so was Martin's lawyer whose name I can't remember. He wrote poetry." We fished for a while and then one of us remembered the lawyer's name: Saul Touster. I said that Aaron Rosen (who had been assistant to Arts and Letters Provost Eric Larrabee) had, indeed, called about Leslie's arrest, but the person he wanted to talk with was Saul Touster the lawyer, not Martin Meyerson the president. Leslie had been arrested in May, which would have been far too late in the academic year for Martin to have been courting Warren for an academic job that began in September. Warren thought for a moment, and then said, "The brunch with Martin was in the fall. You and Saul were in the spring!"

We immediately realized that he had melded two events, both of them Sunday brunches in the same room in the same Charles Bullfinch Beacon Hill house, both of them linked to Warren's pending move to Buffalo. The first was the courtship breakfast with Martin Meyerson; the second was Warren's networking breakfast with me during Saul Touster's visit. Warren had taken what was important to him from the two events nearly three decades earlier and had collapsed them into one story.

This story of Warren's story has a second act. In February 2003, nine years after that dinner with Grace, my wife Diane and I had dinner in Santa Monica with Warren and Grace and Grace's daughter Nina and her new husband Joshua. Leslie Fiedler had died two weeks earlier. We told them about Leslie's great delight when his work and name had become the subject of a family argument in the December 1 episode of the HBO series *The Sopranos*. We talked about Leslie for a while, then Warren recalled for the newlyweds the story of how he had been having brunch with Saul Touster and Martin Meyerson in 1967 when a man who was the assistant to Eric Larrabee, the provost of the faculty of Arts and Letters, called to say that Leslie had been arrested on a drug charge.

"What was that guy's name?" Warren asked me. "Aaron. Aaron something."

"Aaron Rosen," I said.

Warren finished the story, then, he looked at me and said, "I did it again, didn't I?"

"Yes," I said. "You did."

"What?" Grace's daughter asked.

"I subtracted the least important person in the story," he said. He told them who that was. Everyone laughed, and then Warren said, "It does make a better story that way."

As Warren pointed out, knowing about this process doesn't protect you from it one bit. We do some things because that's how we're hardwired. Unless something gets in the way—a tape recording with the words that were really said, a photograph that shows what was really worn, or someone who remembers the event differently—we go for the better story, with "better" meaning, the story that best makes one's point, or the story that is most efficient, or any of countless other possibilities. Lamenting the wiring is pointless—but knowing about it may be useful.

Sticking to the Point

You and I make these narrative changes without necessarily thinking about them, but we're no more born with the ability to compose and tune stories than we are with the ability to ride a bicycle or drive a car with stick shift. Storytelling is a learned skill, just like playing the piano or dancing, and some people never get it right or are never comfortable with it, no matter how many lessons they have. Just as some people are good at telling jokes and other people never learn that the punch line hinges on timing and placement at the end, some people are good at telling stories and other people never learn that stories have beginnings, middles, and ends, preferably in that order.

But sometimes what we think is a bungled story may seem bungled only because we don't understand the real story that is being told. We've all had the frustrating experience of asking someone "What happened?" and getting in response a rambling farrago of words about the car, the children, the dinner, the shoes, the guy who shot the clerk, the problem at work, what cousin Elmo said the time the dam broke, the. . . . We've wanted to scream (and sometimes have screamed), "Can't you stick to the point?"

I now think that in many of those rambling and digressive narratives, the person *is* sticking to the point, only it's not the point we'd choose. From the narrator's point of view, our incessant questions going back to that one moment when the gun went off and the person fell down is missing the point.

That is, sometimes when we think a teller is not getting the story right, it means that the storyteller is not telling the story we would prefer to be told or that we think is being told. Digressions and misdirections may not be errors so much as the enactment of another story entirely, one that is being told but one that we're not quite able to hear. The folklorist Ilhan Basgöz found that among Turkish traditional storytellers, digressions can make the traditional story contemporary and change the meaning of motifs, episodes, and attributes of characters. Digressions, he said, express the ideology, values, and worldview of the performer, and they bring current social economic and political topics into the performance.

Someone transcribing recordings of the several recitations and cutting out the digressions and asides as transient deviations from the so-called real narrative may very well wind up with several similar texts. But they would be the wrong texts, because in the transient parts, the variable parts, the real action was taking place. The ostensible story for such narrators is like the stand that holds the violinist's sheet music: there, necessary, but in itself unimportant and insufficient.

Endings

I've said that all our stories have beginning, middle, and end, but I didn't say all of them were fixed. Joyce's *Portrait of the Artist as a Young Man* ends with Stephen Dedalus going off to forge in the smithy of his soul the uncreated conscience of his race, but our spoken narratives about our lives are far more protean, far more mutable. Not only can our stories be longer or shorter, or made to start or stop at an earlier or later point in time. When the beginning or end changes, the importance of everything between the beginning and end changes, too. Sometimes things that were previously highly important are now of only passing interest or mere background, and things that seemed barely relevant or weren't even included before are now major plot elements.

The way you describe your first sexual encounter, for example, gets narrated differently a day after the event, ten years after the event, and ten years after that. The thing that's probably most worthy of note a day after the event is that it happened at all; in time, other elements may take precedence, like with whom you did it, or what you caught, or how different the next time was.

The Elian Gonzalez story in 2000 was first about the heroic rescue of a five-year-old boy found alone at sea. The small outboard-motor boat in which he and his mother had tried to escape Cuba had gone down in high seas. Then it turned into an international custody drama, and then into American farce as various members of Congress and candidates for president made speeches about giving the boy citizenship. The endpoint was the famous raid or rescue (depending on your point of view). And now it's just one more barely remembered incident in the long and goofy relationship between the United States and that small island ninety miles south of Miami.

Barabas Stories

Some of our stories seem to change very little in form, words, or delivery. They might as well be on film or made of wood.

Andy Golebiowski, one of my graduate students, spoke of attending a screening of a film about a photographer that was prefaced by the photographer talking about himself. "He told these stories about himself," Andy said, "and then they ran the film, and he told exactly the same story in exactly the same way."

Another student in the seminar asked, "And what do you think of that?"

"I think maybe the story was a shield, that rather than exposing something to us it was shielding him from us."

Andy was onto something. Politicians famously latch on to a few key anecdotes that they tell again and again. (I'll discuss one of these a little later in "The Story of Chuck.") The function of such stories in personal situations, as Andy intuited, can be to keep other people from taking the conversation somewhere dangerous. The rigid story doesn't only bring in information; it also keeps other information out. It's as much screen as it is window.

I call those preemptive strikes of personal narrative "Barabas stories" after the protagonist of Christopher Marlowe's *The Jew of Malta*, who is stopped on the road by Friar Barnadine immediately after Barabas has set fire to a convent in which he thought his daughter was sleeping. Friar Barnadine points a finger at him and says "Barabas, thou hast committed—" The homicidal arsonist Barabas famously picks up and continues the sentence with a different narrative entirely: "Fornication? But that was in another country; and besides, the wench is dead."[6]

Truth

Even our highly polished and tuned stories are variable and various, though perhaps on such small levels you wouldn't notice without recordings of different performances to compare. Storytellers learn after a while what works and what doesn't, what moves people and what bores them. We discard and embellish, we polish and prune, we tweak and we tune.

I never consciously altered the narrative that Peter Fonda told about his father. David Tereshuck never consciously replaced the steel helmet with a red beret on the British paratrooper firing at him in Northern Ireland. Warren Bennis didn't deliberately remove me from his story about Leslie Fiedler's arrest. I doubt Andy Golebiowski's photographer consciously decided which of his personal narratives would be cast in stone and which would remain variable.

One consciously thinks editing thoughts when one is working on a legal brief or on an essay or a novel, but that's not how it works with the stories we tell again and again. What happens is more similar to the way our favorite clothes come to fit us over time. They adapt to the way we're shaped, to the way we move, to what we're doing at the moment. The problem is, absent someone else to say, "I was there, and I remember it differently," or a tape, photograph, or some other record, the mind works its economies silently and seamlessly. Our narratives seem as free of interference and manipulation as does the beach that was just washed smooth by the incoming tide, the beach that only moments before showed the clear marks of my feet and perhaps yours.

Eyewitnesses in television legal dramas regularly tell the story of what happened. With rare exceptions, that occurs in real courts only when the attorney is totally incompetent. Experienced trial lawyers will tell you that eyewitnesses reporting what they remember are the most unreliable evidence they can present in a case. Real-life lawyers put someone in the witness box and ask very narrow questions, the answers to which they know beforehand. The last thing in the world they want is someone telling the jury this week's version of how he or she thinks those chaotic facts fit together.

If our stories are always in flux, what can they ever tell about the truth of anything? That depends on what you mean by "truth." If you mean "exactly what happened at that moment," then stories alone may not help you much. If you mean "a primary indicator of what's happening now," they will surely do that.

Our personal stories, like the films and novels I mentioned earlier, are not just about something, they are something; they don't just report facts, they are facts. The facts of the past are of far less importance in our stories than the construction of the past in the present.

All those family narratives hauled out in long or short form at weddings, funerals, holiday dinners, and reunions are true stories all right, but they're at least as much a story of our regard for the family now as they are a report of what happened then. In effect, they're more a story of the family we are than the family we were.

Facts and stories only coincidentally have anything to do with one another. Stories are about truth, not facts. "All stories are true," goes an Italian proverb, "and some of them even happened."

Rachel's Crab, Again

Now let me get back to Hermie, Rachel's starved and desiccated crab. I said earlier that I'd tell you what I thought was going on and so I shall. What I think happened was this: Michael's report of the giant coconut crabs on the island of Diego Garcia in the Indian Ocean triggered not just a memory for Rachel, but a sequence of memories. A sequence of memories is like the geometer's points: two can define a line, the ends of which in theory extent to infinity; three can define a shape, four an object with physical volume. Rachel remembered her pet crab, Hermie, at first with pleasure, and then she remembered the nasty crab in the store, and then the way she let her pet crab Hermie die. Probably she remembered something of how she felt when her mother found the desiccated shell in the basement on the day they left that house forever. Those memories didn't happen at once, they were serial, they happened in the telling, in time, and the emotional object they defined grew more complex with each resonant extension of that first simple line: "I had a crab once."

Were the tears she shed that Sunday afternoon in February 2001 shed for the crab Hermie who died such a dark and lonely death twenty-three years earlier? I doubt it. Rather, I think those tears were for the little girl who did and didn't do those things, the little girl who that woman telling the story once was, the little girl neither she nor anyone else will ever see again.

She was telling a story about something that happened in the life of a young girl, but the story she performed wasn't about a young girl at all: it's about a young woman, near the end of her first year as a lawyer, the first year she'd been more or less on her own, sitting with her older brother and with her father and stepmother. It's a thirty-one-year-old woman's story, not an eight-year-old kid's story. It's a story in which Rachel, in the telling, sensed something we all at some point learn about growing up and about growing older: you can talk about what happened back then, but you will never in this life go there again. You will never again be that person, in part because that thing happened to you.

Marco Polo's Bridge

There's a danger in what I've done here, in retelling and then trying to figure out the meaning of someone else's story. It's the danger that I never fully appreciated until I realized how much I had altered the character and probable function of Peter Fonda's story about his father at the pool. I can analyze the story and its function, but so can you, and there's no guarantee we'll arrive at anything like the same place when we're done, or that the meanings at which we arrive will have anything to do with the meanings of that event for the Fondas when Henry was practicing his draw for *Warlock* or for Peter when I heard him tell it in 1976 or for Peter now.

So I ran my take on what happened the night we talked about the crabs by Rachel. When I was done talking about it, I saw she again had tears in her eyes. "There's nothing to cry about," I said, "it's a story about growing up."

"Growing up?" she said. "What's sadder than that?"

How do you talk about such understanding? I don't know if you can. But you can tell stories in which such things are enacted—I said "enacted," not "depicted." Every story has two parts: what's in it and how it is performed, and they are no more the same thing than the texts of novels and films are the same as the experiences we have each time we encounter them.

We all contain libraries of the small things that happen or the things we do that take us over a boundary across which we can never return. These defining moments are sometimes encapsulated in the smallest narrative utterances that will forever carry more meaning for us than we could ever express in any way but telling the story itself. All explanation is partial and reductive, and all our stories contain more than can be abstracted or extracted from them in any single, transient moment. Buddha and Christ had good reason for teaching in parables.

In time, how we tell our story depends not so much on what happened then, but on what we know of the world now. And that is why the story of that time told at this moment means at least as much, and perhaps more, about this world now than that time then. And that is why these stories we tell again and again remain forever new.

So what is it that really matters—what the story is or what the story does? The memory or the utterance? The text or the encounter?

Marco Polo describes a bridge, stone by stone.

"But which is the stone that supports the bridge?" Kublai Khan asks.

"The bridge is not supported by one stone or another," Marco answers, "but by the line of the arch that they form."

Kublai Khan remains silent, reflecting. Then he adds, "Why do you speak to me of the stones? It is only the arch that matters to me."

Marco Polo answers: "Without stones there is no arch."[7]

3 The True Story of Why Stephen Spender Quit the Spanish Civil War

The symmetry of form attainable in pure fiction can not so readily be achieved in a narration essentially having less to do with fable than with fact. Truth uncompromisingly told will always have its ragged edges; hence the conclusion of such a narration is apt to be less finished than an architectural finial.

HERMAN MELVILLE, "Billy Budd"

Spender's War

When I was a graduate student, I drove Stephen Spender to the Indianapolis airport from Indiana University at Bloomington, where he had given a reading. I had read some of Spender's poetry, but I knew little about him other than that he was a famous and highly respected poet. Spender talked about several things during that sixty-minute drive, but what I most remember him talking about was the Spanish Civil War.

Two of my college teachers at Rutgers had fought in it. I remember one of those teachers in particular—John O. McCormick—who, whenever he could, referred to it in our European Novel class as "the last good war." World War II, McCormick said, "was there, you just went and did it. And Korea, well, who understands Korea? But Spain . . . ah, Spain. . . ." And he'd get wistful and nostalgic.

I wasn't long out of the marines then. I didn't understand Korea either. I envied McCormick the foresight and luck that let him, as a young man, take part in "the last good war."

It wasn't just John O. McCormick's fond memories. The Spanish Civil War had great songs, like "Viva la Quince Brigada," that were part of the repertoire of the Weavers, a musical group that was popular at the time. The Spanish Civil War had occasioned a painting I'd been fascinated by since I was twelve years old: Picasso's *Guernica*, which was then in the Museum of Modern Art. I visited *Guernica* in Madrid in December 2001, and it still is for me the best painting in the world about man-made chaos and disorder and violence. It continues to have great symbolic power for others: when U.S. Secretary of State Colin Powell spoke on February 5, 2003, at the United Nations in an attempt to get support for the impending U.S. invasion of Iraq, the Security Council's tapestry copy of *Guernica* was covered by a blue curtain, in front of which was placed a row of blue flags. Someone, either in the American delegation or on the UN staff, thought it would be inappropriate to have that famous painting visible on television while the U.S. Secretary of State was speaking in praise of war.

I didn't tell Spender about my fascination with *Guernica* or my affection for the Weavers, but I did tell him about John O. McCormick and how he always referred to the war in Spain as the "last good war."

"I'm sure it was," Spender said in a voice that was dry and flat. He was silent for a while, then he said in a lower and different voice, "I'll tell you about Spain."

I don't know what I expected: a story about privation or a story about heroism or a story about blood and guts or a story about how the Brits who volunteered for that war were every bit as idealistic and true-hearted as the Americans who had volunteered for it. Whatever it was I had expected, I got something else.

A meeting was called by the officers of his unit, Spender said. There was discussion of that day's battle and the casualties inflicted and suffered. That was followed by a description of the engagement planned for the following day. Then someone from a higher level of authority, a man Spender had never seen before, began talking about financial problems. Contributions from England had declined significantly, the man said. Something had to be done to get the contributions from England coming in again because that money paid for weapons and food and trucks and medical supplies.

Everyone agreed.

The British, the speaker said, were a sentimental people, so if the right pitch moved their hearts, they would be stimulated to contribute again.

Everyone, including Spender, agreed with that, too, and said so.

"We think," the speaker said, "that they would be deeply moved by the death of a young poet in combat; don't you agree?"

He was looking directly at Spender, so Spender answered him: "I certainly do. They would be very moved by that."

"So," the speaker said, "tomorrow, Stephen, you'll go out with your unit but you won't come back."

"Where will I go?" Spender asked.

There was, Spender told me, a curious silence in the tent. He later realized that everybody else had gotten the speaker's point, and some of them, no doubt, had known of it beforehand. They all waited until Spender got it.

"You were supposed to go out and get killed?" I said.

"I was supposed to go out and get killed. And if I wasn't successful, they would kill me."

"To increase British contributions?"

"To increase British contributions."

I said something totally inadequate, like "wow" or "Gosh." Then I said, "So what happened?" At that moment we were approaching Indianapolis, Indiana, so it was obvious that he hadn't gotten killed by foes or friends.

"That night," Spender said, "after everyone was asleep, I packed my things, and I left the camp, and I kept going until I got back to England. My war in Spain was over."

I recall our long silence after that—I, because I could think of nothing to say other than "wow" or "gosh," which I'd already said, and he, maybe because he'd said what he had to say about Spain, and now he wanted to think about something else. I drove; the cornfields were replaced by houses and the houses by industrial sheds with corrugated roofs, and soon we were at the Indianapolis airport, and that was that. I never saw or talked with Stephen Spender again.

But I held on to his story. I told it and I retold it. At first I told people because his story illustrated for me the silliness of politics and the cruelty of the managers of war and the way such people are careless of people of principle and dedication and artistic sensibility. I thought Spender was, in telling me that story, inviting me to join him in that ironic perception.

In time it occurred to me that perhaps Spender was trying to do something else with that tale: blow a hole in what for me was a very good and romantic war. Maybe he was telling me that what characterized all the other wars also characterized the war in Spain. Words like "glory" and "honor" are not only fragile, but perhaps deceptive. In the moment, no war is romantic—the romance may be before or after, but in the moment people suffer agonizing mutilation and death, and that bears thought.

After even more time, I decided that the story wasn't something Spender had spun out to deliver as parable to a graduate student he'd met only earlier that day and who, in all likelihood, he would never see or hear from again. It was his current story about how and why he abandoned the ideal fight, why he had left the so-called last good war. It was a story about how the last good war had failed a young British poet. It was a story about how all our wars, good and bad, ultimately betray us. Whatever Spender meant it to mean to me, I came to believe that for Stephen Spender it was a story about how the young poet—that long ago was he himself—came to be practical and cynical about political parties and agents and causes.

Would Spender have told that same story that same way to you? Or to me on another occasion? Of course not.

These stories of ours, these reports of our lives, are, as I noted earlier, protean. They wax and wane in detail and emotional shading, depending on when and where and to whom they are being told. Different listeners elicit different versions of the narratives, and the same listener elicits a different version at a different time.

The psychologist Roger Burton told me that research with court testimony by very young children suggests that before children are capable of telling stories, they make very good witnesses; but after they reach the age of narrative ability (I think it's about four), their reliability as witnesses declines. It's not because they start lying once they know how to tell stories; rather it's because once they understand the idea of story, they think events should make sense, so they subconsciously tune their narratives to reconcile irreconcilables or provide links for situations that would otherwise remain unconnected. They clean up the clutter. Adults do the same thing. In criminal trials for violent events, eyewitness testimony—people telling the story of what they saw—is often inaccurate and untrustworthy. It's not that people lie; rather it's that people are very good at making sense, even if they have to create it. That's one of the jobs our stories have: making sense where none may otherwise exist.

Pete's Take

In March 1997, I told the folksinger Pete Seeger, who had been the driving force of the Weavers musical group, that I'd just finished the rough draft of an article on storytelling in everyday life. Pete said he was very interested in such stories, and he asked if I would send him a copy of the draft. The draft (which would develop into the chapter in this book titled "The Stories People Tell") included the Stephen Spender story. A few days after I faxed it to Seeger, I got a postcard from him which read:

> Bruce—thanks! For letter & article "The Stories People Tell." I'm going to quote from it.
> Keep on,
> Pete.
> P.S.—I can't believe any leading communist being so stupid as to talk that way to Spender. I think it was a rank and file soldier's way of getting rid of a dangerously poor soldier. They were sure he'd go AWOL. They wanted him out of their way.

Three weeks later another postcard from him arrived:

Bruce—Just read in *Jewish Currents* mag of Steve Spender insisting that T. S. Eliot "has not an ounce of anti-Semitism in him," when some of Eliot's poems contradicted this. So now I don't trust Spender. Pete.

A few months later a third postcard arrived:

Bruce—I still don't completely trust Spender's story. He's the one who passionately declared that T. S. Eliot hadn't an ounce of anti-Semitism in him. I still think it was a soldier's rough joke to get rid of an undependable colleague. Pete.

Pete Seeger's sense of what was happening on the ground in the Spanish Civil War was clearly not as cynical as Stephen Spender's. More important was that Pete was able to accept all the details of Spender's story but rejected Spender's interpretation of those details. Pete didn't question or argue any of the events in my report of Spender's story, only who was doing what to whom and why. In effect, he was saying that our narratives, like the obelisk mounted in honor of a military hero or the diary of a public figure, are facts in and of themselves. Whatever intention the maker has for that thing, we—you and I—can accept it for the fact of utterance that it is in the same moment we reinterpret whatever meaning it may contain.

Whose Story Is This?

I included my memory of Spender's story in an article on personal narrative that was published in the summer 1997 *Antioch Review*. Three years later, on December 21, 2000, I received the following email:

Dear Mr. Jackson,
Today I have seen your story about Stephen Spender on the Internet. I must point out that in the 'telling and retelling' of it you have it confused it to the point of total transformation.

You will find the authentic account in chapter 4 of *World within World* (1951) to be republished as a classic by Random House in 2001, and in *The God that Failed* (1949), edited by Richard Crossman.

In the 54 years I was married to Stephen I did not ever hear him deviate from these well-documented accounts. The facts you have misremembered or erroneously reconstructed are:

1. Spender was never a soldier nor "attached to any unit" in the Spanish Civil War.

2. As a civilian he visited the Front where a young soldier "Nathan" predicted his own death. But Spender himself was not in any meeting where he was expected to take military action. The conversation you describe is invented.

3. The young soldier 'Nathan' (not 'a committee') invited Spender to linger at the Front as a visitor but he left.

4. At a later writers' congress an English novelist in private's uniform who claimed to be a general told Spender that as an officer in the Republican Army he had sent a cowardly soldier to a place in the Front where he knew the soldier would be killed. Spender disbelieved the story and thought the novelist was merely showing off.

I would be grateful for an acknowledgement and public correction of these errors of established fact.

Yours, etc.

Natasha Spender

I publish Natasha Spender's letter in its entirety here to honor her request that her arguments with my article be made public. I wouldn't think of arguing her reports of what Spender did and did not tell her during their long relationship. Nor would I argue the fact of what he wrote in his wonderful fictionalized autobiography, *World within World,* or his carefully considered reflective essay on the discarded politics of his youth in *The God that Failed*.

She is right that Spender was not a soldier and not part of any military unit in Spain. He was there as a journalist. He was with units, but not part of them. When he told me he was with a unit, I assumed that he was there as a soldier; it wasn't until I received Natasha Spender's letter and read *World within World* that I realized he was there as correspondent for the British *Daily Worker*.

But the capacity in which he served is a minor part of his story and mine. The cynical plan to capitalize on the death of a young British poet works whether Spender was carrying a rifle or a notebook. Her other three numbered points, though interesting in their own right, tell us nothing either way about the story I remember Spender telling me.

Natasha Spender takes her husband's narrative writings as unambiguous and unquestionable proof of what did and did not happen. She says things didn't happen because he didn't mention them to her. How many things have you never told people very close to you?

More important, I wasn't reporting what did and didn't happen to Stephen Spender in Spain in 1936 or 1937. I was reporting what I remembered of what Stephen Spender said to me in a car in Indiana in 1961 or 1962. The only information Natasha Spender has about that conversation is in my *Antioch Review* article. She says the fact that he didn't tell her the story I remember him telling me and the fact that he didn't publish it means he never said it. How could she possibly know?

I'm not the only one who remembers Spender telling this story. The Mark Twain scholar Victor Doyno remembers him telling it at a college visit in Massachusetts about the same year I heard him tell it on the highway between Bloomington and Indianapolis. "And I remember him saying someone else was with him," Doyno said. "Auden, maybe."

Stories Poets Tell

Two or three years after the conversation in the car on the way from Bloomington to Indianapolis, I worked on a book about poets, and I wrote Spender to ask if I might use the story he'd told me about leaving Spain. I wanted to be sure I had it all right; if it was, in fact, okay with him for me to use it, I hoped he could take a few minutes to write out for me what he'd told me in the car that morning.

Spender's reply came quickly. He said that it would be fine with him for me to include his story about Spain in my book, but would I please write him and let him know which story about Spain it was. He remembered our having had a conversation, he said, but it was a long drive, wasn't it, and didn't a lot of things get said?

I got involved in doing another book, so I never wrote back to Spender and, he, therefore, never wrote the letter that would have clarified all of this, the letter saying, "Oh, that story, well, we were . . ." or the one saying, "I never said any such thing. . . ."

What's the truth? What really happened to Spender in Spain? What didn't happen or happened differently, and what did I misremember or forget? What did Vic Doyno misremember or forget? What did all three of us get right? What things did Spender choose or not bother to tell his wife? Could what he never said to her or what he published in an admittedly fictionalized autobiography in 1951 disprove anything about a conversation he had in a car in central Indiana and a lecture he gave at a Massachusetts college?

Nobody knows, nor will anyone ever know. Sometimes memory is perfect; sometimes it is not. Things fall out of memory. Things are polished and honed in memory. Things in memory melt and meld. Things told one time one way can be told another way at another time.

We may tell a story once or twice because it fits what's going on at the moment, and then the moment may never be right again, and that story, therefore, may never be told again. We don't tell stories just to make sounds; we do things with stories: we make points, we court favor, we entertain, and we bond. All stories happen in the service of some end, and that end influences what story is told and how it is told.

As I said in the conversation with John Coetzee I told you about earlier, the only thing you ever know for sure about a story you tell or that someone tells you is, at that point in time, the story got told that way.

The novelist has the great luxury of not having to deal at all with truth (not that kind of truth, anyway), only with plausibility. What meaning would there be in saying of a narrative by Cervantes or Camus or Faulkner or Solzhenitsyn or le Carré, "That's a good story, but that's not how it really happened"? The novelist promises us a good story, not an historically exact one. We all have more in common with our novelists, and they with us, than we usually admit or suspect.

The same is true of our autobiographers. The "I" in an autobiography is as much a construct of the writer as the "I" of first person fiction. There may be a difference in the claim to truth, but not less in the craft and art.

To that point, let the last word on these stories about Stephen Spender—by Stephen Spender, Victor Doyno, and me—go to Spender himself, from the preface to *World within World*:

> An autobiographer is really writing a story of two lives: his life as it appears to himself, from his own position, when he looks out at the word from behind his eye-sockets; and his life as it appears from outside in the minds of others; a view which tends to become in part his own view of himself also, since he is influenced by those others. An account of the interior view would be entirely subjective; and of the exterior, would hardly be autobiography but biography of oneself on the hypothesis that someone one can know about himself as if he were another person. However, the great problem of autobiography remains, which is to create the true tension between these inner and outer, subjective and objective, worlds.[1]

4 The Stories People Tell

What Words Do

A story is not the sequence of events only; it is also the specific words with which that sequence is given utterance and the way in which those words are uttered. The plot is only part of the story. I think I first became aware of this when I tried to deal with a conversation I had in 1964 in the ward for terminally ill convicts on the top floor of the old state prison hospital in Huntsville, Texas.

A dying old man named Pete McKenzie told me that many years earlier he had received a death sentence. I asked McKenzie what he had gotten the death penalty for.

"There was a gunfight of three, four plainclothes officers and myself," he said. "I wasn't committing any crime, though I was on escape from here. I was armed; that's where I violated the law. But I wasn't committing any crime. I wasn't trying to commit any crime. I was attending to my own business, but the situation developed to such an extent where there was a gunfight, and the gunfight put wounds in my legs, and I started shooting after I had been shot."

"Did you get any of them?" I asked him.

"A chief of detectives was killed."

I asked McKenzie what he had been serving time for when he had escaped from the penitentiary.

"Murder," he said.

"And what were you carrying when the police came up on you?"

"I had a Luger and a .38."

"So you were carrying two guns, you were escaped from a murder sentence, and you killed one of the cops trying to bring you back to prison."

"That's the way they said it was!"

I maintained my nearly neutral interviewer's face, and we continued with the conversation. Later, when I was working with the transcript, I realized that what was really screwy about what he had said wasn't in the substance, it was in the diction: "[T]he situation developed to such an extent where there was a gunfight and the gunfight put wounds in my legs and I started shooting after I had been shot. . . . A chief of detectives was killed."

It's nearly all in the passive voice or intransitive mode. Things happen; no one does them; no one is responsible for them. McKenzie wasn't saying he didn't kill anyone or that he was innocent. But neither was he admitting culpability. He was instead using the exquisite subtlety of language to cast that shootout and murder of a policeman into a narrative in which he was merely an agency, a prop. It happened, he got the death penalty for it, but he was no more responsible for the event than the two pistols that happened to be in his hands. Pete McKenzie was using the storyteller's art to make the past reasonable and bearable and manageable. He wasn't lying, but he wasn't telling the truth, either.

What Pete McKenzie said to me that day is a special story, but the technique isn't at all special. All detectives and judges I know have versions of it:

"Why did you shoot him?"

"The gun went off."

"Whaddaya mean the gun went off?"

"It just went off."

"You mean the gun you took out of your pocket and were pointing at his eye when you were robbing him, that gun?"

"Yeah, that one."

The device is common in political discourse. ABC News personality Diane Sawyer asked Theresa Leport, creator of the infamous Florida butterfly ballot in the disputed 2000 presidential election, if it was true that she was so upset over the heat she was getting for providing the instrument that gave Florida's electoral votes to George W. Bush that she was going to switch her party affiliation from Democrat to Republican. "That's something that was said in the heat of the moment," Leport replied.[1] Skilled academics take refuge in the passive and intransitive when they get into trouble they cannot rationally explain. In June 2001, for example, Joseph J. Ellis, author of the Pulitzer Prize winning *Founding Brothers: the Revolutionary Generation*, was exposed for having lied to his Mount Holyoke College students and reporters about his military service as a platoon leader in the 101st Airborne in Vietnam and his work as an antiwar activist after he got back. Neither claim was true: he spent his military service teaching history at West Point, he was a grad student at Yale the year he said he was in Vietnam, and there is no evidence of him taking part in any antiwar activities. In his written statement after the *Boston Globe* ran a big story on these alleged activities, he took refuge in the passive: "Even in the best of lives, mistakes are made.[2] I deeply regret having let stand and later confirming the assumption that I went to Vietnam. For this and any other distortions about my personal life, I want to apologize to my family, friends, colleagues, and students. Beyond that circle, however, I shall have no further comment." (I'll have more to say about faux-Vietnam vets in the penultimate chapter of this book, "The Storyteller I Looked for Every Time I Looked for Storytellers.")

Politics

It's not only crooks and poets and kids who tell personal experience stories purposefully and well. They are frequently used by politicians to embody ideas, often in ways that are unchallengeable.

It's not that the idea is unchallengeable, but the story seems to be. To get at the idea, you have to bully your way through the story, and sometimes you just can't do that without appearing heartless or aggressive and accusatory.

For example, at the 1996 Democratic Convention, vice-presidential candidate Al Gore justified his recent opposition to the tobacco industry by telling the story of his smoker-sister's painful death by lung cancer. It was a moving and awful and tender story, one that gave reporters real pause before they could bring up the fact that for years after her death, Gore and his family received substantial payments from tobacco companies that rented the Gore land on which to grow tobacco for cigarettes.

In 1990, at the start of the First Gulf War, the Bush administration brought before the House Human Rights Caucus a fifteen-year-old girl who told of having seen premature babies dumped out of respirators by Iraqi soldiers who then shipped the medical equipment to Baghdad. The girl's name was not given; she had family in Kuwait, it was said. She feared for their lives and her own were her identity made public. She was taking a mighty risk in bringing this dastardly truth to the American people. It was one thing for George H. W. Bush to say that Iraq was the evil enemy, but quite something else to have the specificity of a young, anonymous eyewitness who saw helpless babies left to die by vile men in a fit of lust for hardware. Bush quoted and summarized her testimony in at least five speeches.

The young woman was later revealed to be Nayirah al Sabah, the daughter of the Kuwaiti ambassador to the United States, and she had seen nothing. Her story had been manufactured for her by the public relations firm Hill and Knowlton, a fact known by the members of Congress who took her public testimony. They also knew her identity. Nayirah al Sabah wasn't just telling a story—she was also lying.

Some personal stories are true, some are not, and sometimes the difference is all but impossible to discern. You can't tell from a story alone whether it's true; you can only tell whether it's a good story.

The story of abused children frequently surfaces when violent official action is involved. Britons learned of Germans bayoneting babies in Belgium before they got into World War I, and Americans saw images of Japanese bayoneting babies in Manchuria at the start of World War II. Clinton administration Attorney General Janet Reno explained the precipitous and disastrous 1993 assault on the Waco compound of the Branch Davidian group by citing vague narratives of children being abused within the compound. The FBI, she said at the time, went in to save the children; it was only bad luck that the assault wound up killing most of them.

In August 2004, the presidential contest between George W. Bush and John Kerry became a war of stories and counterstories, of evidence that exploded counterstories, and revised stories designed to explain the exploded stories. Vietnam was one of the key issues in the campaign. Vice President Dick Cheney had received five draft deferments during the Vietnam years and, thereby, avoided military service entirely. President George W. Bush avoided Vietnam by joining the Air National Guard (which, in those years, was a guarantee of not being sent to war); he was moved ahead of hundreds of other applicants because of his father's political influence. After a year as a National Guard pilot, he failed to take his required flight physical and was banned from flying. Furthermore, he seems never to have reported for duty at all during his final year. John Kerry, on the other hand, had enlisted in the Navy, volunteered for Vietnam, and had been awarded a Silver Star, Bronze Star, and three Purple Hearts. Neither Bush nor Cheney attacked Kerry's war record directly; how could they? They attacked instead through a group that called itself "Swift Boat Veterans for Truth," which received its initial funding from two Texas supporters of Bush and Bush's father. The group had as its legal counsel one of the chief lawyers to the Bush campaign (who resigned from the campaign when his double affiliation was revealed) and seemed motivated primarily by their thirty-three-year-old rage at Kerry for having joined the antiwar movement on his return from Vietnam and for eloquently testifying before the Senate Foreign Relations Committee in April 1971.

All the stories put forth by the Swift Boat Veterans for Truth in August 2004 were contradicted by military documents from the time the incidents in dispute occurred and by other eyewitness veterans (the Swift Boat Veterans for Truth, who attacked Kerry's version of what happened to him in Vietnam, weren't there at the time or never served with him at all). The whole episode was a ploy designed to divert the political conversation from issues of the moment—such as the Iraq War, the faltering economy, the Bush record on the environment, and other crises. But the mainstream press covered hardly anything else for three weeks leading up to the Republican convention in New York. The stories, and later stories about their falseness, occupied prime time newscasters and front page editors not because they were true, but simply because they were stories.

Some political use of personal narratives is true, honest, and revealing rather than false, mendacious, and obfuscatory. When I think of examples of this behavior, the morally murkier are the first to come to mind. The point is the same in any case: sometimes it's easier to trust a good story than a person; a story that makes sense on its own seems to make sense in its application, and that is why politicians and the rest of us love them so.

Family Affairs

We all use stories to texture and contextualize our worlds. Stories are the primary devices by and with which families define themselves. Who and what is this family? Listen to the stories going around the table—that's who and what this family is.

Many, maybe most, families have at least one story about the relative in a prior generation who missed the chance to make or who lost a fortune by making a bad choice or by selling out too early or by not buying X when he or she had the opportunity. In my family it was my father's father, a tinsmith, who, at some never-quite-specific time in the first quarter of the twentieth century, presumably sold out his company to what became the American Can Company for $25,000. His wife (my grandmother) spent the entire amount in less than a year. That story was told only by my mother, never by my father, and it was a long time before I understood that it was more about my father's inability to make money than his parent's inability to hold onto it.

At major gatherings of my wife's family, someone always tells about the time Diane's nephew Scott, then five or six, dumped a glass of water on my head as I sat having adult talk with other grownups in the dining room. He then ran outside and jumped into the middle of the twenty-four-foot-above-ground circular pool. Scott was wearing a bathing suit; I was wearing shoes, jeans, shirt, watch, and wallet. According to the story I pursued young Scott into the pool without removing clothes, watch, or wallet and dunked him roundly, and as a result he never again assumed watery invulnerability. Scott is now over thirty, and the pool is long gone, but the story is still told at least once a year. It is one of our dwindling links with a long-ago time that now seems sweet and easy.

When Diane read my notes for that paragraph she said, "There's a lot of things going on in that story: Bruce the wild one, Bruce the kid, Bruce the patriarch acting like a kid, the family as fun, Scott who doesn't have a father getting Bruce to act silly and like a father."

I said that was true and very interesting.

"What's really very interesting," Diane said, "is nobody has to say any of that. Nobody does say any of that. It's all there inside the story. You take whichever thing you want that time."

Most families have such narratives—narratives that seem simple but contain more about the family than anyone could or would ever say overtly. These stories aren't always benign. A friend spoke of an anguished afternoon when she was playing with her very young son. She realized that a family story her parents always told with great amusement contained the explanation of why her memories of her own childhood were so confused and difficult:

> My family moved to Mexico right after I was born. The story that my parents always told and everyone thought was so funny as I was growing up was that I spoke only Spanish as a child and I would run around speaking Spanish with a Mexican accent.

When I was about five and a half years old we moved back to the States and I learned English but spoke it with a heavy Spanish accent. We'd go to the store and my mother would be slightly embarrassed because I'd come running up to her and I'd say, "¿Mamacita, mamacita, cómo se dice . . . cómo tu hablas?" How do you say this the way you talk? And she would tell me. They all thought it was hilarious that here I was this little tow-headed blonde midwestern-looking child who spoke just like a Mexican child. It was the story I heard all the time I was growing up.

I didn't think that much of it until I had a child of my own. I was sitting on the stoop one day watching him as he explored the world in front of our house. He would go and pick up a bug and bring it back to me saying "bug." Then he would pick up a flower and do the same thing. I realized how important verbal language is as a tether, as a connection. He felt safe as long as he could see me and talk to me. So he would wander a couple of yards away, pick up something, and bring it to me. We verbalized everything. He was learning the world through me.

As I sat there on the stoop this sunny day watching him, I suddenly remembered the story and began to cry. I didn't understand why I was crying until I realized it was because the story meant that my parents had never talked to me. They were both Americans—English-speaking Americans—and I had not even learned their language. This meant that the only people talking to me were the maids. My parents would not have been comfortable speaking to me in Spanish. So they had essentially not talked to me until we came back to the States and there were no maids.

It was a story I had heard all my life, but I never interpreted it until then, sitting there on the stoop and talking with my son. I was thirty-one years old.

Her eyes filled with tears as she talked, twenty-three years after that morning on the stoop with her young son. I asked what in the story her father found so funny. "I don't know," she said, "but he still does. He told it the last time I saw him."

Family stories aren't just a way of reminding us who we are; they are also a device for dealing with newcomers. Family stories introduce the newcomer to the family's image of itself because the presence of that new person at the table provides an occasion for telling family stories in greater detail than usual. They're also a test of the newcomer: Do the responses of that new person indicate that he or she understands what these stories are really about, who we really are? The same stories may also exclude newcomers or document their outsiderness. A psychiatrist-friend who married a man with three grown children told me that the first few times her husband and his children got deep into family storytelling she was interested because she felt she was learning about the family she'd joined, but after a time, she felt exactly the opposite. The father and children's energetic "these-stories-that-are-us" engagements simultaneously said to her, "You, who have not partaken of the reality that was the reality for these stories, are not one of us, nor will you ever be one of us."

Was their storytelling an act of exclusion, as she said, or was her negative reaction to the family stories evidence of her alienation from and perhaps antagonism toward his children from a prior marriage? Did her sense of the storytelling as exclusionary represent something they were doing or her own sense of, and perhaps preference for, being an outsider in that group? I don't know, and I suspect neither may she, but either way, the stories are active elements in defining the family unit.

So, at both the private and public levels, stories are strategic. They're told for reasons overt and covert, understood and not understood, articulated and not articulated.

Res ipsa loquitur: Stories as Affidavits

My daughter Rachel called one evening in the summer after her first year in law school. She'd been clerking for the public defender in Toledo, Ohio. She'd spent the day in court helping her boss, Lou, in a felony crack-possession case in which the client, against all advice, had insisted on a full jury trial rather than taking the offered plea bargain. Lou's summation ran for more than an hour, a grand performance full of citations and enthusiasm and innuendo and eloquent questions on the quality of the prosecutor's evidence. The prosecutor was more parsimonious: his summation ran five minutes, Rachel said, ten at most.

In late afternoon the jury went into the jury room, the bailiff closed the door behind them, and immediately the court clerk said, "So Lou, how's July second for sentencing?"

Lou examined his calendar and said that July second was fine for him. The prosecutor said it was fine for him as well. "Good," the clerk said, "I'll put it down." Lou made a note on his calendar. The prosecutor made a note on the outside of the case folder.

Diane was on the extension, and all three of us laughed at the absurdity of the situation. Here was the full armamentarium of the court at work: the long days of testimony, the long afternoon of Lou's carefully reasoned and eloquently phrased summation, the prosecutor's terse summation, the judge's instructions to the jury on points of law, the jury sent off to begin its solemn deliberation. Then, as soon as they're out of hearing, the court clerk acts on the assumption everyone in the room shares, except perhaps the defendant—that the jury will render a guilty verdict—and goes about arranging the next step. No conditional, "If they come in with guilty, how would July second be?" Just an unmediated, unmodified interrogative: "So Lou, how's July second for sentencing?" Everyone, even Lou, the attorney who just made the interminable, impassioned speech for the defense, accepts the court clerk's economy.

"There's more," Rachel said. "The jury was back in twenty minutes with the conviction." At that point, the prosecutor crossed the room and shook Lou's hand. He said he was congratulating him for beating the old record for shortest time in the jury room before a guilty verdict. Everybody in the courtroom said the same thing, or at least nodded in agreement: the clerk, the bailiff, the judge, the deputy who would momentarily take the former defendant and now convicted felon back to lockup. "Shortest time any of them knew for a guilty verdict by a jury," Rachel said.

"What did the defendant say?" Diane asked.

"He didn't say anything."

And the three of us laughed at that, too.

In that simple little story is much of the structure of ordinary public defense: you don't get many cases you can win, you get few cases worth taking to trial, when you go to trial you're likely to lose, and everyone in the room knows it. The only issue is how good a job you do on the way down: how you keep the prosecutor from getting all the jail or prison time he wants. No one, except a naive defendant, thinks ill of a public defender for losing cases, because no one, except a naive defendant, expects much else. So, save for the moments they're attacking one another's cases in summation, the attorneys in the courtroom are generally friendly, and everyone gets along with the judge's clerks, and everyone is amused at absurd variations in the pattern.

That's what the story was saying, but it's not what Rachel was saying with it. She had just done very well in the first year of law school after several years of floating in the world, and she was letting her dad, who had done a lot of criminal justice work, know not only that she understands the game very well now, but she's a player in it and knows how to extract from ordinary events the kind of representative anecdote that wraps it up for insiders and outsiders alike.

The story is fun on its own, it says more than the words in it seem to say, and it does something complex for both the teller and the listener. It's a young woman telling her dad that she's doing just fine in a way that saying "I'm doing just fine" couldn't approximate.

I doubt Rachel ever thought about her motive before she called and told us about her day in court. Rather, she was just telling me a story she knew I'd understand and Diane and I would like. The rest of it just came along for the ride.

Hard Copy

Our own family storytelling repertoires can be extended to include not only stories told by others, but stories told in print or film. I realized this not long ago when I became aware of a pattern to the novels my daughter Jessica and I mailed to one another from time to time. Jessica is an executive in Manhattan and lives in New Jersey with her husband and two small children. She's always busy with one of the three, but gets to read on the bus commuting to work and back home again each day. We see one another only a few times a year, but we talk frequently on the phone, and the talk frequently concerns what we've been reading. We both read a lot, and the novels we are most likely to talk about are those that relate to what we've been talking about, and the novels we're most likely to mail one another are not only the best, but also the most apposite of that group. Those long fictions have become part of our story-telling relationship, one way of bridging time and distance.

The Psychiatrist Who Maybe Killed His Father

Our personal storytelling is sometimes carefully situated in a way that lets a possibly dangerous story be told in a place that is especially safe.

Larry Beahan, a retired psychiatrist taking my graduate Faulkner seminar, was giving an oral report on *Wild Palms,* one part of which deals with a doctor whose bungled abortion of his lover leads to her death by septicemia. Larry knew that this report was strictly oral, no handouts for the class or written report for me. Nonetheless, he handed out to the class Xeroxed copies of the full text of his oral report. As the stapled packets were going around the seminar table he said, "I didn't know if we'd get to me today, so I xeroxed this up for you." At first, I thought this was just compulsive behavior on the part of a retired psychiatrist. His report on the novel was excellent. Then he got to the part I'm about to quote. You should be aware that there was no change in tone or body language when he got to this and, because he went to the trouble of making the text available to everyone, I'm quoting for you his exact words, not my memory of them:

> I am an MD and that makes it easy for me to identify with a certain corner of Harry's problems, his surgical treatment of Charlotte. Doctors are advised not to treat themselves or their relatives. It is said that, The Doctor who treats himself has a fool for a physician.
>
> Yet when ever I consult an MD or some one in my family sees one, my brain goes into gear and I come up with my own diagnosis and treatment and compare it with what the other guy says. I know that my judgment may be off because of my emotional involvement but I have great difficulty in keeping this impulse under control.
>
> Once a neurologist diagnosed my father as having a stroke. I diagnosed a peripheral facial nerve inflammation and had it treated by an ENT guy. The neurologist praised me for taking a better history than him and my Dad recovered well.
>
> On the other hand just before my father died, ten years later, I thought that a certain antidepressant would help his mood and appetite. He was then gradually dying of kidney failure. The Doctor in charge prescribed the drug which I had suggested and my father immediately died of heart attack which may well have been produced by my medicine.
>
> I know Harry's troubled mind after he killed Charlotte with his abortion. There is nothing like standing along side the body of some one you loved and wanted to help and believing that you are responsible for their vacant eyes and their still, pale flesh. Which may not have been the point of the story but it was one angle of it that got to me.

During the first part of Larry's presentation, when he was summarizing the novel, I was listening but not at a very deep level. When he got to his personal narrative, I began listening very carefully. I also watched the room more carefully.

The other students went into what I can only call a semi-catatonic-I'm-here-but-for-god's-sake-don't-call-on-me mode. They heard what he was saying but, I think, they didn't want to hear it; they didn't want to know it. No eyes met his or mine. When Larry was done and I said my usual, "Any comments or questions?" there was silence for longer than usual. Finally, the conversation went to things earlier in his report, and there wasn't very much of that. We soon went on to another report, and then to our scheduled discussion of the assigned reading.

I went home and told Diane about what had happened in class. Her response was, "He told you he did what?"

"He prescribed medicine he thinks killed his father."

"And what did the other students do?"

"Changed the subject."

"And what did you do?"

"Let them."

"Interesting," she said.

I called a good friend of mine, a surgeon, a pal I can tell anything, and told him the story of the class.

I said "What do you think I ought to do about this story? Do you think I should address it?"

He said, "Do nothing. It should not be addressed. It was important for him to say it; he said it in a place he could keep it safe, leave it there."

The next week I said to Larry, "Have you done anything with that story you told last week?"

"What do you mean?" Larry said.

"That thing about maybe prescribing medication that maybe killed your father. Have you ever dealt with it in therapy or talked about it to anyone?"

"Oh, that. No, not in therapy. And I don't think I've talked about it either. But I did write about him. Would you like to see the article I wrote about him?" I said I would. A week later the article arrived in my campus mailbox: it was about something that happened on a long ago vacation when the father was alive and the psychiatrist was a boy.

Well, what shall we make of this? I don't want to engage in facile psychologizing, but I believe my surgeon friend was right: Larry found a time and place where he could safely tell a story he very much wanted to tell and, more important, needed to tell. He made sure his audience got the story right by handing out copies of it in a forum where no handouts were needed or even wanted. He wasn't taking any chances on any of us being on autopilot during his presentation. I don't know if telling and printing the story accomplished what he wanted, but I am certain that it was important for him to tell the story in an absolutely protected way, and that our class gave him that protection.

I showed Larry the final draft of this chapter—it is identical to what you are reading now except for this paragraph—and asked him if it would be all right with him for me to tell that story here and, if it was, if he preferred a pseudonym or his own name. "Please go ahead and use my name," he wrote. Then he wrote two sentences that, in a way, go to the heart of this book: "I am sure I don't know all of what is going on when I tell a story like that" and "A thing that I have discovered about it is that confession interests listeners."

David's Choice

I said earlier that stories are devices with which families characterize themselves. Individuals use them the same way. I'll give you two examples, one having to do with the leadership guru Warren G. Bennis, whom I mentioned earlier, and the other with the late civil rights attorney William M. Kunstler.

In 1969, a few hours after we had been tear-gassed in a campus anti-Vietnam War demonstration, Warren told me that as a young lieutenant in World War II he had expressed despair at what seemed to him an astonishing number of logistical screwups within the American army. "What I don't understand," he told his captain, "is why we're winning the war."

The captain, Warren said, "spat out a few drops of Red Man tobacco, looked at me, like a beagle dog might look at a foolish human, and said—these are his exact words: 'Shit kid, they've got an army, too.'"

I always liked that story, and I was pleasantly reminded of it a few years ago when one man among a group of businessmen at a table next to ours in a neighborhood restaurant in Buffalo told it to his companions; his voice got so loud at the punch line that I heard him over the room noise and the conversation at my own table. As his group was leaving I asked him if he'd read that story in one of Warren's books. "No," the man said, "I've heard him tell it!" He didn't say how recently, but I assumed it was fairly recently, which meant that more than thirty years after Warren told me that story and a half-century after the event, Warren was still telling it.

Not long after that brief encounter I saw Warren in Santa Monica, where he now lives. I told the restaurant anecdote, and we talked about how we keep some of our stories for a long time. Warren said he loves the army story because it expresses perfectly the stupidity of the bureaucratic mentality.

His professional career has focused on the ways organizations behave and how people can perform rationally and excellently within them. But Warren knows full well that always at the edge of the bounded discussions of organizational behavior is the disorder and irrationality of the real world. Warren's story of what his captain said to him contains what is maybe one of the deepest and darkest organizational secrets he's got to tell: at a certain point you can't whip or even cope with the idiocy within or the chaos at the edges, so just go ahead and do what you know how to do as well as you can. If the law of averages is working today, the clutters will neutralize one another because "they've got an army too." The story is maybe Warren's way of saying to corporations asking him for sophisticated management advice just what his captain was saying to him a half-century ago: "Beyond this point of explanation, I don't know. Keep walking." It's also Warren saying the same thing to himself.

At a 1977 conference on heroism, I heard William Kunstler tell what in subsequent years I decided was his most important personal story. When he was a young man, he had wandered through the Galleria dell'Accademia in Florence and had stopped briefly before Michelangelo's *David*. He started to move on when an elderly man standing nearby told him to pause awhile. This statue, the old man said, was the only depiction of David in the critical moment before he became a hero. All the others showed David triumphant; Michelangelo depicts a shepherd boy, not the warrior who would soon be king. Some time later, Kunstler said, he learned that the elderly man had been Bernard Berenson, the famous art historian.

Kunstler told that anecdote whenever he could—at graduations, conferences, meetings. He particularly liked telling it to groups of young people. Toward the end of his life, Kunstler dropped Berenson from the narrative, and the unique aspect of Michelangelo's David moved into his own voice. The last time I heard him tell it was at the 1995 University of Buffalo School of Architecture commencement, just a few months before he died. His subject was ethics and the erosion of the Bill of Rights in recent years. He ended with Arthur Hugh Clough's "Say not the struggle naught availeth," a poem about the critical significance of the individual in large battles. Just before he read the poem, he told them about David:

> [T]he people I really talk to and really look for are those who are like the David of Michelangelo's statue (which you have in the Delaware Park here). Michelangelo's David is a good example for all of you. This is the only representation in art of David before he kills Goliath. All the rest—Donatello's bronze, the paintings—show him holding up the severed head of Goliath. Michelangelo is saying, across these four centuries, that every person's life has a moment when you are thinking of doing something that will jeopardize yourself. And if you don't do it, no one will be the wiser that you even thought of it. So, it's easy to get out of it. And that's what David is doing right there. He's got the rock in the right hand, the sling over the left shoulder, and he's saying like Prufrock, "Do I dare, do I dare?" I hope many of you, or at least a significant few, will dare when the time comes, if it hasn't come already.

That's a fine parable for young men and women about to enter employment in which they will be frequently confronted with ethical choices. Still, I have no doubt that it was also Bill Kunstler talking about himself. It was he reflecting on defendants early in his career who were nice people with cases that were morally clear—the Mississippi Freedom bus riders, Martin Luther King, the American Indians at Wounded Knee; and it was he reflecting further on recent defendants who weren't at all nice and whose cases weren't at all clear, like the 1993 World Trade Center bombers, mobster John Gotti, a 16-year-old charged in the 1989 brutal assault of a woman in Central Park, 1986 Bronx cop-shooter Larry Davis, and El Sayyd Nosair, accused of murdering militant rabbi Meyer Kahane in 1990. All of these were cases for which he'd gotten flak not just from the old foes of the right but also from old friends of the left.

Kunstler often made general statements about who in American society benefited before the law from social position and power and who did not, and why he thought the most unsavory defendants were most in need of excellent legal counsel. That was his public explanation for taking those unsavory clients and cases. What he never discussed publicly was the personal cost of making such choices. Kunstler was boisterous and public about his cases, but not about his private self; to talk about the personal aspect of silent moral choice would have been unseemly for him. But he could talk about the boy David standing there, looking at the giant Goliath, pondering his options.

The David story had another secret part. Kunstler was very much aware of it, and I think it's the reason he needed to tell it so often and for so many years. The biblical David met one Goliath one time. Kunstler knew that in real life you meet Goliath again and again, and though the confrontation may get familiar, it never gets easier. When he was telling those kids to remind themselves of David's choice, he was telling the story to himself as well. After he left whatever podium gave him that occasion for telling about Michelangelo's David, he went home where the message machine tape was always full of pleas from desperate people asking him to take their case. And he would, once more time, choose.

Both stories are grounded in a key long-ago understanding that continued to have current importance and current resonance. The meanings and use of both stories may have changed over time, but the stories continued to fit the tellers, like an old pair of boots. Such stories aren't just vessels containing advice for others; they're also articulations of the tellers' deepest perceptions about themselves. Stories like these are the way we tell people who we are, and they are the way we express what we are. "Character," Bennis said in a conversation about the stories I've been recounting for you here, "character is so hard to define. Maybe it's in stories like these where character is defined: 'You want to know who I really am? I am the person who tells a story like this one.'"

The Doctor's Story

The front page of the Christmas Day 2006 *New York Times* featured an above-the-fold article about surgery performed a year earlier for a dissecting aortic aneurysm on 97-year-old Dr. Michael E. DeBakey, who pioneered such surgery half a century earlier. I read the article online a little after midnight and immediately emailed it my friends Warren Bennis and Howard Lippes.

I sent it to them for different reasons. Warren was then getting over recent neck surgery and I thought the story of 98-year-old DeBakey back at work after far more serious surgery might cheer him. He responded twelve minutes later: "A thrilling story. Thx for sending it on. Will call tomorrow. Love, W."

Howard, an endocrinologist and internist, loves interesting medical stories, and frequently tells them, so even though I was pretty sure he got the *Times* I sent the DeBakey story along just in case. He responded in an email a little after noon on Christmas day with a story of his own:

I had occasion to speak with Dr. DeBakey. It was a very terse exchange. I was a new intern at the Buffalo General Hospital and it was 1977. My assignment was the ICU and C1 ward service. It was late November around 7 pm and I got a call from the emergency room resident. A patient was being admitted to my service. He asked me to come and get him and if possible move the patient to the ward quickly because the emergency room was overflowing with patients and they needed beds. When I got to the emergency room the resident said to me, "Howard, I don't know what this guy's got, but he's got something, and I am admitting him." I went to see my new patient. He was lying supine on the gurney with his legs about a foot longer than the end of the gurney; nearly 7 feet tall. He was about my age, in his late 20's. He appeared quite comfortable.

I started with the usual questions as I wheeled him to the ward. He told me that he had been working out in the gym about a week earlier when he experienced a stabbing pain in his chest. He felt dizzy and lay down on the floor. After a half hour he felt well enough to ride his bicycle home. The stabbing pain waxed and waned all week. He went to see the nurse at the Roswell Park Cancer Institute infirmary where he was a graduate student. The nurse could not find his blood pressure in right arm and blood tests were done and were normal. The day of his admission he was in the Main Place Mall Christmas shopping when the pain became worse and the dizziness returned. He lay down on the floor. Someone called an ambulance, and thus we met.

I remember that Mohammad Ali was fighting that night and my patient asked if there was a TV so he could watch. When we arrived at the ward I set about doing a physical exam. The diagnosis still eluded me. He had peculiar physical features. A very narrow face, long thin fingers, and pigeon bone like rib cage and sternum. He had a high arched palate. He had a faint heart murmur. I listened to his carotid arteries with my stethoscope and there was an even louder bruit [an abnormal blood flow sound heard through a stethoscope]. It was then that I realized my patient had a dissecting aorta. I also realized that he had Marfan's syndrome; which explained his physical features and the problem with his aorta.

I recall a feeling of dread came over me and I had to sit down for a moment with the realization of the mortal danger that the patient confronted. I thought the aneurysm and dissection were probably not something that could be repaired, and that my patient would not survive.

I called the resident in charge of the ICU, and who was supposed to be supervising my work that night. He wasn't much help. I called the chief of Cardiology, Dr. David G. Green, who I'd been told was the first person to perform Cardiac Catheterization in Buffalo and had trained at the Karolinska Institute. He was a stern, demanding and imposing figure. I presented the case to him and offered my diagnosis. He told me to call the nurse in charge of the Catheterization Laboratory, and to have the patient there in 20 minutes. The procedure demonstrated a Cooley's Type I dissection (the dissection begins in the ascending aorta, just above the heart and involves the great vessels leading to the arms and brain). I stood in the back of the room out of way of the nurse assisting Dr. Green. When he finished the procedure Dr. Green peeled off his surgical gloves and turned to me. "His only chance is to send him to Houston and have Dr. DeBakey fix it" is all he said, and then he wrote one sentence in the patient's chart and left. The resident and I were dumbstruck. There were several distinguished cardiac surgeons at the Buffalo General then, but we had no instructions to call them.

We transferred the patient to the ICU. It was around 11 pm and Mohammed Ali's fight was over. I asked the hospital operator to get the number of Dr. DeBakey in Houston. A few minutes later I was on the phone with the operator at the hospital in Texas. I explained that I was a physician and that I needed to talk to Dr. DeBakey. The phone clicked and Dr. DeBakey answered. I presented the case and related the Catheterization findings. Dr. DeBakey's response was, "Send him down here and we'll fix it. Thanks for calling." He then said good night and hung up.

We spent most of the rest of the night arranging the patient's transport to Houston. Since he had no insurance this was no easy task.

The patient returned to Buffalo and visited the nurses that had cared for him in the ICU and one who volunteered to accompany him to Houston. A few years later I read a paper that the patient had authored in the Journal of Biological Chemistry.

I was surprised that the article in the Times did not mention Dr. DeBakey's collaboration with Dr. Denton Cooley.

Howard

Dr. Howard Lippes's story is about a young physician's brief encounter with an internationally famous surgeon, but it is also about relationships in the hospital community between intern, resident, attending, nurse, and patient. It is wonderfully specific: thirty years later he names his two assignments, the time of year, the hour of day. It describes an instance of the detective work at the heart of much of the best medical diagnosis. It is about an event that took place in more than one kind of "real time." One is suggested by the Muhammad Ali fight, which began and ended while the fight to save this patient's life was going on; another by the article by the patient that Howard read "a few years later," which tells us that the Buffalo diagnosis and Houston trip worked out well enough for the patient to return to a productive life. Both of those temporal groundings further indicate that, to Howard, the patient was more than a case to be dealt with, written up, and forgotten, but rather a human being situated in a specific part of the real world, and the doctor was paying attention.

And finally there is Howard's comment on the *Times* reporter's failure to mention the fact that DeBakey's early important heart work had been in collaboration with Dr. Denton Cooley. The two separated under friendly terms in 1962. That friendship ended in 1975, when Cooley implanted an artificial heart in a patient. DeBakey said the design was his and he hadn't done an implant yet because he didn't think the device was ready. Some medical researchers think Cooley's end-run around DeBakey cost DeBakey a Nobel Prize in Medicine. Cooley was censured by the American College of Surgeons and the two men didn't speak to one another until 2004 (the story is on-line at http://blog.kir.com/archives/000563.asp). That Texas medical relationship was, for Dr. Howard Lippes, very much a part of the story.

Dr. Lippes does here something all the great physicians I've known do when they narrate memorable cases: he locates the medical event in at least two life narratives, one the patient's, the other the physician's. For him, as for those other physicians, the medical event is about human beings, not merely organs or conditions or techniques or technology. Organs and conditions and techniques and technology don't come alive in a story; people do. Organs and conditions and techniques and technology don't give a damn that nobody got to see that Mohammad Ali fight, but Dr. Howard Lippes and his patient did.

In the world of story, beginnings and endings are important, and tellers treat them with care. It makes no difference if the story is in the rapid and unrevised space of an hasty email, the give and take of a conversation, the considered and edited space of a novel or a movie screen. Homer and Virgil, Faulkner and Tolstoy, Howard Hawks and Howard Hughes, the author of the New York Times story on Dr. Michael E. DeBakey's recovery from heart surgery and Dr. Howard Lippes in his recounting of a medical event that led to a two-sentence encounter with DeBakey 30 years ago—they all knew where the beginnings and endings of their stories were.

Howard Lippes's brief comment on his surprise about the omission of Dr. Denton Cooley is a critique of the story that had prompted his own that says, among other things, "That reporter wasn't telling you the whole story. There's more to medicine than that. For instance, these other things, those other people." What are those other things and where might a hint of them be found? Amid all those complex relationships, insights, and pleasures of the hunt in Dr. Howard Lippes's own narrative about the very tall guy with the very ruptured aorta who missed the Ali fight but who got to write a paper Howard Lippes read a few years later in the *Journal of Biological Chemistry*.

9/11

On May 21, 2006, several friends and relatives gathered at my house for a dinner celebrating my seventieth birthday and what would have been the eightieth birthday of the poet Robert Creeley, who had died fourteen months earlier in Texas, where he'd been a writer-in-residence at the Lannan Foundation. Diane was there, as were our children—Michael, Jessica, and Rachel—as well as Jessica's younger daughter, Ali. Only a few hours earlier we'd ended a two-day celebration of Bob's life and work that consisted of numerous poetry readings, film screenings, and musical performances, so among the other guests were the British poet Tom Raworth, who'd given one of the readings the previous night, and Penelope Creeley and her children with Bob—Will and Hannah.

People were making toasts, during the course of which Jessica said, "I've always wanted to thank my dad for talking me down when I started hyperventilating when I watched the first tower go down."

Explaining what towers or what day she was talking was not necessary. Certain events, like certain celebrities who are identified by one name (Dylan, Fidel, Clint, Marilyn, Bill, Jack), need hardly more than a word to be brought into the present conversation.

"Where were you when it happened?" someone asked her.

Twenty years ago, an adult who was asked that question would have told where he or she was in the early afternoon of November 22, 1963. The same question now is answered in terms of the morning of Tuesday, September 11, 2001.

"Twenty-fifth floor of the Grace Building. Someone said come look what's happened. I went across to the south side of the office and looked, and that's when the second plane hit. I stood there until the first tower went down and that's when I started having trouble breathing. We"—she nodded toward me—"were on the phone five or six times that day."

"Until the phones went down," I said.

"After a while you couldn't make calls any more," Jessica said.

"Were you able to get home?" Pen asked her. I knew from previous conversations that Pen had been crazy worrying about Will and Hannah that morning. Both of them were in lower Manhattan, and it was a long time before she was able to make contact with them. Pen knew that Jessica had two small children at home, both of whom surely knew what had happened and would, therefore, be fearful about their mother.

"No," Jessica said. "A friend was in town from our Columbus office, and she had a hotel room so I spent the night there."

"How far away is the Grace Building?" someone asked.

"The window I was looking out of is on 42nd Street."

"So you were quite a ways uptown."

"It didn't seem very far away," Jessica said.

"No place in New York was very far," Will said.

"Will was only a few blocks away," Penelope said.

Will told how he was walking toward the towers when the second plane hit and of the astonishing rumbling of the ground when the first tower went down. "I never felt anything like that. And the tower was so big; I didn't know if it would fall all the way to where I was. I just ran. I kept running, feeling the ground rumbling."

Diane said that when she saw on our kitchen TV the report of the first plane having hit, she'd called upstairs to tell me about it. I was at my desk checking my email. I said I'd assumed it was just some idiot who'd run his private plane into a tall building and that I hadn't even gone downstairs to look at the news reports that were coming in. I told them about when I was nine years old and the front pages of the *New York Daily News* and *Daily Mirror* had photographs of a B-25 bomber that had plowed into the Empire State Building in the previous day's fog. "I thought it was like that," I said, "but it wasn't." Diane said she called me a second time, saying Rachel was in the kitchen with her now, and that another plane had hit, and they were big airliners, not small airplanes, and that I'd better come down. I said that we'd then gotten on the phones, landlines and cellular, trying to find Jessica.

We all talked about how we heard, where we were, what we did next, how we got in touch. We told our 9/11 stories for a long time, and at one point or another, nearly everyone at the table weighed in.

Whatever you think of what America did and became after that day, whatever you think of the Bush administration and its so-called war on terror, that day stands alone, outside of politics. On that day most of us sensed a vulnerability we had never before experienced, and a day when we felt a unanimity rare in modern life. It's a day when we all, in one way or another, tuned in, watched, and waited. It's a point in time we share as we share almost no other. Just as a family can sit around a table and reaffirm itself by telling this or that family story, or as old friends can get together in the presence of someone new and reaffirm or recreate the old relationship by telling the old tales one more time, so, I think, can we all look to 9/11 as a day lifted out of all the others, a day that binds us together. We may not understand why or how, but we have those stories of where we were and what we did that morning to prove it.

I doubt that anyone thought, when Jessica offered her birthday toast, that we would wind up bonding over 9/11, but that's what we did. Four of the twenty people at that dinner knew nothing of Bob Creeley's poetry, so they'd been out of our earlier discussions, but they, too, had something to say about the morning of 9/11. So, too, did Tom Raworth, the English poet, who knew Bob and his poetry very well, but who also had that day clearly in his memory. Everyone there, except eight-year-old Ali, had something to say about the morning of September 11, 2001, and had Ali not been out back playing with the dogs, she might very well have had something to say as well.

George Beto's Mare

We don't only tell stories that make sense of the past or illuminate the present; we also imagine stories that help us move into the future. Not just Hollywood scriptwriters make up stories and not just actors act them; we all do it, only we get to be writer, actor, director and, later, when we're looking back, editor or historian. That is, our stories aren't only our histories, our version of what happened; sometimes they're our scripts, our map of what's going on now and what's going to happen next.

Some years ago I was visiting my friend George Beto at his ranch, Wit's End, a few miles out of Huntsville, Texas. It was a place to which George said he went to think. He walked a lot and tended his small herds of Black Angus cattle and Nubian goats. We were sitting on the porch talking when George became quiet and looked off into space. At first I thought he was thinking about something serious, then I realized he was looking at something in the distance. I followed his gaze and saw a slanted plume of dust moving our way along the road from town.

The road was not paved; part of it even went through a stream a mile or two toward town that sometimes got hubcap deep. Every few years the Huntsville city fathers offered to pave the road and even build it up over the stream, but George always talked them out of it. He told me his reason: "If there's a good road people will come out here, and the reason I have this place is to get away from people."

It wasn't long before we made out a white Ford pickup at the head of the plume of dust. It stopped at the road coming into Wit's End, a few hundred yards from the house. The driver got out, opened the gate, drove up a few yards, stopped, got out again, closed the gate, then got back into the cab and drove the rest of the way up to the house.

He was a tall man, older than I but younger than George. He wore rancher's work clothes, but it was a Saturday and around there a lot of the men wore rancher's clothes on Saturday who wore business suits or doctor's coats or judge's robes on weekdays. George stood up to greet him. The man said he was out this way and thought he'd stop by to say hello. George said he'd have been insulted if he hadn't. George introduced us, then invited the man to join us for a beer. The man said that would be nice because it was a hot day and the drive had been dusty. He sat in a chair next to me, and George took the chair the other side of him, and the three of us then looked out into the east Texas afternoon.

We talked about the dust, the lack of recent rain, and the recent election. The man asked me what it was like this time of year in

Buffalo. I told him this weather was very hot for me; he said it was very hot for everybody today. George provided another round of longnecks. There was talk about Austin politicians. The man complimented George on his Nubians, several of which had just trotted into sight in the pasture. George loved those goats.

Then the man got up, said it was good to have had this chance to say hello to George; it was nice having met me. We all shook hands. He stepped back into the cab of his white pickup.

We watched him reverse his arrival: he drove to the gate, stopped a few yards our side of it, got out and opened the gate, got back into the truck, and drove out to the road, got out and walked back to close the gate, got into his truck and drove toward town. A moving, slanted plume of dust followed him. Soon we couldn't see the truck any more, just the plume, and after a while we couldn't even see that.

When the noise of the truck had attenuated to nothing and the dust had dissipated, George said, "He's not going to get that mare for what he thinks he's going to get her for."

"What mare?" I said. "I don't remember him saying anything about a mare."

"He didn't," George said. "He won't get around to saying anything about her until next time, or more likely the time after that. But he's still not going to get her for what he thinks he's going to get her for."

What I like about the story is that it shows how people see themselves in a narrative. It's not like the story of a car crash or what happened in the hospital. It's a story as it is happening. Both George and his friend are looking forward and backward, weaving their narrative through their daily life. Both are looking back at scenes already played and ahead to scenes as yet mapped out only in general terms, and heading toward a denouement both almost know. The mare will be sold, but at what price is uncertain. Other encounters will lead up to the first mention of the sale, and there will, after that, be discussions of the sale itself. When or where those will occur neither man knows, nor does either man know exactly what will be said on those occasions. The human script will be written on the fly, but in terms of a plot very much in place.

The plot is not rigid. It's not that kind of script. The mare might die. Someone else might come along and make an offer to George that cannot be refused. The man I met might find another mare he wants more. This is real life, not Shakespeare. In real life, the last act of any story isn't written until after it's been played.

I told a few people what you've just read. Hearing myself tell it, I began to wonder if maybe I was reading too much into their scripting of the ongoing events of their lives. Then, in December of 1991, I met that man in the white Ford pickup once again. I was in Austin for George's funeral. It was a big formal affair with a herd of politicians and ranchers and state officials and people from the university where George taught the last fifteen years of his life. A man came up to me after the service and said hello. That I didn't remember him was obvious. "I met you at Wit's End twelve or thirteen years ago," he said, "the day I went up there to buy George's mare."

Dream Weavers

Speech is linear and one-dimensional, but the meanings of our stories are neither linear nor one-dimensional. The wonderful thing about a good personal narrative is this: its message isn't exhausted all at once. You hear it and you think or ask, "What does that mean?" You come up with an answer that makes wonderful sense. Then you hear it again or remember it and ask again, "What does that mean?" You once again come up with an answer that makes wonderful sense; only it's not necessarily the same answer you came up with last time. I think such stories serve best when the situation demands more than one idea or point of view at once, like the story of young Scott getting me into the twenty-four-foot-above-ground pool fully clothed.

Tellers may not even know they're telling parables when they're telling amusing or interesting stories about themselves. Stephen Spender was a very intelligent and sophisticated man, but I doubt that he thought through the levels of meaning and applicability of the story he told me in that car moving north on Indiana State Road 37 in 1962, and he surely was unaware of the way Pete Seeger would reconsider that story in 1997. I doubt that Pete McKenzie gave consideration to which narrative voice he used to tell me exactly what happened on the day he earned his death sentence. I doubt that Larry Beahan thought the inclusion of the story about his father's death in his report on Faulkner's *The Wild Palms* was anything but a personal gloss on a complex plot that would help his fellow students better understand what he was talking about. I doubt Rachel cast about for a narrative that would at once let me know she had her life on track and she had some sophisticated insights of her own in an area in which I had worked for many years. I doubt that Howard Lippes, responding in an email to a *New York Times* article I'd sent him in the night, thought he was sending me a comment on the complex relationships within the broad medical community and between individual patients and individual doctors. I doubt those of us sitting around the dinner table on May 21, 2006, recalling where we were and what we did on the morning of September 11, 2001, thought we were doing anything but telling one another about a morning that wouldn't be forgotten. And I doubt that George Beto thought of himself as writer, director, and actor in a personal narrative that hot and dusty afternoon we sat on his porch drinking beer and talking about the world.

Professional dream weavers—like trial lawyers and politicians and men of the cloth—spin stories deliberately and consciously, seeking to manipulate us. Professional reporters link facts deliberately and consciously, seeking to inform us. We all know that. At least as important is the fact that we all, all of us, do the same thing all the time. We are more skilled than we know. While doing one thing deliberately, we do another subconsciously; no matter, we can do both. A story that serves one end today serves another tomorrow; no matter, the story is protean, living. We've learned how to do it by a lifetime of managing language without conscious thought, just as we know that a plural subject takes a plural verb, just as we unconsciously know that right now is the right time to say, "there was a gunfight in which a chief of detectives was killed" or "the plate fell on the floor and it broke" or "they've got an army too" or "he's not going to get that mare for what he thinks he's going to get her for."

5 Acting in the Passive, *or,* Somebody Got Killed but Nobody Killed Anybody

Remember Pete McKenzie? He's the man in the Texas prison hospital who said, "[T]he situation developed to such an extent where there was a gunfight and the gunfight put wounds in my legs and I started shooting after I had been shot.... A chief of detectives was killed." I want to spend a little more time with that use of the passive voice ("It is thought that") and intransitive ("The plate fell") as an avoidance device. With the passive, something happens but nobody's doing it; with the intransitive, something happens but the verb has no consequences. It's a major narrative element, one you'll hear politicians and scoundrels using all the time once your ear gets tuned to it.

I encountered the construction in early 1988. A woman friend of a killer named Jack Henry Abbott sent me a copy of a document Abbott had sent a New York judge. Abbott was asking the judge to set him free.

Jack Henry Abbott spent the nine years prior to his eighteenth birthday in Utah reformatories. He was free for six months; then he was sent to the Utah penitentiary to do time for writing bad checks. He earned more time three years later when he stabbed one inmate to death and injured another in a prison brawl. He robbed a bank during a brief escape in 1971; that added a nineteen-year-federal sentence on top of the state time. He was then twenty-five years old.

In 1978 Abbott began a lengthy correspondence with Norman Mailer, who was at the time writing *The Executioner's Song* (1979), a fictionalized biography of executed murderer Gary Gilmore. Mailer got some of Abbott's letters published in the prestigious *New York Review of Books*, which led to publication of Abbott's first book, *In the Belly of the Beast* (1982). When Abbott came up for parole, Mailer wrote a strong letter on his behalf. Abbott was transferred to a New York halfway house in early June 1981. If he had stayed out of trouble for eight weeks, he would have gone on parole.

He didn't make it. Six weeks after he got to New York, he stabbed to death a waiter named Richard Adan. Because of his previous record, Abbott received the maximum sentence: fifteen years to life. Back in prison Abbott wrote a second book, *My Return* (1987), which reminded me of a politician who had been out of office for a while and who had been reelected to his former position. I didn't like the book and said so in a review, which is what prompted his girlfriend to send me the appeal I'm telling you about now. In her cover letter she told me that, like nearly everyone else, I'd failed to understand his sensibility. Had I read his brief carefully, she said, I might have a better understanding of the kind of man Jack Henry Abbott was. In that, she was correct.

In the entire document Abbott wrote in the hope his sentence would be set aside, he never referred to Richard Adan by name. He referred only to "the deceased." These two sentences especially caught my attention:

> There was never sufficient evidence presented at my trial to support a finding of intent to kill. The deceased in this case was inflicted a single wound under circumstances which would have demanded the infliction of more wounds, if the single wound had been inflicted with the intent to kill and not merely to repel him.

I'll translate that into English for you: "They never proved I meant to kill the guy. If somebody like me really wanted to kill a guy like that, you think I'd stab him only once? Moi?" But that's not what Jack Henry Abbott wrote. Instead, he wrote:

> There was never sufficient evidence *presented* at my trial to support a finding of intent to kill. The *deceased in this case was inflicted* a single wound under circumstances which *would have demanded* the infliction of more wounds, if the single wound *had been* inflicted with the intent to kill and not merely to repel him [emphasis mine].

Neither Jack Henry Abbott nor Pete McKenzie was in a position to lie about the facts of their killings (there were witnesses to both); the only issue was the meaning of those facts. For a long time what impressed me about McKenzie's statement was how astutely he had used language so he could talk about what happened without admitting his guilt.

Did Pete McKenzie consciously decide to utilize the passive voice as a way of containing or managing his guilt for the murder of a policeman? Hardly. Pete couldn't have told you what the passive voice was, let alone consciously decide when to incorporate it into our conversation. He didn't have to: he just did it, just as he killed that cop and Jack Henry Abbott killed Richard Adan. That's how language works. We don't think, "I'm switching into the passive now" any more than an experienced driver thinks about when to move the right foot from the accelerator to the brake pedal.

And it's not just in speech that killers use the passive voice or intransitive to change the subject into an object. "I am sorry those people had to lose their lives," Oklahoma City bomber Timothy McVeigh wrote in a letter to the *Buffalo News* published June 10, 2001, "but that's the nature of the beast. It's understood going in what the human toll will be." Those people didn't "lose their lives"; Timothy McVeigh murdered them. They surely were not party to any understanding. "It's understood"—by whom? And "going in" to what? Mass murder? McVeigh says he's sorry for their loss—but not for his action. He could write a letter using the same diction about mountain climbers killed in an avalanche, a shipwreck in the Pacific, or an earthquake in India.

After I reread McVeigh's letter, Abbott's statement, and thought back on the conversation with Pete McKenzie, I understood that there was in language a way to acknowledge events without in any way accepting responsibility or accountability for them. Language, I realized, has profound moral power that can appear to recast the very facts its users purport to present.

This aspect of the structure of language—to say and do things that are different from what the words seem to be saying—is not limited to the management of guilt. Here is a more benign example. At 8:38 P.M. on July 16, 1999, a Piper Saratoga piloted by John F. Kennedy Jr., took off from Essex Airport in Fairfield, New Jersey. The plane was supposed to land at Martha's Vineyard about ten P.M. Early in the morning of July 17, the family notified the Coast Guard that the plane hadn't arrived. A search was started, and all the major networks cut their usual programming to cover the search for Kennedy, his wife, and her sister. The reporters were uniformly careful to remain at least open to the possibility that the plane had crash-landed and there were survivors. At 2:15 P.M., while talking about the plane Kennedy was flying, NBC aviation correspondent Robert Hagar said, "It was a very good airplane." The first confirmed reports of luggage washing up off Gay Head were hours away, but Hagar's shift in tense—"It was a very good airplane"—said what everyone was assuming but not saying.

Diction is part of substance, not a vehicle for it. Our stories exist not only in what we tell, but in how we tell them.

6 The Story of Chuck

I wrote earlier about the way politicians use stories. I want to tell you about one politician and one story in particular.

New York Senator Charles (or "Chuck" as he prefers to be called) Schumer is a relentless performer at college and university commencements. During the May graduation season, he traverses New York State appearing on stages as an announced part of the program or turning up as a surprise visitor. Some days he'll catch multiple commencements, like a dog hitting every tree and hydrant. He made two commencement stops in Buffalo in May 2006. The first, on May 6 at Buffalo State College, came as a surprise to everybody, including the invited speaker, New York's junior senator, Hillary Clinton, who was visibly annoyed at his presence on what she'd assumed would be her individual platform. (It was an event, said a trustee who had been there, in which "Hillary got Schumered.") The second was twelve days later at University at Buffalo, where I teach.

The three primary reasons Schumer and Clinton, and politicians like them, adore college and university commencements are (1) they don't look like the campaign stops they, in fact, are; (2) somebody else does all the work of getting people there; and (3) just about everyone there is happy: the kids because they can go out into the world for what they think will be freedom from adult supervision; the parents because they're proud of the kids and now they can move into a period of paying off the bills rather than seeing them accumulate; and the faculty and administrators because commencement is one of the few markers of something having happened in an industry that is, on the whole, far more about process than product.

Politicians piggyback on all of that. Commencements are events in which, with rare exceptions, they owe nothing. It's not like appearing at a union or party dinner, which is entirely about who owes or will owe what and to whom. Politicians appearing at a commencement can at once stroke supporters and reach out to people who would never otherwise hear them performing live. Commencements are about one of the fundamental processes in a free society—education—and politicians performing at them are often given a pass on ideology or party or position, unless they introduce such matters into their speeches, which Chuck Schumer is careful never to do.

The new graduates and their parents know perfectly well that they're hearing a campaign speech for an election that won't happen until next November or the November after that, or, in the case of a senator, as many as five Novembers away. But, because of the occasion, few people seem to mind. Perhaps they also realize that, just like the shark—which never stops swimming because it begins to die the moment it is still in the water—politicians never stop campaigning. What matters to the audience isn't why that particular politician is there, but rather whether he or she is interesting. If the politician is just blowing smoke, people are annoyed and feel exploited; if the politician tells a good story well, people take it as part of the day's entertainment and feel fine.

Chuck Schumer, like most politicians who frequent commencements, always gives the same commencement speech. The introductory lines vary, but not the central narrative.

I've heard him give the speech six times now, most recently at the May 6, 2006, University at Buffalo commencement before an audience of 6000 new graduates and their families. When we were in the platform party robing room, forming a line to march into the arena, I said, "You're going to give that same speech again, aren't you?"

"Of course," he said.

"We're all going to recite it with you, Chuck," I said, waving toward the rest of the platform party.

"You've heard it before, Professor," he said cheerfully. "'They"— he pointed to the corridor through which we would shortly walk to reach the auditorium where the students and their families were— "haven't." I groaned. "But I've changed it," he said.

"I don't believe you," I said.

"I did. But people complained so I changed it back."

After some introductory bits about the school or town in question (his staff finds out the favorite student bar and pizza joint, which he names; if there's a local athletic team, he tosses that in as well), Chuck tells the graduates they will never make friends as good as the ones they are with now and says nice things about the parents (the 2006 UB graduation fell on Mother's Day, so he riffed on that). Then he tells The Story of Chuck.

The Story of Chuck, which never varies, goes like this: When Chuck Schumer graduated college, he had a scholarship that would provide him a year-long trip around the world, but he'd fallen in love so he declined the scholarship and stayed home while the girl spent the summer abroad. He never explains why he didn't go with her or why she didn't stay home with him. She came back, and he met her at the airport. "As soon as she got off the plane and I saw the expression on her face, I knew it was over. She dumped me before Labor Day. I made the wrong choice, and I paid for it with my heart and my head—no scholarship, no trip around the world, no girl."

Then he went to law school. When he got his degree, he decided that instead of going into a well-paying New York law firm, he wanted to do something that would give him satisfaction in life, so he ran for the New York State Assembly. He had three opponents— "the party machine candidate, a neighborhood activist, and my mother, who went around the district asking people to vote for anyone but her son." But he won, becoming, at twenty-three, the youngest person elected to the Assembly since Theodore Roosevelt. His advice to the graduates is, he says, "Go for it." In closing, he always reads Rudyard Kipling's "If," which ends as follows:

> If you can talk with crowds and keep your virtue,
> Or walk with kings—nor lose the common touch,
> If neither foes nor loving friends can hurt you;
> If all men count with you, but none too much,
> If you can fill the unforgiving minute
> With sixty seconds' worth of distance run,
> Yours is the Earth and everything that's in it,
> And—which is more—you'll be a Man, my son!

Six or seven years ago, he tried changing the last line to "you'll be an adult, my child," which was politically correct but awkward. He soon went back to Kipling's line, usually with a brief explanation that it, of course, replied to sons of whatever gender. For the University at Buffalo 2006 performance, he folded into his opening routine mention of the Buffalo Sabres hockey team, which a few nights before had won the quarter finals of the Stanley Cup playoffs. He waved a small, pink saber-toothed tiger, which he placed on the right side the lectern, and a small replica of the Stanley Cup, which he placed on the left side of the lectern—upside down. It's an easy mistake to make, since the Stanley Cup is small at the top and wide at the bottom, but it's a mistake few people in a hockey-crazed town like Buffalo would make, or miss when someone else made it. A professor of classics sitting next to me on the platform said, "He better fix that. He's inviting bad karma." A trustee passed a note to the university president telling him about the inverted icon and suggesting that he remedy it when he went up for the next part of the ceremony.

Several years earlier, Chuck had spoken of a bill he was going to introduce in Congress to make college tuition fully deductible for parents; this time he referred to the legislation "I passed" creating a $4000 tax deduction for college tuition. Basically, he just changed the verb tense for that part of the speech. Chuck does a riff on technological change that ends with "In 1993 when most of you were in elementary school, there were thirteen web sites on the World Wide Web. That's it: just thirteen. Today there are more than"—at which point he plugs in whatever his staff has found to be the current number of web sites. It was 80 million for the 2006 versions of the speech.

Many old hands in the platform party bring pieces to read during the boring parts of the commencement ceremony. You can't do that if you're in the front row, which is where university officials and honorees sit. But the TV cameras and the audience can't see what the deans and the SUNY distinguished professors in the second and third rows are looking at when they're looking down. The physician two seats to my left was reading a medical report; the classicist was listening to Shakespeare on his iPod; the literature professor to my right had the *Sunday Times Book Review*; I had my BlackBerry, on which I planned to do email and look at the *Times* headlines.

We were all, however, listening attentively during Chuck's speech, waiting for the parts we knew, looking for the variations and fresh bits. Occasionally we'd look at one another and nod or smile.

When he got to the end of the jilting story, most of us were saying the line along with him, but I noticed something I hadn't noticed previously: by the time he got to the third part, much of the audience had joined in too. Whether or not they had ever heard it before, they knew how the sentence had to end: "[N]o scholarship [pause], no trip around the world [pause], no GIRL." He'd drawn us all into his performance with that one line: the honorees, big shots and professors behind him, and a huge portion of the 9000 students and their families and friends in front of him.

When he finished the speech, Schumer turned and shook hands with University Council chairman Jeremy Jacobs and Provost Satish Tripathi. He beamed; he had his full Jack Horner face on. He was as obviously delighted with himself as he had been every other time I'd seen and heard him deliver the speech. He turned to the row behind him, beamed at us too, waved, and then turned again. Then, as he had done previous times, he hunched over and left the stage, as if no one would notice him going down the front steps in full view of everyone in the auditorium.

As Chuck had tried to tell me in the robing room, the people in front of the stage who hadn't heard the speech before loved it. The people on the stage, nearly all of whom had heard the speech before, also loved it—not because it was new but because it wasn't. They were appreciating this performance, just as people going to a concert adore that performance of a particular piece they know well.

Afterwards, at the lunch for the platform party, Chuck's speech came up again and again. People quoted it, recalled other performances, and told jokes about it and about his "I'm not really doing this" stage exit strategy. But they weren't angry jokes. Nobody minded.

I asked the university president, John Simpson, "Did you know Chuck was coming?"

"This time we did," he said, "but we always have a chair for him, just in case."

We were, in various ways, all participants in that performance of The Story of Chuck. It was as much a comfortable part of the day as the tunes the university band played while students and faculty marched in and out of the auditorium, and as the inflatable beach ball bounced from row to row as the names were read aloud and the graduates got to shake hands and be photographed with the president.

The ball rose and fell, sometimes disappearing briefly then rising again, moving, always moving. It was just like Chuck Schumer who was on his way to, or perhaps already at, another school's commencement. There he would give The Speech, changing only the names of the local bar and pizza parlor and athletic team. And if the school was in or around Buffalo, he would only have to change two of the three.

7 Commanding the Story

When storytellers are telling stories, they're active, fit for description: they're talking, fluttering their hands, moving about. Their listeners aren't so easy. With few exceptions, a storyteller can get to them only after the narrative moment is over, by which point they are themselves telling a story about an event in which they were among the listeners.

But there is no story—told, written, filmed, sung, or otherwise performed—without story listening, seeing, or reading. Every fiction writer, alone in a room, posits a reader or hearer. That, as Primo Levi says, is part of the fiction writer's art: the ability to tell a story and to imagine a responsive listener who is not there.[1]

Another part is imagining the response of the listener who is there, making the act of storytelling part of the story being told. No surprise in this: storytellers in any medium are aware of story listeners. Primo Levi's lines on the fiction writer's art are from a novel with two characters: the first-person narrator, who is a listener, and the talkaholic mechanic, to whom that narrator listens. Homer used that narrative relationship in the *Iliad*, as did Mary Shelley in *Frankenstein*, Dashiell Hammett in *The Maltese Falcon*, and William

Faulkner in *Absalom, Absalom!*, each of them in a different way and to a different end.

Iliad: The Worst Storyteller in Homer

The *Odyssey*'s Homer loves storytellers. Odysseus has a different identity and different story for nearly every person he meets. The four books he spends in Phaeacia, telling Arete and Alcinous about his marvelous adventures, is perhaps the most fabulous first-person narrative of antiquity. In book 1, Mentes (really Athena in disguise) tells Telemachus that years ago Odysseus visited his father, the king of the Taphians, to get poison for his arrows. Nestor and Menelaus tell Telemachus about their adventures getting home, Helen tells the story of the Trojan Horse, Penelope tells Odysseus the story of how she kept the suitors at bay by weaving and unweaving the shroud for Laertes, Odysseus' father. Even the dead tell stories: Agamemnon tells Odysseus the story of his own death, and Amphimedon, one of the dead suitors, tells Agamemnon the story of Penelope's weaving trick and the battle with Odysseus and Telemachus. There are more.

The stories told in the *Odyssey* are informational and instrumental. Some are told to get people to act: Odysseus's long tale, for example, is told to convince Arete to provide him a ship with which to get home, and Athena/Mentes' story of Odysseus's early travel is told to prod Telemachus to go off on his own journey. Some are informational for us as much as for the characters: Agamemnon telling Odysseus about his murder and Menelaus telling Telemachus about his encounter with the Old Man of the Sea. And some are ostensibly told for entertainment but become important plot elements: the performance of the Phaeacian minstrel Demodocus moves Odysseus to tears and sets the stage for his own narrative.

But Homer's other great epic, the *Iliad*, has only one storyteller: Phoenix, an old man who appears in the second part of book 9. He appears nowhere else in Homer, and he is never mentioned by any other character. Phoenix tells two stories, one about himself and the other about Meleager. He tells the stories to convince Achilles to return to the fighting. Unfortunately, he tells the stories so badly the results are exactly the opposite of what he intended.

The *Iliad* begins and ends with a ransom—for the living daughter of the priest Chryses in the first book and the dead son of the King Priam in the twenty-fourth. In the course of that first exchange, Agamemnon, leader of the Argive forces, ignites the wrath of Achilles. A plague has afflicted the Argive camp, and Agamemnon has no idea what to do. Achilles, the best of the Argive fighters, asks the seer Calchas what's wrong. Calchas says the plague is the result of Agamemnon's refusal to accept Chryses' offer of ransom for his daughter, Chryseis. In a rage, Agamemnon accuses Calchas of always giving him bad news. He insults Achilles for asking Calchas's advice, and then says he'll return Chryseis to her father. If he's going to lose a female toy, though, he'll get a replacement: Achilles' captive, Briseis.

Agamemnon violates almost every principle of leadership and makes a farce of the reason the Argives have been fighting the Trojans. They've come to Troy to get Helen, wife of Agamemnon's brother Menelaus, who was taken by force from her home by the Trojan prince Paris. Here Agamemnon is committing the same misdeed: taking by force a woman from Achilles. Agamemnon is the leader of the forces, but he never thinks—as a good leader would—to go to the seer for advice. He leaves that task to someone else. When he doesn't like the seer's advice, he insults his best fighter. Agamemnon and his brother and the other kings have come because they have an agreement about Helen dating back to her wedding. The younger fighters are there only for plunder. Briseis was one of Achilles' payments, and here is Agamemnon taking back what he'd given. In a few lines Homer lets us see him failing in the secular, sacred, interpersonal, and military realms.

Achilles is ready to kill Agamemnon on the spot, but the goddess Athena stays his hand. The gods in Homer meddle in human affairs, but their meddling usually gets people to act the way they'd act anyway. Achilles is angry, but he is the son of a king and is aware that regicide is a major offense. In the Greek calculus, Achilles has cause to be angry at Agamemnon, but not sufficient cause to kill him. (This situation is pushed to its extreme in *The Libation Bearers*:

Orestes is bound to kill his father's murderer, but the murderer is his mother, so the requisite revenge involves matricide and regicide. He is in what prisoners in Texas call a "switch": whatever he does, he loses. Athena has to invent the jury to resolve the issue in *The Eumenides*; the resolution comes from outside.) For Achilles, reason triumphs over rage. Athena, the goddess who stays Achilles' hand, has two primary functions—reason and war—and both are in play here.

He withdraws from the battle, vowing to put his Myrmidon soldiers on their long ships and head for home. For seven books, the battle rages back and forth with large battles, small battles, even individual combat between Menelaus and Paris that Aphrodite interrupts by whisking Paris back to Helen's bedroom before Menelaus can hurt him. Events are going so badly for the Argives that, in the first part of book 9, Nestor argues that Agamemnon should send an embassy to Achilles' tent to ask him to return to the war. Agamemnon agrees, saying that he never intended any of this, rather it was *ate*, or madness, that made him do it. Which is to say, he did it, but he's not actually responsible for it.

In Homer, anger alone does not explain or justify impaired judgment. Quite the contrary: anger is seen as volitional, but *ate* comes from without; it is a state one endures and for which one usually pays, but it is not a state one selects or discards at will. On numerous occasions, Achilles and Agamemnon are asked to "give over" their anger; no one is ever asked to give over his *ate*. One is responsible for the consequences of one's *ate*, but not for the fact of it. Anger is another matter entirely. As the embassy to Achilles will reveal, there is in Homer a profound logic to anger.

Agamemnon prepares an offer he hopes Achilles cannot refuse. There will be lavish gifts now: as much plunder as Achilles wishes should they win the war. Furthermore, if they get home, Agamemnon will give Achilles his choice of his three daughters in marriage without a bride price, and for dowry he will bestow on the couple seven wealthy and well-populated cities.

Odysseus, Phoenix, and Aias, along with two heralds, go to the Myrmidon camp to present the offer of reconciliation. They find

Achilles in his tent, strumming his lyre and singing songs of fame. Achilles listens to Odysseus' listing of Agamemnon's promised gifts and then tells him the offer is meaningless: he has already seen Agamemnon take back gifts given in the field, and he's the one getting the plunder anyway because Agamemnon doesn't do much fighting. More important, there is a prophecy that if he received glory in Troy he would die there, but if he received no glory he would go home and live to a ripe old age. If he reenters the war, his only permanent prize will be death. Achilles' response is followed by Phoenix who makes his argument with two stories, the first of which is about himself.

Phoenix's mother urged him to seduce the mistress of Amyntor, his father, so the girl would turn against the older man. When Amyntor learned of the affair, he asked the Furies to make sure Phoenix never has children of his own. The request was granted. Phoenix decided to murder his father, but his anger was checked when he considered his reputation: he did not want to be known as a parricide.

Phoenix isn't very bright: who but a dolt would seduce his father's mistress to make his mother happy and then expect a happy family after it's all over? There isn't even the usual intimation of meddling by the gods or claim that *ate* made him do it. The mother and son considered only the young woman's response—she would be so much happier with a younger man that she would abandon the older one—but neither gave thought to the older man's passion and pride. They made Agamemnon's error. Sterile young Phoenix eventually flees his home and gets refuge from Achilles' father, Peleus, who makes him nursemaid and trainer to young Achilles.

Phoenix uses the story to show that it's not good to anger powerful men. From Achilles' point of view, however, Phoenix has the wrong powerful man in mind: Phoenix wants Achilles to identify with Phoenix himself, but Achilles identifies with the father. Phoenix means his story to weaken Achilles' resolve by showing the price of anger, but it reinforces Achilles' resolve by demonstrating the utility and potency of appropriate anger. Young Phoenix insulted his father in a profound way. He usurped the older man's position and, thereby, brought down Amyntor's wrath; he dishonored a man to whom he owed significant respect. Amyntor's curse worked perfectly, and at this point, Achilles likes to hear about curses by dishonored men, which worked perfectly. Amyntor limited his anger; he didn't kill his son the moment he found out. Likewise Achilles didn't kill Agamemnon the moment he was shamed by him.

Then Phoenix tells the story of Meleager, who was angered, refused to fight to help his city, was promised great rewards, entered the battle because of those promised rewards, but didn't get them. The people who promised the rewards were annoyed that Meleager had forced them to offer him rewards. The Meleager narrative is garbled and rambling, clumsy in a way matched by none of the narrators in the *Odyssey*. Like Phoenix's first story, this narrative misses the point: Agamemnon has already taken back a prize awarded to Achilles; now he's making grand promises about what he'll do in the future. As an incentive to act now, Phoenix tells the story of a man almost exactly in Achilles' position who does what Agamemnon is asking him to do—and who gets nothing for it.

Phoenix's narratives fail perfectly. In the first, Achilles identifies with the king rather than the foolish son; in the second, Achilles hears a story about a hero not given a promised reward rather than the cost of waiting too long before accepting an offer. Homer is acutely aware that sometimes our stories produce exactly the opposite of the intended result. It's not only important to tell stories well, it's also important to tell the right story at the right time to the right person.

Frankenstein: The Believable Absurd

(Mary Shelley uses three narrative voices to tell *Frankenstein*:)

the explorer Robert Walton's in his letters to his sister, Frankenstein's in his conversations with Walton, and the creature's in his conversation with Frankenstein as Frankenstein reports that conversation to Walton. The most lucid of the three is also the most improbable: the long first-person autobiographical account, a fifth of the novel, told by the creature.

Hardly anyone questions the creature's story of how he acquired language, his ability to read and write, and his familiarity with technology. Shelley embeds his narrative within the other two. The effect is rather like what they say about a frog in a pan of water over a fire: if you increase the heat slowly, the frog never notices what is happening, even to the point of death. Shelley moves us farther and farther from the ordinary. By the time we are reading about the utterly fantastic and improbable, we don't notice it at all; we only notice the conflict between the characters, which is why the novel works so well.

The novel begins with four letters—dated December 11, March 17, July 17 and August 19—from Robert Walton to his sister back in England about his attempt to reach the North Pole to study magnetism. Presumably, the first three letters are given to ships sailing south, or they're posted at ports where Walton's ship stops for supplies. The August 19 letter cannot be mailed because by the time he writes it, he is beyond civilization and in a world of Arctic ice.

Everything he writes seems reasonable enough. He's a rich young man off on an ambitious expedition to a place no one knows. The novel is set in an unspecified year in the eighteenth century. In Shelley's time, as in antiquity, people thought that once you got past the Arctic ice the world turned tropical. It would be more than a century before the first European reached the North Pole and told people back home what a brutal clime it was, that it just kept getting colder all the way up.

In the fourth letter Walton tells of picking up a man stranded on the ice, which also seems reasonable enough. He then reports the story the stranger, Frankenstein, told him about his creation of and relationship with the creature. If the story had begun in Frankenstein's voice, we might have dozens of questions, we might cavil at what was obviously left out ("How did you DO it?"), but we're getting the story via Walton. If any questions are to be asked, they are to be asked by Walton, not us. Walton is a firewall protecting Frankenstein's plausibility. Frankenstein talks in his own voice for ten chapters, then we get the creature's story. It is embedded in Frankenstein's story, long past the point where we ask questions about technical possibilities. The creature talks for six chapters, then Frankenstein picks up the narrative for another eight.

After that, Walton resumes his unfinished letter to his sister with passages dated August 26, September 2, September 5, September 7, and September 12. Walton reports Frankenstein's death and his own encounter with the creature. With that, the two embedded narratives are grafted and ratified; nothing in them is questionable because the most trustworthy and ordinary narrator in the book sees the creature with his own trustworthy and ordinary eyes.

The stories, folded in upon and wrapped around one another, become mutually validating. The epistolary frame is a common convention and easily accepted. We don't question the most fantastic part not because it is believable, but because by the time we encounter it we are at home with the narrative.

The Maltese Falcon: The Flitcraft Story

The narrative voice in Dashiell Hammett's *The Maltese Falcon* belongs to an omniscient narrator who explains nothing and who, with one exception, tells us nothing that the central character, Sam Spade, doesn't see and hear. Hammett's narrator never goes inside the consciousness of Spade or any of the other characters. The novel occurs completely on the surface of Sam Spade's world, and Sam is present for everything that happens in it. The only information that could not be provided equally well by Sam are the few brief descriptions of Sam's facial expressions.

Near the end of novel, Sam tells Brigid O'Shaunessey, the woman who involved him in the search for the Falcon, that he intends to turn her over to the police for the murder of his partner Miles Archer. She asks how could he, isn't he in love with her? He says he probably is, but other factors weigh more heavily: as a professional detective he's obligated to do something about the murder of his partner; only by turning her over can he convince the police he wasn't involved with Caspar Gutman, Joel Cairo, and Wilmer in their nefarious plots. Most important, he doesn't know when she'll decide he's no longer useful and will kill him or have him killed. She argues that love should be enough to assuage those doubts. They embrace, the police arrive, and he hands her over.

John Huston used Hammett's dialog almost verbatim for that scene, as he did for most of the movie. Houston did amend the ending. The novel ends with Sam in his office, his secretary Effie Perrine angry at him for having handed Brigid over to the police, and Miles's widow, Iva (with whom Sam had an affair before the action of the novel starts), about to come in to give him a hard time. The film ends with Brigid and Lieutenant Dundy going down in the small elevator. Sam and his detective friend Tom Polhaus stand in the corridor and watch them descend.

Tom, holding the enamel-covered lead figure of the falcon, says, "Heavy. What is it?"

"The stuff that dreams are made of," Sam says. (Huston said that Sam's Shakespearean response was Humphrey Bogart's idea.)

"Huh?" Tom says, as the two begin walking down the stairs. Music up and fade out.

Huston made two other important changes. He deleted an episode involving the daughter of Casper Gutman. Her function in the novel was to send Sam on a wild goose chase, which Huston does more economically (in terms of film time) with a telephone call.

He also omitted a long story Sam tells Brigid soon after one of the many times he catches her lying to him. The story occurs about a third of the way through the novel. It is about a man named Flitcraft whom Spade encountered years earlier when he worked for a detective agency in the Northwest. Huston may have dropped it from the script because Brigid has virtually no reaction to it, and it is never mentioned or alluded to again in the novel. Even if it had figured dramatically, he very well might have dropped it because the telling takes six or seven minutes, without any pauses, an eternity in screen time, and that would have stopped the plot dead in its tracks.

(Print is different. Print permits digression. Print has parentheses, such as the pair we're within now. Print lets you set things down for later reference. Fiction and film are both linear experiences, but they're not the same kind of linear experiences. Parentheses in film are usually disjunctive or gags, such as the famous scene in François Truffaut's *Shoot the Piano Player* when the gangster says to the kidnapped boy, "If I'm lying may my mother drop dead," whereupon there is a small insert in the upper right corner of the screen showing a motherly woman in a kitchen suddenly flopping to the floor. The experience of a film is always in real time: a two-hour movie takes two hours, though it may feel longer or shorter depending on the editing and the story and everything else. A three-hundred-page novel can take as long as you like, and you can easily go back to a whole section or a single sentence. Few of us read novels at a single sitting: real life interrupts our immersion in long fiction. Authors of fiction and essays can better afford digressions and explanations than directors of films.)

Sam begins the story with no introduction. His voice is level throughout, "though now and then he repeated a sentence lightly rearranged, as if it were important that each detail be related exactly as it happened."[2]

Sam is a detective and getting the facts right is the heart of his business. At first, Brigid is hardly interested, Hammett tells us, "her curiosity more engaged with his purpose in telling the story than with the story he told." But then "it caught her more and more fully and she became still and receptive."[3]

Flitcraft had abandoned his family, job, and house in Tacoma and had set up an almost identical life in Spokane. In Tacoma he had a real estate office, did well financially, had a wife and two young sons, played golf at four in the afternoon; in Spokane he had an automobile business, had a wife and one young son, played golf at four in the afternoon.

He tells Spade he rearranged his life because one day he was almost hit by a falling beam at a construction site and realized that what he thought was an orderly world was instead an absurd world, a world in which beams could fall at any moment. Before the beam fell, "The life he knew was a clean orderly responsible affair. Now a falling beam had shown him that life was fundamentally none of those things. He, the good citizen-husband-father, could be wiped out between office and restaurant by the accident of a falling beam.

He knew then that men died at haphazard like that, and lived only while blind chance spared them."[4]

Flitcraft made an inference: "Life could be ended for him at random by a falling beam: he would change his life at random by simply going away. He loved his family, he said, as much as he supposed was usual, but he knew he was leaving them adequately provided for, and his life for them was not of the sort that would make absence painful."[5]

Flitcraft traveled for a while, then settled in Spokane. "His second wife didn't look like the first," Sam tells Brigid, "but they were more alike than they were different."[6]

Then no more beams fell, and Flitcraft reconstituted his old life. He went back to being what he always had been, only in a new place. "He wasn't sorry for what he had done. It seemed reasonable enough to him. I don't think he even knew he had settled back naturally into the same groove he had jumped out of in Tacoma. But that's the part of it I always liked. He adjusted himself to beams falling, and then no more of them fell, and he adjusted himself to them not falling."

Brigid reacts to the story with three words—"How perfectly fascinating"—then changes subject and mood: she moves close to Sam, her eyes are open wide, and she toys with a button on his coat.

Sam says to her, "Don't let's confuse things. You don't have to trust me, anyhow, as long as you can persuade me to trust you."[7]

Brigid should have listened more and coquetted less. The Flitcraft story undergirds Sam's decision to hand her over to the police for murder at the end of the novel. It's not a story about the vagaries of the world; that's Flitcraft's story. Sam tells it because it's a story about the constancy of character. Flitcraft exemplifies Spade's belief that people return to what they really are once the extraordinary recedes, and, therefore, it suggests the likelihood that Brigid will betray and possibly even murder him should it ever seem useful to her to do so. Sam tells her that in a few lines in the final chapter, but this long narrative told much earlier in the novel is his theoretical underpinning.

Sam's theory for knowing what people are going to do is grounded in this narrative: he knows what people are going to do because most of the time, they do what they did last time. He's rarely surprised in this novel, and nobody surprises him twice, including Brigid O'Shaunessey.

This is like the story Athena/Mentes tells Telemachus in book 1 of the *Odyssey* about Odysseus having gotten poison for his arrows many years earlier. Nothing more is made of this incident in the poem—but in the great battle scene with the suitors in book 22, every arrow shot is fatal. It's not as if Homer thought arrows were always deadly: in the *Iliad* only some arrows kill. The difference is the poison tips, about which Homer says nothing after that brief redaction by Mentes. If you remember from book 1, you know why the arrows in book 22 are so deadly; if you don't remember book 1, then, well, they're well-aimed arrows. The same is true of Sam's list of reasons for turning Brigid over to the police in chapter 20 of *The Maltese Falcon*. The list makes sense on its own, but the reason Sam is impervious to Brigid's argument about love is explained in the Flitcraft narrative, back in chapter 7. She heard the story he told, but she didn't know what the story was saying, and that, too, is part of her character and why Sam hands her over.

Documentary filmmaker Frederick Wiseman is often asked if he is concerned about people acting, posing before his camera. He always says no, that if people are going to act, the characters they'll play are just exaggerated versions of the characters they know best: themselves.

When Sam hands Brigid over it is indeed for all the reasons he spells out for her. But it is mostly because she is what she is: liar, thief, and killer. He gives us the rationale for that not in an abstract discussion, but rather in a story that he doesn't gloss in terms of her world at all. It's out there, not just for her to hear, but for her to respond to. She doesn't respond to it. She doesn't get it. She immediately plays the seductive girl and turns to her own concerns. The story is not only the rationale for his final action with her; it is also one of the tests that prove him right.

Absalom, Absalom! Whom Can You Trust?

William Faulkner's *Absalom, Absalom!* is, on first reading, the story of Thomas Sutpen, a man who wanted to found a dynasty but lost everything to fratricide, incest, and murder. Most of the story is told to Harvard-bound Quentin Compson by his father, Jason Compson III, and a spinster named Rosa Coldfield, who was Sutpen's sister-in-law. Nearly everything the elder Compson and Rosa Coldfield tell Quentin has been told to them by other people. Part of Quentin's knowledge of the story is presented to us in dialogue: we read his direct quotations to his Harvard roommate, a Canadian named Shreve McCannon, several months after the novel begins. The most important parts of the story of Thomas Sutpen and of the novel are imagined by Quentin and Shreve in their Cambridge room.

Thus, we are told a great deal about the life and career of Thomas Sutpen, but very little of what we are told is certain. Faulkner relates hardly any of the novel in the one fictive voice we can usually trust—the third-person omniscient author. Nearly the entire novel is quoted or reported narrations by characters we can't trust at all: the angry and vengeful spinster (Rosa Coldfield), a man in the process of drinking himself to death (Jason Compson III), the drunk's obsessive son who will commit suicide a few months after the action of the novel ends (Quentin Compson, whose suicide takes place in the second section of *The Sound and the Fury*), and a Canadian (Shreve MacKenzie) who has no primary knowledge of any of the action and who has never been within a thousand miles of where the action took place, but who nevertheless vigorously makes up some of the key parts of Sutpen's story in the course of a late-night, winter conversation in an unheated Harvard dorm room. The spinster, the drunk, and the future-suicide include in their narrations stories told to them by other people. Much of the narrated information reaches us second- and thirdhand.

Do we take what each of the characters say as true? Then *Absalom, Absalom!* is a novel about a dynasty that never happened.

Do we take what each character says as truer about the characters themselves than the stories they are telling? Then it's a novel about how several people of varying degrees of unreliability create a story of Thomas Sutpen to fit their own needs, which means it is a novel about people telling, creating, manipulating, and utilizing stories rather a novel about Thomas Sutpen. Read one way, *Absalom, Absalom!* is about Thomas Sutpen; read another, it is about Quentin Compson.

The genius of the novel is that both possibilities exist at once, all the way through; Faulkner never loses control of the double narrative. *Absalom, Absalom!* is like the famous trick drawing that is two faces or a vase, which depends on how you look at it and what you're thinking at that moment. It's not just either of those things; it's both of them. The only difference is your perception.

Phoenix's wrong story is told to the wrong person. Frankenstein's creature's improbable autobiography works only because it is told to a listener we trust who is embedded in the narrative of a listener far easier for us to trust. Sam Spade's disregarded Flitcraft parable has meaning only when we realize that the person to whom Sam tells it doesn't listen to it as carefully as we do. Thomas Sutpen's unknowable life takes shape only in refraction through stories told, heard, retold, and reheard. In each of these, as in the stories we tell one another, meaning is predicated on both the utterance and the reception.

Remember Italo Calvino's Kublai Khan in *Invisible Cities* asking the young Marco Polo, "When you return to the West, will you tell your people the same tales you tell me?"

Marco Polo replies, "It is not the voice that commands the story, it is the ear."[8]

All stories are collaborative, either in the moment (all stories told to or performed for people in the storyteller's physical range) or serial (all stories in which the listeners or watchers experience the story after the storyteller has wrapped it up—a film, a novel, a story on the evening news). That collaboration, whether momentary or serial, can be repeated, but the character of it is never the same

because we are never the same And that is why we can, with pleasure and engagement, experience again and again the novels or
movies that speak to us most, or tell and listen to, year after year,
those family stories that never, miraculously, get dull.

II   Public Stories

*Facts and truth really don't have
very much to do with one another.*

—WILLIAM FAULKNER

8 Stories That Don't Make Sense

[I]t's in a story's Ending that its author pays (or fails to pay) his narrative/dramatic bills. Through Beginning and Middle the writer's credit is good so long as we're entertained enough to keep turning the pages. But when the story's action has built to its climax and started down the steep and slippery slope of denouement, every line counts, every word, and ever more so as we approach the final words. All the pistols hung on the wall in Act One, as Chekhov famously puts it, must be fired in Act Three. Images, motive, minor characters—every card played must be duly picked up, the dramaturgical creditors paid off, or else we properly feel shortchanged on our investment of time and sympathy, the willing suspension of our disbelief.

JOHN BARTH, *On with the Story*

I've said several times now that stories are devices we use to make sense of things, or they're the verbal objects that articulate the sense we've made of them. That's true, but it's not the whole story. Not all stories make complete sense, and some stories don't make any sense at all.

Many years ago I got roped into being the adviser for an M.A. student whose thesis was a novel. I don't teach writing, and I didn't want to do this one, but her novel was about police and gangsters and the head of the writing program asked me to do it as a personal favor because, he said, "You know about that sort of thing."

The student didn't show me anything until the very end of the spring term when she delivered the entire manuscript. It was awful. The wooden dialogue was uttered by caricatures, and not one of the major plot points was motivated. Things just happened, unexplained and senseless, and her caricatures had to deal with them until something else equally unexplained and senseless came along, whereupon they shifted their attention to that.

I told her this, at more length and I hope with more delicacy and tact than I'm summarizing it here. She got mad at me anyway. She said I was an idiot. She said I didn't know what I was talking about. She said, "My husband's a cop. I got all those things from him. Every word in that manuscript is true!"

After a pause, I told her what fiction-writing teachers always tell their students: one key difference—maybe the key difference— between narrative fiction and real life is narrative fiction usually has to make sense but real life is under no such obligation. One event may follow another in real life, but only once in a great while will the relationship between the two be causal.

In most narrative fiction—written or oral, the kinds we read and write or the kinds we tell and hear—*because* (or some equivalent) must be there, explicitly or implicitly, or the story doesn't work, it doesn't have what we call "verisimilitude," the appearance of reality. To give the appearance of reality in fiction, we have to provide something that in reality is elusive and rare: connections that seem to make sense.

I say "seem" because sometimes in fiction we and the characters we're reading about think we know what's going on, but it turns out we're both wrong. In such novels as John Le Carré's *The Spy Who Came in from the Cold*, John Fowles's *The Magus*, or Faulkner's *Absalom, Absalom!* or any good piece of detective fiction, things make sense until new facts come into play and what we thought made sense wasn't at all right. Then the new situations in their turn are explained. It's a continuing condition of clarifying, muddying, and clarifying again until we get to the denouement, the point at which there are no further questions to be asked. In that, too, real life tends to be frustratingly deficient.

True Stories

On the seventeenth of December 1967, a Sunday, Harold Holt, the prime minister of Australia, was on holiday in the resort town of

Portsea, Victoria. He swam in the ocean. He was a good swimmer. He disappeared in the ocean. His body was never found. Australia got a new prime minister. That's it. No "becauses," no "therefores." He went into the water, and nobody ever saw him again. The prime minister of an entire continent was gone.

If you or I were writing a novel or a movie script in which the prime minister of an entire continent went into the ocean and didn't come out, we'd maybe have submarines and underwater spy swimmers making it happen. We've seen all the James Bond movies, so we know how such events can be handled. Perhaps we'd have as the prime minister's fishing companions people of dubious character or secret lovers of whatever gender. We wouldn't—couldn't—just have him go into the water and not come out of the water. Things like that—a major character disappearing on an innocent Sunday swim—don't just happen in movies or novels.

In real life, such things happen all the time. In January 1998, U.S. Congressman Sonny Bono, a very competent skier, died after he slammed into a tree on an ordinary day on a trail he knew very well. Unlike Michael Kennedy who died the same way a week earlier, there was no ski patrol person to testify that the deceased had been playing ski football after having been warned that the slope was too icy and, therefore, too dangerous for such frivolity. Bono, so far as we know, was just skiing downhill. Why did he collide with the tree? No one knows. An accident, it just happened.

Sometimes there's enough information to posit a comfortable story. William E. Colby, retired director of the CIA, came up missing when he was canoeing alone in the fall of 1995. Colby's body was found a few days later. The autopsy showed no evidence of foul play, and the coroner opined that he'd suffered a heart attack and had fallen into the water. It wasn't a perfect explanation, but neither was it sloppy enough to excite the conspiracy theorists, especially since Colby was retired and presumably hors de combat. Unlike the bodiless Holt story, Colby's had closure and seemed to make sense. Unlike the senseless Bono story, there was an explanation.

When we can't figure out the plot in real life, people say, "It's senseless, just senseless." And that may be true; it may be senseless.

Sense is a product of our intelligence, not a condition of the world. But few of us are satisfied with "it's senseless" as an explanation. We want bottom lines. We want villains and conspiracies and plots like those in movies and novels; we want to live in a causal universe, a universe in which things make sense.

How do we make sense of Lee Harvey Oswald—who before November 22, 1963, was as insignificant a person as one might imagine—murdering John F. Kennedy? One way is by enveloping him in opulent plots (as in Mark Lane's *Rush to Judgment* and Oliver Stone's *JFK*) or documenting his life in a thousand pages of micro-detail (as in Norman Mailer's *Oswald*) or folding him into a 900-page government report (*Report of the President's Commission on the Assassination of President Kennedy*, better known as "The Warren Commission Report").

Sometimes we shift responsibility away from the secular: "God called him home" and "It was God's will." I think the power of the Book of Job is in the idea that when preposterous and undeserved things happen there is a reason, even if that reason is nothing more substantial than God and Satan, who though omniscient, conduct an empirical study to resolve their argument about the human heart. As the story reveals, they don't seem to know it as well as one might have hoped. When Job asks why he allowed all those abominations to occur, God responds with non sequiturs: Where was Job when the earth was being made? Do Death's Portals open for him? Can he control the heavenly constellations? Could he have made and controlled Leviathan? Job gets the point: God is real, and his reasons are beyond ours. That's all the explanation Job needs or is going to get.

People who live in what anthropologists used to call "primitive societies" believe the world is perfectly causal: things happen because someone or something makes them happen. The closest mindsets to that of primitive thinking are found, perhaps, in paranoid-schizophrenics and scientists. For both groups, all things are presumed to have a logical explanation. For both, the fact that we can't figure out why X happened means only that we haven't uncovered who or what was responsible. Paranoids always have perfect stories for why things happen. If scientists don't have one, they're looking.

For the scientist, our inability to explain random or gratuitous events resides in the inadequacy of our science rather than the irresponsibility or silliness of nature. Einstein famously said, "I cannot believe that God would choose to play dice with the universe." Not that God couldn't do it, only that he couldn't believe that God would do it. The belief in a rational universe is the bedrock of all scientific inquiry.

How can you study science if you don't believe that if you research long and diligently enough you'll be rewarded with an explanation? Chaos Theory specifically seeks to provide order for disorder, logic for the random. I know no scientist who will tolerate the final answer "It's unknowable." They can live with "I don't know," which is for them just a transient condition.

Scientists' answers are presented as stories: "Here's what I did in the lab from beginning to end; here's the plot in which the facts I found seem to fit." Henri Korn, who was for a long time director of research in neurobiology at Institut Pasteur in Paris, told me that facts are just clutter until he fits them into a narrative that makes some kind of sense, that goes from here to there. A research scientist gathers discrete bits of data and notices that some do not fit the current theory, the story. At first the odd bits are somebody's fault: someone copied the results incorrectly, did not wash the test tube thoroughly, didn't zero the measuring instruments. After a point, the discrepant data can no longer be ignored or dismissed or explained away, and there's a scramble for a new narrative or theory that incorporates everything.

"All theories tell a story," wrote Roald Hoffman in *American Scientist* (2005):[1]

> They have a beginning, in which people and ideas, models, molecules and governing equations take the stage. Their roles are defined; there is a puzzle to solve. Einstein sets his characters

into motion so ingeniously, using entropy to tease out the parallels between moving molecules and the energy of light. The story develops; there are consequences of Einstein's approach. And at the end, his view of light as quantized and particular confronts the reality of the heretofore unexplained photoelectric effect. The postscripted future, of all else that can be understood and all new things that can be made, is implicit. . . .

A young man of 25, Einstein had mastered the old stories. In this paper, "On a Heuristic Point of View Concerning the Production and Transformation of Light,"[2] he combined the ways others looked at the world, and trusting analogy as much as mathematics, made something new. Science is an inspired account of the struggle by human beings to understand the world. Changing it in the process. How could this be anything but a story?

The Place of Stories

Stories, as I said earlier, are how we know and how we learn. Stories are forms into which scattered or new pieces of information are poured so they can make sense. A friend who did ethnographic research among Eskimos told me that when new things happen, the Eskimos regularly look for a traditional story that's sort of like what just happened, and they interpret change in terms of that old story.

Stories central to the culture don't have to be told all at once to make sense. A Yoruba or a Cree could tell a story about the trickster spider Anansi or Coyote and the tribal listeners could appreciate it, not just because of the immediate details and performance characteristics of that recitation, but because nearly everyone in the audience knows the stories, facts, and characters already. The stories are protean, cumulative, alive. You don't have to explain why Anansi or Coyote does something that seems nonsensical—it makes sense because the listener knows about Anansi or Coyote from other stories. It's similar to our knowing what to expect from the traveling salesman joke or the one about the Irishman, Jew, and Black in a rowboat. Cultural categories are all in place before the finish of the first sentence.

Members of a group—family, tribe, platoon, private club—share a mass of information, so a name or reference that is meaningless or opaque to an outsider conjures up for the insider a congeries of relationships. To an outsider this myth or folktale or anecdote may make little or no sense, but that's how we know who's an outsider and who isn't: outsiders are the people to whom we have to explain the things everybody who is one of us already knows.

Stories Told in Pieces

Popular stories—stories so long and various they seem without beginning or end—may also belong to a group. I know people who talk about characters in soaps as if they had been together for lunch or had gone to the same prom. In 1979 on death row in Texas, I met men who would not leave their cells for a rare visit when *As the World Turns* was on. The late literary critic Leslie Fiedler wouldn't have missed a daily episode of *The Guiding Light*, and fierce and fearless culture critic Camille Paglia had the same relationship to *The Young and the Restless*. Diane and I will not miss the HBO series *The Sopranos*.

A friend who had a role in one soap for fourteen years told me strangers frequently talked to her as if she were the character she played:

Hollywood actors [she said], people talk to them because they're stars. They say, "Hey, Dustin Hoffman," not "Hey Tootsie." Soap actors, people talk to us because we're X, Y, or Z. They think they know me, and in a way they do, because they're not talking to me as a person, they're talking to that character I play. If they miss a week or a month they can come right back in because they know us as family. Whatever X has done for the time you missed, she's still X, the same way you know cousin Charlotte even if you haven't seen her for ten years. Character is the core of what we do.

Some events are so drawn out or so big it is impossible to deal with them as stories, so they take on the character of a frame. We don't tell the story of it so much as it is the place where we find stories to tell. Nobody reports a war; we report what happened in that village on that morning to those people.

CNN broadcast round-the-clock coverage of the 2003 Iraq War. Reports poured forth all day, but it was episodic and often contradictory. Wolf Blitzer, CNN's primary on-air anchor, often spent long periods repeating what had just been said, trying to parse sense or broader meaning from fragments of detail. He was rarely successful. The most interesting bits of coverage were the small, separate stories that had their own coherence, framed as stories by reporters in the field.

Framing applies equally well to fiction: twenty-two of the twenty-four books of Homer's *Iliad* deal with a week in the tenth year of the Trojan War. Soaps and long wars are worlds of perpetual middle. That's what reporting from Vietnam and Kosovo was like, and it's what reporting about the O. J. Simpson trial and the Clinton impeachment became.

The physicist Richard Feynman liked to talk about how busy the universe was. He said it's only because our human physical sensors were so limited that we were unaware of how much was going on constantly around us. Spaces like the one in which I'm writing, and the one in which you're reading swarms with invisible activity. In addition to cosmic rays, ground radiation, body heat, and sound vibrations, we're surrounded by signals for radio and TV stations, cellular phone calls, beepers, and other activity about which we know nothing. If we could see and hear all the supervisual and subsonic waves, they would blind and deafen us. It doesn't happen like that. The stuff we don't want might as well not be there. When we do want it, we just turn on our radio or TV set or beeper or cell phone, and we are tuned in and in touch.

That's what a long-running story is like. We tune in when we want it; we tune out when we don't. The story is there, we know it's there, we know it when we see it, we know the characters that populate it, we know where to find it, and we enter and exit at will.

O.J.

In our culture most people probably get more stories from the print and electronic press than anywhere else. The story the American popular print and electronic press focused on more than any other from 1995 to 1997 had to do with legal events occasioned by the June 12, 1994, murders of Nicole Brown Simpson and Ron Goldman in Brentwood, California. Three related events taught me how deeply the O. J. story was embedded in public consciousness:

- The first occurred one morning before the trial started when I was home when the mail came. Our mailman, Don, and I almost never encounter one another. When we do, the conversations are about something for which I have to sign or the Buffalo winter. That winter morning, he was putting mail in the through-the-wall milk box we use for a mail drop. We looked at one another through the rectangles and Don said, "So whaddaya think?" "Guilty as hell," I said. "Goddamned right," Don said.
- The second was a few weeks later, at the beginning of the spring semester. I walked into the first meeting of a new class of forty-eight undergraduate students, only a few of whom had I ever met before, and said, "Guilty?" Almost every hand went up. "Not guilty?" Four or five hands went up. "Undecided?" Maybe ten hands went up, all of them people who had voted previously.
- The third was a month or so into O. J.'s trial when my wife and I went to dinner with two friends, Bruno Freschi and Vaune Ainsworth. On the short walk from the car to the restaurant, I heard Vaune (a clinical psychologist) say to Diane (a university English professor), "I hate that new hairdo. I didn't see any reason for that new hairdo. It's just giving in, don't you think?" Although Vaune was talking about prosecutor Marcia Clark's most recent makeover, she never said, and Diane felt no need to ask.

Every time Clark got a new outfit or changed her hair-
style, it was covered in detail by both print and television
reporters.

In none of the three encounters did any of us specifically name,
or need to name, the O.J. trial. Simpson's trial was one of our major
stories.

Two years later the Clinton impeachment trial, which went on
for a full year, produced the same phenomenon. Would anyone, in
the United States in 1988 or 1989, have needed to ask "Monica who?"

Judge Lance Ito said several times at the beginning of the O.J.
trial that all the key players would be searching for the truth. Judges
say that sort of thing. Nearly all of the lawyers in the O.J. case said
something similar to the jury and in interviews. I doubt any of them
believed it. Trials are about winning, not truth, and the instrument
of winning is the development of a plausible story. The defense attorney's job is to screw up the narrative the prosecutor puts before
the jury in his opening statement and summation. "In every jury
trial," writes Sam Schrager in his excellent study of trials as performances, *The Trial Lawyer's Art* (1999), "the attorneys construct rival
stories from testimony and evidence whose meaning is unclear. A
trial is a competition over the framing of this ambiguous material:
how should the jury interpret the testimony and evidence? And it is
also a competition over the authority of the lawyers: *whose* account
of the meaning of this material deserves to be believed?" (emphasis
in the original).[3]

Usually, criminal cases are about actions none of the people in
the courtroom would do. They've seen characters in movies and
television rape, murder, and steal; they've read in newspapers about
people who have; the person in the dock has been accused of such
crimes—but the jurors have neither done nor probably would ever
do them. Neither have or would the attorneys, the bailiffs, or the
judge. We may swipe a pen from the office, but we won't hold up a
bank. We may fantasize about an erotic encounter with an attractive

stranger, but we won't engage in such activity or want it at knife-point in a darkened hallway. The idea doesn't occur to us or if it does, it's like all those other transient fantasies that never get past our first censor.

So juries aren't just sitting there trying to decide if X committed that crime. They're trying to decide whether the prosecutor's story about how and why X did it makes sense. If the prosecutor's story works for them, X gets indicted by the grand jury and convicted by the trial jury. If X did it but has an acceptable reason why—that is, if his *because* makes sense and is also legal—X will probably go free. And if the prosecutor's story doesn't make any sense at all to the jury, X will surely go free. X doesn't even have to come up with a counterstory.

Five Situations in Which It Is Okay to Tell Stories That Don't Make Sense

My granddaughter Leah, then about twenty-eight months old, telephoned and said, "We're going to see you guys. We're going on an airplane. Daddy can't go. He's too big." Maybe her father said he was too busy to go, and she misheard and translated it as "too big." In any case, she and her mother were coming to Buffalo and Daddy wasn't, and the simple fact that he wasn't coming wasn't adequate. Leah needed a reason, something to make his absence make sense. For a girl of her age, bigness worked as well as anything else. She was doing something we all do nearly all the time: look for some causal factor that makes sense of the world.

I can think of only five situations in which it is permissible to tell stories that don't make sense, stories that openly violate the basic principle of storytelling so nicely expressed in the quotation from John Barth with which this chapter began. In these five situations, having holes in the narrative is permissible, even necessary; as are discordant parts or parts absolutely counterintuitive that must be accepted on faith:

One is *myth*. With myths, we accept the otherwise unacceptable because that's what myths are about and what they do. Myths are the stories we use to manage life and death and thunderstorms and tidal waves and winter. Every single one of them requires a leap of faith.

A second is stories told by *paranoid psychotics*. We accept psychotic disjunctions because—by definition—psychotics are adults who tell stories that make no sense to us. The stories told by paranoids have an internal lucidity based on a double premise of hostile intention and perfect causality: when bad things happen, it's because a malevolent person was behind it, and those malevolent persons are always at work on new bad things. The paranoid, like the primitive, envisions the world as perfectly orderly always. The true paranoid, psychologists like to point out, never lies. (The best film depiction I know of this is Ron Howard's 2001 film about Nobel laureate John Nash, *A Beautiful Mind*, based on Sylvia Nosair's 1998 book of the same title.) Curiously enough, the real danger for them may be reason: some psychologists think the most probable time for suicides by paranoids is when the delusional structure begins to crack.

A third kind of story that doesn't make sense is stories told by *very young children*. Very young children don't know how to make stories; they only know how to make sentences. Therefore, they can, in perfect comfort, utter incompatible sentences. I once listened to my granddaughter Leah when she was playing with her doll house. She was several characters. They spoke. She used voices: high-pitched, low-pitched, sweet, harsh. Sometimes what they said connected to something else said; sometimes it didn't (at least to me). I recognized some of the lines as having originated with her mother or with me or a character in her favorite videotape that month, *Aladdin*. There was no end; it just went on until she got hungry and went into the kitchen. Everything fits in little kids' narratives because there is no organic structure that keeps anything out. For that reason, as I noted earlier, they make excellent witnesses. When they learn how to tell ordinary stories (as we tell), they become unreliable witnesses (as we are).

A fourth is *dream*. Dream is a land where all rules of narrative and physics are suspended. In a dream, you can go to a public meeting or interview the president stark naked and no one but you will notice. A room can be full of people and, in an instant, empty of everyone but you. Most of the time, a dream is not screwy inside the dream; it gets bizarre only later, when we're outside, when we're in the land of the Awake. (I am fully dressed right now, right?)

The fifth place it is okay to tell fragmentary and contradictory stories is the *daily press*. Stories in the daily press are not bound by rules of external consistency; they are bound only by attribution and accuracy. What happened doesn't have to make sense. Only the reporting does. In the daily press, we don't have to explain or understand why Harold Holt disappeared, why Lee Harvey Oswald shot John Fitzgerald Kennedy, why movie executive David Begelman, with a salary in the millions, risked it all to skim a hundred thousand. People quoted in the news stories may speculate on the puzzlement, the contradictions, but the reporter has no obligation to resolve any of them. Contradictions in reported utterances extend rather than limit the reporter's story, since opposing statements are facts, just as the time the fire alarm was turned in or the train left the rails is fact. The reporter is obligated to include whatever "facts" seem to be of moment and not to tell any lies; the reporter is not obligated to reconcile the apparent facts or the contradictory utterances.

This obligation doesn't mean news reporting is by its very nature more objective than other narrating or writing. All of us are always busy selecting what we think matters: we hear some people better than others, we're more sensitive to some issues than we are to others, we have attitudes that help or get in the way of what we see and hear. But whatever its shortcomings, the daily press, perhaps more than any other venue, is the place where things are described, people get quoted, and there is no need to reconcile apparent irreconcilables.

The daily press is maybe the only place in which it is okay for conscious and sane grownups to tell stories in which nothing important is resolved or even explained. News stories are not private, as are dreams and psychotic utterances, and they are not formless, as are the protostories of children. Unlike myth, they are not responsible for providing connections among things that otherwise do not connect. And unlike the stories of court, they don't have to have a bottom line, a conclusion that can be accepted only at the exclusion of all other conclusions.

A student in my introductory humanities class wrote, "Our stories are the dots we use to connect the parts of our lives." She's onto something. Sometimes the lines connecting the dots produce a picture that is lucid and enlightening. Sometimes they produce what seems to be a scribble. Sometimes the dots don't connect at all. No matter. All our stories—senseless and sensible—do the work they're supposed to do: they help us deal with a world that cruelly refuses to provide us the *because* we so passionately desire and desperately need.

9 The Real O. J. Story

Family Feud

A few evenings after O. J. Simpson was arrested for the murders of his wife Nicole Brown Simpson and her friend Ron Goldman, a waiter at the Mezzaluna Restaurant in Brentwood, California, my wife Diane and I had dinner with our friends Bruno Freschi and Vaune Ainsworth at Just Pasta, a restaurant on Buffalo's West Side. Like nearly everyone else around here that summer, we talked about the murders and the preliminary hearing on probable cause, which was just beginning. O. J. had played for the Buffalo Bills in the seventies, and he was still a local hero. A lot of people here partied with O. J. in those glory years, or know people who partied with him, or had heard stories about people partying with O. J.

Bruno is an architect, so he spends a good deal of time moving pieces of information around, trying them out in different juxtapositions and combinations, making them big, making them small, seeing what seems to work and what doesn't. The two of us got to spinning scenarios that seemed consistent with what we then knew about the murders and O. J.'s movements. We came up with what we thought were three or four plausible narratives. We did not insist that these narratives were true or even likely—just plausible.

The first was the most obvious: the movie actor ex-husband finds the sexy ex-wife with a Hollywood hunk and in a jealous rage slaughters everything in sight, then rushes home, cleans up, and catches his plane to Chicago where, in his hotel room the next morning, he receives a phone call about the murders from the Los Angeles police and feigns shock.

Nearly everyone we knew was already repeating this scenario, so Bruno and I concentrated our imaginative plot-making energies on alternative narratives. We were playing with pieces, just like discovering the many different things you can make out of a fixed number of Erector Set or Lego pieces.

We were so deep in play that neither of us realized until it was far too late that Diane and Vaune were seething with anger. They were saying things like, "But you know he's guilty! We all know he's guilty! Why don't you admit that you know he's guilty?"

"All we're saying is there are other ways the same evidence might be explained," Bruno said.

I said that we weren't talking about truth; we were just playing with the very small number of ostensible facts that were at that time available. "We're being hypothetical," I said.

Diane and Vaune had no interest whatsoever in play or hypotheses. Diane said, "What happened can't be explained like a game. It isn't a game. You two are just making stories. You know he's guilty!" Vaune concurred. It got rough, there on the Just Pasta patio on that warm evening in June 1994.

Later, I realized that the four of us were having two totally different—and mutually exclusive—conversations. Diane and Vaune were talking about what they believed had happened; Bruno and I were behaving as if we were filmmakers or novelists or lawyers in court, so we were talking about what we thought might or could have happened. We were all using the same words and the same apparent facts, but we weren't talking the same languages or imagining the same kinds of stories.

Kinds of Talk

The two kinds of talk, *might-have-happened* talk and *real-life* talk, aren't the least bit compatible. Sometimes they coincide, but when they do it's just luck.

In fact, neither Diane nor Vaune nor Bruno nor I, nor any of the television stars commenting on the murders or reporters reporting on them knew what actually happened in front of Nicole's condo at 875 S. Bundy Drive in Brentwood the night of June 12, 1994. We didn't know it then; we don't know it now. The only living person who knows for sure is the person who murdered Nicole Brown Simpson and Ron Goldman. No one has come forward to say, "I did it." No one has said, "I saw that person do it." Every living person (but one) who has touched or been touched by this story has been operating on assumption, hypothesis, and speculation.

Everyone I knew had an opinion about the case, and it seemed that everyone's political correctness was in harm's way: With whom *should* you have sided if you wanted to be a good person? If you believed the defense, you had to ignore O. J.'s history of stalking, jealousy, and verbal and physical abuse. If you believed the prosecution, you had to send to prison Mister Nice Guy, Mister 2003 NFL Most Rushing Yards in one season, the famous black man who pulled himself up and out of the ghetto and sufficiently decolorized himself to have become poster boy for Hertz, an auto rental company that caters primarily to middle-aged white businessmen. You had to lock up the sweet and long-suffering Norberg from the hilarious *Naked Gun* films.

The emotions erupting at our table in June 1994 were nothing to the emotions that erupted when the trial ended fifteen months later. A caller to Geraldo Rivera's television show a few days after the October 3 verdict said, "As a black man, I felt like I was on trial."

Geraldo asked if he felt vindicated by the verdict.

"Yes," the man said, and then he spoke of Emmett Till, the fourteen-year-old boy lynched in Mississippi in 1955. For that caller, the verdict addressed outrages forty years in the past.

That same week, in a voice I can only describe as full of significance and suspicion, a white Buffalo surgeon said to me, "She had candles all around her bathtub lit that night."

I said, "So what?"

He said, "That means she had something going with Ron Goldman."

I said, "No, it doesn't, but so what if she did?"

He said, "It means we don't know everything."

As far as he was concerned, a complex plot was percolating and "they" were keeping things from us.

Real Life

In real life, as we all know, a more complex plot is always percolating, and we are always keeping things from one another. Think of a half-dozen people you know well: What terrifies those people the most? How much money do they have and where is it? What sexual and political proclivities do or don't you share? Do they bunch or fold the toilet paper and how many sheets do they use at a time? In real life, we know everything about hardly anything or anyone.

The only place we know everything about anything is in fiction, which is one reason we like novels and movies so much. With the novel, we've got the whole world in our hands, between those two covers; with movies, it all happens between fade in and fade out. If we're willing to read or watch all the way through, we can know everything there is to know about those people, everything.

Professors and critics speculate all the time about what this or that thing, present in or absent from, the novel or film means. I'm talking about what we can know. There are no more facts to a novel than there are facts in the novel, and there are no more scenes to a film than there are scenes in the film. All the rest is criticism or speculation.

New versions of films or DVDs with cut scenes restored by the director change nothing about our experience of the original; each is one other version of a story that has to be experienced and evaluated on its own terms. Francis Ford Coppola's *Apocalypse Now*

Redux (2001, 202 minutes) is not just forty-nine minutes longer than Francis Ford Coppola's *Apocalypse Now* (1979, 153 minutes). It is a different film. The new scenes of Willard's grinning theft of Kilgore's surfboard and Kilgore's absurd and pathetic begging on a helicopter loudspeaker for its return don't just add narrative elements; they significantly alter the characters themselves. The killer Kilgore who says "I love the smell of napalm in the morning... smells like... victory" is turned into a surfer buffoon. The long romantic episode at the French plantation further changes not only our sense of Willard, but the film's entire dramatic structure.

Likewise, outtakes and stories that appear on a DVD may or may not be interesting, they may help us understand a film, but they can neither place in a film what is not there nor remove from it what is there. If those supplementary elements are part of the story, then the story they are part of is one that consists of several parts, only one of which is the original. In terms of the original they are, as filmmaker T. Minh-ha Trinh says of all discussion about her own films, "outside." Works of art, whatever information is stacked up "outside," are perfectly self-contained.

Real life is just the opposite: in real life we don't know most things that really happen, and most of the time that is just fine with us. Who wants to know what the prime minister whose speech we are told about in the evening news had for lunch or which toothbrush he or she used today? When we hear about real life, we just want to hear what matters. To know what matters, we—just like the writer of fiction—have to know what story we're telling.

Movies

Another important difference between real life and fiction is this: in real life what seems to have happened nearly always is what happened. We're guided by probability, you and I, because on the whole probability works very well. But in movies and popular novels, what seems to have happened is often just obscuring what "really" happened, and the task of the hero is getting beyond the deception of the obvious.

In real life, that which seems peripheral usually is peripheral. The dark Mercedes sedan with smoked windows and high-beam headlights, three cars back on the thruway, that keeps changing lanes, in all likelihood, has absolutely nothing to do with your life. But if the protagonist in a movie looks into his rear view mirror and twice sees those high beams, that car changing lanes, we know some interaction is pending. In movies, in dramas, everything matters, and the things that seem out of place matter more rather than less because they are the clues to what comes next or to the invisible. If that weapon on the wall in act one isn't fired by the end of act three—to put a slight twist on Chekhov's famous dictum— somebody better give us a good reason why.

In real life some, perhaps most, things happen randomly. People are hit or missed by falling objects knocked off a window ledge by someone with whom they otherwise have no connection. People win the lottery or they don't. They slip in the bathtub and catch themselves in time or crack their skulls and die. They fall in love with the right or wrong person. They cross with the light after looking both ways, but a drunk driver runs the light, crosses the white line, and runs them down anyway. There is, most of the time, no meaning to such events; they're just luck, good or bad.

Luck hardly exists in popular media. Popular media is a lot like what anthropologists call "primitive thought." In primitive thought, if something happened, it's because someone or some thing made it happen. There is no random event, no random violence, no mere accident. In primitive thought, every fact matters. Our inability to figure out the meaning of a fact means only that we haven't yet figured out its meaning, not that it doesn't have any meaning.

Trials

I tell you all this because I think criminal trials are far more like the world of popular fiction and primitive thought than the world of everyday life. Prosecuting attorneys try to bring the jury to a place where everything, every apparent fact, must make sense, must have been deliberate, must be connected to something else. Defense attorneys do the opposite: they try to convince juries that the prosecutors' narratives don't really hold together after all.

Claims by judges and attorneys notwithstanding, a trial is neither a search for truth nor a search for justice. A trial is a search for victory, and all the participants know it. What goes on in the trial is the development of a narrative internal to the courtroom. The judge doesn't tell the jury to decide what actually happened, but rather to answer this question: "Has the prosecution proved its case beyond a reasonable doubt?" The jury is asked to evaluate a narrative. In a trial the truth of the narrative matters far less than the plausibility of it.

Why O. J. Wasn't Convicted

O. J. Simpson's lawyer Johnnie Cochran offered a counternarrative to the prosecution's narrative: If the labs handing the evidence in the Simpson-Goldman murders were sloppy, if L. A. Detective Fuhrman was a racist, if Fuhrman said he found the blood on O. J.'s Ford Bronco, and if some blood matching O. J.'s wasn't discovered until weeks after the murder, then the lab and Fuhrman were in cahoots with the guy who planted the blood, right? It's a plot hatched on the street at five in the morning by Los Angeles Police Department, the Los Angeles Medical Examiner, the FBI, the state crime lab in Sacramento, and who knows who else. Otherwise, how could all those things make sense? If you don't think collusion is the right explanation for all the separate facts, then you come up with a better theory and it better not be called "coincidence."

You don't have to understand or even believe all that, he told them. You just have to believe that it's possible. If it's possible, then you've got reasonable doubt about the prosecution's case.

Cochran didn't keep repeating this line of thinking. Instead, he reduced it to a one-line mantra that he said again and again: "If it doesn't fit, you must acquit. If it doesn't fit, you must acquit." Cochran was referring to the disastrous moment in the trial when prosecutor Chris Darden allowed O. J. to try on before the jury a pair of gloves. O. J. wore protective rubber gloves so he wouldn't contaminate the evidence, even though the gloves he was trying on weren't the actual gloves from the crime scene. No one made sure that the two pairs of gloves were the same size. Simpson, a professional actor, seemed to struggle with the glove and couldn't quite get his fingers all the way in. He made a face for the jury as if to say, "See what the white establishment is telling you is evidence against me?" In interviews after the trial, several jurors repeated Cochran's mantra to help explain their votes: "It didn't fit so we had to acquit." They had reasonable doubt.

Or they were given a phrase that let them claim reasonable doubt for a decision they wanted to make anyway. "To go by the post-trial interviews," a criminal defense attorney said to me, "the jury in the O. J. Simpson case didn't like prosecutor Marcia Clark and they didn't much like Nicole Simpson either. They were angry because one of the prosecution's chief witnesses had lied on the stand about having made racist remarks. They were charmed by Johnnie Cochran and to several of them O.J. Simpson was still a hero." It may be that in the confines of the jury room the jury members were moved to a state of reasonable doubt by Cochran's mantra. Perhaps they wanted to acquit long before summations began, and they just used that mantra as their justification.

In retrospect, the verdict in the O. J. case seems inevitable. The police were clumsy with the evidence. Los Angeles county D.A. Gil Garacetti shifted the trial from Santa Monica to downtown Los Angeles for reasons that seem to have had more to do with his convenient access to the press than anything connected with the trial. Prosecutor Marcia Clark ignored her own jury-experts' sound and considered advice, and she made a poster boy key witness of— and never adequately distanced herself from—an L.A. cop who not only lied on the stand but left an audiotape trail proving it. Her colleague Chris Darden allowed Simpson's glove performance before the jury. Judge Lance Ito was bedazzled by being on national television and buffaloed by Johnnie Cochran.

But maybe that's only because history is always inevitable when we're looking back. That's what history is—what actually happened, not the alternatives that didn't. In the moment, when the end is still in the future, when the bits and pieces have not yet coalesced into narrative, things are far less certain. That's what makes the stock market work and what lets hope spring eternal in the human breast. It's also why no trial attorney predicts the outcome of a jury trial until the judge says some local variant of "And is that your verdict, each and all?" and every one of them says "Yes, your honor, it is."

The enormous rage that manifested itself among many whites after the trial perhaps occurred because they thought the worlds inside and outside the trial were the same. The enormous satisfaction that manifested itself among many blacks after the trial occurred in part because they knew the worlds outside and inside the trial weren't the least bit the same.

"The nigger gets it."

Some of O. J.'s defense attorneys were fond of calling it the "trial of the century"— a grandiose claim, given that the twentieth century's trials included those of John Scopes for advocating evolution in 1925, Bruno Hauptmann for kidnapping and murdering the child of Charles and Anne Morrow Lindberg in 1935, the Nazis for war crimes at Nuremberg in 1945, and Julius and Ethel Rosenberg for treason in 1951.

It was, however, great television, and it was a great celebrity event. I knew we were out of real time and into show time long before the trial started, on June 17, 1994, the day of the "slow speed car chase." Nobody was really chasing anyone: it was a parade, not a pursuit. A squadron of police cars delicately followed O. J. and his friend Al Cowlings around the L.A. freeway system, past the airport, and finally to O. J.'s Brentwood house. Everyone sat still for hours, except some of us TV watchers who occasionally went to the kitchen or the toilet. During the vehicular parade, the cameras occasionally cut to the people bunched up along the freeways and at exits, cheering O. J. on. Some had signs that said, "Go Juice."

"Juice" was O. J.'s football-player nickname. His initials stand for Orenthal James. How can you say "Go Orenthal James?" "Juice" it was—when he was a Heisman Trophy-winning football star running back at USC, when he helped pull the Buffalo Bills out of the cellar and onto *Monday Night Football*, and when he did those lucrative Hertz commercials.

On the football field "Go Juice" maybe meant something, but heading north on I-405? Where was Juice to go now? What was he to go to? Finally, O. J. drove back to his house, got out of the car, and allowed the L.A. police to arrest him and take him to jail.

The episode reminded me of one of my favorite scenes in Mel Brooks's *Blazing Saddles*. The good folks of the small western town of Rock Creek are about to lynch the black sheriff just sent to them by the governor. The sheriff draws his pistol and points it at his own head. He says in a gravelly voice, "The next man makes a move, the nigger gets it." The lynch mob freezes in its tracks.

The white mayor says, "Hold it, men, he's not bluffing."

The black sheriff says, in his gravelly voice, "Drop it, or I swear I'll blow this nigger's head all over this town." Then he says, a quavering octave higher and with eyes rolling, "Oh lawdy lawd, he's desperate! Do what he say! Do what he say!"

Pistols drop to the ground. A woman says, "Isn't anybody gonna help that poor man?"

Someone says, "Hush, Harriet. That's a sure way to get him killed."

The sheriff drags himself toward the jail. He says, in his quavering, faux darky voice, "Oh, oh, hep me, hep me, somebody hep me! Hep me! Hep me!" Then in his gravely voice he says to himself, "Shut up." He obeys his command, pulls himself inside the jail, shuts the door, holsters his pistol, and says in his real voice, "Oh, baby, you are so talented. And they are so dumb."

My Wife, the Addict

I didn't watch the O. J. trial as a matter of course. My wife—who has a Ph.D. from Johns Hopkins University, wrote her thesis on Blake's composite art, and who is a Distinguished Teaching Professor at SUNY Buffalo—did. Every day, when she had the time—and many days when she did not—she planted herself in the kitchen and watched the trial on the TV set over the sink. Sometimes when I'd come in, she'd pretend to be doing something else: reading books or newspapers or grading papers. Other times she'd ignore me entirely because something particularly wonderful was going on, which trumped the need for excuse or explanation. Sometimes, during a break, she would regale me with descriptions and analyses of courtroom minutiae, much as if she were doing a deep analysis of a poem by Blake or Milton.

I teased her about this mercilessly until I noticed that when I did it in front of friends—many of them academics or professionals—I was getting far less reinforcement than I thought I deserved. I learned that an extraordinary number of people I liked and respected either watched the trial or watched the *Court TV* replays at night and followed it in newspapers and news magazines. One elderly society woman told me she had been forced to abandon her decades-old weekly luncheons with three other elderly society women because lunchtime in Buffalo was court time in California. "One must choose," she said.

Moreover, I came to realize that I was riding a horse higher than was perhaps appropriate, for I did not remain pure. I couldn't pass through the kitchen, where Diane was feeding her addiction, without sitting down next to her. Like the victims in Homer's Lotusland, I was transfixed until rescued by the midmorning break or noon recess (three P.M. our time). Only then would I remember that I had come into the kitchen only to refill my coffee cup and, let's see, how long ago was that?

Addicts and Writers

When the trial ended, my friend Ronald Gottesman, who at the time taught at USC, suggested, I presume in jest, an "O. J. Withdrawal Kit," which could be advertised on TV for $49.95 ($44.95 if you order in the next hour). The kit would contain a leather glove, a pair of black socks, a knit cap, a stiletto, a map of Brentwood, and grounds plans of the Bundy house and O. J.'s Rockingham Road estate. People in withdrawal could open the box and touch whichever object offered the most solace, just as young children are given comfort by certain stuffed animals or remnants of certain blankets.

The only thing wrong with Ron's idea was there was no need for it. The O. J. action continued, night and day. Instead of the continual and nearly open-ended form of the courtroom, it metastasized, exploded into the world of books and talk shows. Marcia Clark's agents got her a $4,2 million advance, the third largest advance in American publishing history, trailing only Generals Colin Powell and Norman Schwartz-kopf, who had received $6 million and $5 million advances respectively for their memoirs. Then Johnny Cochran's agents announced that he had received an even larger advance, so Ms. Clark was pushed back to number four, whipped by Johnnie C one more time.

Nearly everyone with a major role in the case published a book about it. First out of the gate was Alan Dershowitz with *Reasonable Doubts*, a Jack Hornerish explanation of how and why the case had really been won by Dershowitz's pre-trial work. The book was published on February 1, 1996, two days short of four months from the verdict. Within weeks of the 1998 verdict in the civil case filed against Simpson by Nicole's family, Dershowitz had a revised version of *Reasonable Doubts* on the stands, this one with a commentary on the civil verdict. Most of the attorneys on both sides wrote about the inferiority of the other attorneys. Jurors published books explaining their verdict. Cable talk show hosts like Geraldo Rivera and Charles Grodin were still feeding regularly off the O. J. table two years after the criminal trial ended. Johnny Cochran got a talk show on *Court TV*. The supermarket tabloids continued to report O. J. sightings even into the new century.

Once the trial was out of the way, O. J. said he was going to devote himself to finding the real murderer of his wife and her friend. He would deliver the justice that hadn't been delivered and clear his good name. So far as I know, he hasn't started his detecting yet. Every so often there's a brief TV story about something that happened to him when he was playing golf. Usually the story is about people who were assigned him as a fourth. Some people refused to play with him; others did play with him and reported that he was really just like anyone else, not at all like a superstar or a multiple-murderer. Sometimes we see O. J. smiling, sometimes not. He usually seems to be working very hard to look like he's having a good time. He also seems to know we're looking at him and thinking bad thoughts. He's like someone with an enormous scar on his cheek who knows we're thinking about the scar even when we're trying very hard to maintain eye contact or look at his necktie or the wall over his shoulder.

Nobody Gets Off

It is part of the nature of our criminal justice system that nobody once charged gets off free. Even to those who are innocent and acquitted, the costs are phenomenal. Once charged, you will pay. Do you know any physicians who've been charged with malpractice? Guilty or not, the insurance rates go up, and the reputation is smeared. If nothing else, you are changed by the experience. Someone once said that after Jesus resurrected him, Lazarus was ostracized because he'd been to a place to which no one else had ever been, a place from which no ordinary person would ever return. Lazarus wasn't dead any more, but neither was he like anybody else.

The same is true for anyone tried for a felony.

The same is true for O. J. Simpson.

Simpson, after all these years, remains a prisoner in a very narrow world. He can't go out or travel as he once did; he can't go to places he used to visit or see most of the people he used to see. He can't work.

One of William Faulkner's great novels, *Light in August*, is about a man named Joe Christmas who does not know if he is white or black, nor can he ever know. Faulkner said that Joe Christmas was the most tragic figure he could imagine because his was the saddest condition to inhabit: not to know what you are or who you are.

In early November 1995 O. J. called Associated Press reporter Linda Deutch to report that "everywhere I go . . . people are totally positive." He made this statement after he was dumped by his talent agency of twenty years, kicked out of his country club, and had his second book proposal rejected by his publisher. He had watched his girlfriend Paula Barbieri bail out of their relationship on *PrimeTime Live* with Diane Sawyer; someone had planted a sign near his house that read "Home of the Brentwood Butcher." Before he made this statement, an Atlantic City event was cancelled at which he was to have been paid for signing memorabilia ($135 for flat objects, like books; $185 for objects that were not flat and for photos of the slow-speed chase, $124.95 and $159.95, depending on the size). In 1998 he lost an $8.5 million civil suit in Santa Monica for having caused the deaths of his wife and Ron Goldman. A rumor circulated that he might be hired by Fox News as a commentator for the trial of actor Robert Blake, accused of having murdered his wife outside a Studio City restaurant, but nothing came of it.

O.J. and the story of the Brentwood murders continue fading from and then coming back into public view. In late 2006, the New York publisher HarperCollins and the Fox television network announced "If I Did It,'" a book by O.J. with a two-hour companion tv special in which he would describe how he would have killed his wife. The project generated such public scorn that Rupert Murdoch, who controlled both HarperCollins and Fox, cancelled the book and the program. For weeks "If I Did It" and the various people involved in it were prime copy for the talkshows and blogosphere. O.J. later said he had little to do with the writing and that he had never killed anybody, that it was just a gimmick that gave him a chance to raise some money for his kids.

Relevant Fictions

During the Simpson trial, *Othello* was often cited as a literary parallel because in a jealous rage the black Othello stabs to death his white wife. But the parallel goes no further. As soon as Othello killed Desdemona, he took responsibility for it. After the Rockingham murders O. J. took a plane to Chicago. Different story.

But there are literary resonances. I think in particular of Albert Camus's *L'Etranger*, John Milton's *Paradise Lost*, and Jorge Luis Borges's "The Aleph"

L'Etranger takes place in Oran, Algeria. The protagonist, Meursault, is charged with the murder of an Arab on a beach. In prewar

Algeria, a Frenchman killing an Arab was not unlike a white man killing a black in prewar Mississippi: you shouldn't do it, but if you do, it's no big deal.

But there is a problem with this particular killing: Meursault shoots the Arab five times rather than just once or twice. The examining magistrate asks him why so many bullets. Meursault doesn't know how to tell the magistrate that it was because the sun was burning into his skull, so he says nothing. Meursault could have said, "I thought he was about to get up and come at me again with the knife" or "I was petrified and lost control." Any explanation would have gotten him off. But he says nothing; he offers no story at all. The magistrate decides he's guilty because he lacks a story. Later, in court, he explains that he fired the second, third, fourth, and fifth bullets because of the sun. His explanation is worse than no story: it is a story that makes no sense. Senselessness, as I suggested earlier, is a common aspect of ordinary life, the rantings of psychotics and the reports of journalists, but it is intolerable in the courtroom. Everyone connected with the trial decides Meursault is a monster. The novel ends moments before Meursault's execution by guillotine. He's executed not because he killed the Arab, but because he didn't come up with a plausible story in which to contextualize it. In the world of the court, you must present a story that makes sense, else you lose.

The prosecutors in the O. J. case blundered by introducing details that didn't make sense. Simpson's attorneys brilliantly found, and pointed out again and again, details the prosecution had dismissed as mere loose ends. The prosecutors complained that the defense made far too much of those minor and irrelevant details, but they missed the point: a case is won and lost not in the bulk of facts but in the coherence of facts. In real life, if everything fits but one thing, then that one thing is what is aberrant and what is tossed out; in court, if everything fits but one thing (and if you've got a good lawyer), then it is the other side's story that is tossed out. "If it doesn't fit, you must acquit." The court, like the world of drama, requires perfection in narrative. There can be no loose ends. In drama and in court, and in crime, the loose ends kill or acquit you.

Would it have made any difference if Marcia Clark had told the jury what I'm telling you, if she had explained that what they were doing there was about real life, not drama? I don't think so. I don't think the judge would have let her explain. She couldn't say, "This is theater from which this fact and that fact and that fact have been excluded." Had she, Judge Ito would have immediately found her in contempt. Saying the inappropriate truth in court can get you locked up in jail.

A second literary aspect of the O. J. case is how particular stories incorporate extraordinary ranges of human concerns; what may seem like a simple or sensational or unique narrative turns out to have resonances in major aspects of our lives. Milton's *Paradise Lost* is about the Eden myth. In his essay "On Christian Doctrine," Milton wrote why he thought that myth important. The myth, he said, includes:

> at once distrust of the divine veracity, and a proportionate credulity in the assurances of Satan; unbelief; ingratitude; disobedience; gluttony; in the man excessive uxoriousness, in the woman a want of proper regard for her husband, in both an insensibility to the welfare of their offspring, and that offspring the whole human race; parricide, theft, invasion of the rights of others, sacrilege, deceit, presumption in aspiring to divine attributes, fraud in the means employed to attain the object, pride, and arrogance.[1]

A wonderful accumulation. It's as if that story is a crystal, which, if turned this way or that, casts a striking spectrum of light on that wall.

Which brings us to Borges's story, "The Aleph." The Aleph is a crystal in which may be seen everything: all knowledge, all time, all stories. What is seen at any instant just depends on how you look at it, and who is looking.

The O. J. case is an American Aleph. In it, there is a story, a structure, an ethic, an ethos for everyone. And that may be what is most important about the O.J. case, the extraordinary range of issues and conditions it helps or forces us to think about and look at.

Not that this specific and famous deracinated athlete/personality was on trial for the horrific murders of his wife and her acquaintance. But rather that in the O. J. Simpson murder trial we each found some other narrative or narrative element of primary importance. The O. J. case and trial force us to consider anew those forever unresolved questions about appearance and reality, about chronology and history, about how we convince ourselves we're right when we're talking about the past.

What Really Happened That Night in Santa Monica

The Mezzaluna—the restaurant on San Vicente where Nicole Simpson had her last dinner and forgot her eyeglasses, the place Ron Goldman worked and where he found the glasses that he fatefully took to Nicole's house when his shift was over—has gone out of business. In Hollywood there is publicity that nourishes and publicity that kills. Maybe Mezzaluna would have gone belly-up anyway, but I don't think so. It became déclassé for the locals, and places like that can't fill the tables with tourists alone. Nicole's Simpson's Bundy Avenue house has a new owner, its number has been changed from 875 to 879, and the street entrance has a new facade. If the new design and number were meant to confuse tourists, they have nearly succeeded. Some still figure out the place and the correction appears on some star maps, those sheets you buy from street vendors that purport to tell you where everybody who is anybody lives. When I last drove by 875/879 Bundy, there were two groups on the sidewalk across the street, one Asian, the other Anglo, each of them in heavy conversation, pointing, looking at maps, looking up, pointing again, nodding.

A few months after the civil trial ended, I was walking my dog Penelope in the park and I met Ralph, a guy I know from around town. We know one another well enough to say hello when we cross paths, but we've never hung out. and I don't know what Ralph does for a living.

He told me he'd talked to _____, a good friend of O. J.'s in the old days and one of the few local people who still maintained regular phone contact with him. Ralph said that _____ said O. J. was depressed about all the old friends who didn't want to be friends any more, both here and in L.A. I said I could see how that might be depressing.

Ralph looked around to make sure no one else was nearby. Then he said, "I don't want to be quoted on this, but _____ told me what really happened on Bundy. You know him don't you?" I said I didn't. "But you know who he is, right?" I said, of course, I did, everyone knew who _____ was. "All right, then," Ralph said.

His dog went into the lake. Penelope doesn't swim. She yapped at me to continue the walk. Ralph and I stood there, watching our dogs. After a while I said, "So what happened on Bundy?"

"You can't quote me by name on this."

"I wouldn't."

"It's only me telling you what a friend of O. J.'s told me."

"I got it."

"_____ said O. J. went there that night to slash Nicole's tires. He was really pissed off at something that happened earlier in the day at the kid's recital. Maybe because he wasn't invited to dinner with the family. That's why he had that knife, the one with the serrated blade. No one would use a blade like that to kill a person."

I didn't say, Someone did.

He went on: "So O. J. was about to slash the tires on Nicole's car when Goldman showed up. O.J. freaked. Goldman confronted him. O.J. stuck Goldman. Then Nicole came out and saw what was going on. So O. J. killed her because he was afraid she'd tell people about him killing Goldman. Then after O. J. was done with her, he went back and finished Goldman off. It was all just panic. All he wanted to do was her tires."

"Do you think it's true?" I asked.

"True? Who knows what's true?" he said. "It's the story I got, is all."

10 Bob Dylan and the Legend
of Newport 1965

Perhaps the key legend in twentieth-century-popular culture in the United States is the one about Bob Dylan being booed throughout much of his performance at the 1965 Newport Folk Festival. The performance and audience response, many cultural historians have argued, stands out as the pivotal moment in the shift from the folk revival to rock. The events described in the legend never happened, but in popular culture, as in political campaigns and jury trials, facts matter far less than the perception of facts, and the course of events matters far less than the narrative of events.

Before I can tell you about the disjunction between what happened at Newport 1965 and the Legend of Newport 1965, I have to tell you something about what legends are and how they fit into the spectrum of other kinds of stories people tell.

Telling Tales

Folklorists often distinguish three kinds of oral prose narratives: myths, folktales and legends.

Myths are sacred stories. They deal with the origin of things, with big questions such as the origin of death and the nature of the universe. They tend to take place before calendars and clocks and sometimes before the world looked anything like it does now. They are meant to be believed just as they are. Generally, they are told this time just as they were told the last time and the time before that. You don't tinker with the sacred charter of your world.

Folktales also tend to take place outside of time, but they're meant to entertain. Folktales include such narratives as the Märchen published by Jakob and Wilhelm Grimm, animal tales and jokes. Folktales may begin with a formula on the order of, "Once upon a time." What time, exactly? Doesn't matter. Where, exactly? Doesn't matter. The woodsman lives in a forest, the prince in a castle, the farmer in a farmhouse. That's all you need to know for a folktale. The storyline of a folktale may remain fairly constant (how would we otherwise know it was the same tale?), but the actual words can vary a great deal from teller to teller and situation to situation.

Legends, like myths, are grounded in belief, but they mostly take place in what is supposed to be real time and involve what are supposed to be real people and places: how a place got its name, what a saint made happen, what a famous person did, what somebody in this family did many years ago. Like folktales, legends are flexible: depending on the situation and the skill of the teller, they can be long or short, embellished or unembellished.

Myths, folktales, and legends are told because they are useful: people tell them and listen to them because they have reasons to tell and listen to them at that place, at that time. Myths contain or express a culture's worldview. Jokes provide a safe way of dealing with potentially dangerous substances and behaviors. Saints' legends provide moral examples. Family stories describe who and what the family is or was.

Legends may be true, but that's not a requirement. The requirement is that somebody somewhere thought they were true, and the teller is aware of that fact or possibility: "I don't believe this but people around here say . . ." or "I can't vouch for this but I've heard. . . ."

When a legend is obviously untrue but people keep telling it anyway, it is safe to assume that the legend is fulfilling a need better than the available facts. Sometimes the service is as simple as making sense out of something that otherwise does not make sense or to provide a name for something that needs one.

Perhaps the most explicit instance of this in film occurs in John Ford's *The Man Who Shot Liberty Valance*. A young reporter writes down the story told to him by Rance Stoddard, whose killing of badman Valance in a gunfight resulted in his distinguished career as governor and United States senator. But, Stoddard says, the well-known story is wrong. He didn't kill Valance; a man named Tom Doniphon did, shooting a rifle from an alley across the street. The young reporter is delighted with his scoop, but his editor takes the sheets from his hand, shreds them, and tosses them into the fire.

"You're not going to use the story, Mr. Scott?" says Stoddard.

"This is the West, sir," the editor says. "When the legend becomes fact, print the legend."

Dylan at Newport: Legend

Bob Dylan and the Beatles were the only popular music performers of that era whose songs were covered by artists across the entire spectrum of nonclassical catalogues: rock, pop, country, gospel, and folk. In 1965 alone Dylan's songs were covered more than 300 times by The Four Seasons, Chet Atkins, John Baez, the Beach Boys, Leon Bibb, The Brothers Four, Glenn Campbell, Johnny Cash, Cher, The Chipmunks, Judy Collins, Johnny Copeland, Dion, Duke Ellington, Ramblin' Jack Elliot, Stan Getz, Richie Havens, The Kingston Trio, Rod MacKinnon, Manfred Mann, The Mitchell Trio, Gerry Mulligan, Odetta, Peter, Paul & Mary, and scores of other individuals and groups. Dylan mattered.

Dylan wouldn't play a Newport Folk Festival again until 2002. Nearly every print, radio, and television story about it referred to the angry booing that famously accompanied his 1965 Newport performance, when he appeared on stage with members of Paul Butterfield's blues band and Al Kooper at the Sunday night closing concert. The 2002 concert contained no surprises, and the audience seems to have been delighted with what they saw and heard.

The July 25, 1965, audience, the story goes, was driven to rage because their acoustic guitar troubadour had betrayed them by going electric and plugging in. According to the Bob Dylan page on the Rock and Roll Hall of Fame web site, "He was booed offstage after only three songs, at which point he returned with an acoustic guitar and a message for all the folk purists: 'It's All Over Now, Baby Blue.' " The BBC page announcing the British broadcast of Martin Scorsese's 2005 PBS *American Masters* Dylan documentary, "No Direction Home" says, "At a disastrous concert at the Newport Folk Festival in 1965 his electrified instruments set the audience in turmoil."

A host of associated narratives describe turmoil in the wings. "Backstage," wrote Greil Marcus, "Pete Seeger and the great ethnomusicologist Alan Lomax attempted to cut the band's power cables with an axe."[1] Singer Maria Muldaur told Scorsese's interviewer that a third of the audience was booing. "We ran backstage and there was mayhem going on. Pete Seeger and Theodore Bikel and all the old guard, old leftist singing factions, were horrified and thought, 'this is pop music, this isn't folk music.' There was just a big battle raging backstage. And I understand Pete Seeger had an axe and was going to go cut the electric cables and had to be subdued." Folk music critic Paul Nelson said, "Seeger, from all reports, was very, very upset by this. And I had heard that he had tried to cut the wires and that he had gone into a car and wouldn't come out after this whole thing." Dylan himself heard the story: "I heard a rumor that Pete was going to cut the cable," he told his manager, Jeff Rosen, in his interview for the Scorsese documentary. "I heard it later. It was like, 'It doesn't make sense to me. Pete Seeger whose music I cherish, who's someone I highly respect, was going to cut the cable it was like ohhh, god, it was like a dagger, the thought of it made me go out and get drunk."

Dylan was right: it didn't make sense. Moreover, and more important, it didn't happen, none of it. They're all great stories, but not one of them is true. Bob Dylan wasn't booed off the stage at the 1965 Newport Folk Festival. Pete Seeger did not look for an axe with which to cut the power. And neither did he hide in a car and mope.

Dylan at Newport: Fact

I was in the wings during Dylan's Saturday night performance; for six years I was a director of the Newport Folk Festivals. Every time I heard those stories retold, I'd say to whoever was talking, "That's not how I remember it. Nobody made a move for the power. Nobody took a swing at the sound man. It wasn't Dylan the audience was booing."

After Dylan's 2002 Newport appearance occasioned all those retellings of the Legends of 1965, I decided to check both the legend and my memory: I listened to the original tapes made from the stage microphones during that performance. (I have all of the Newport board's audiotapes, save some that Peter Yarrow borrowed from producer George Wein and, to my knowledge, never returned, and some that were made for us by a Providence, Rhode Island, recording company that shortly thereafter went belly-up and disappeared, along with our half-inch, four-track master tapes.)

The entire event, from the beginning of Peter Yarrow's introduction of Dylan to his introduction of the next performer, took thirty-seven minutes. You can hear the audience very clearly throughout. Yarrow's voice is clear, the musicians' performances are clear (although the mix is sometimes overmodulated and muddy), and the audience's responses are clear. No doubt the sound of the people in the front come through more loudly than people far in the back, but there's no reason to assume that they didn't all cheer and boo the same things.

Here is what is on the tape, what people on stage, in the wings, and throughout most of the audience heard:

> YARROW: One, two. Can I have some volume on this microphone? Hello. One, two. Ladies and gentlemen, at this time there's a little microphone setup to be done. Cousin Emmy's a gas, right?
>
> [laughter, applause]
>
> There's someone that's coming on to the program now, as a matter of fact, the entire program tonight was designed to be a

whole group of small performances. You know I will be performing later with the group that I'm a part of, you know. [Yarrow was a member of a pop-folk group named Peter, Paul and Mary.]

[light applause]

And we are all limited in the time that we can be on stage for a very specific reason. The concept of the program tonight is to make a program of many, many different points of view that are together and yet without the huge expanse of the performing of any group. We will be very limited in time and so will each person who comes up. The person who's coming up now—

[a single note from each string of an electric guitar struck by someone apparently checking the tuning]

Please don't play right now, gentlemen, for this second. Thank you.

[three more guitar notes]

The person who's coming up now is a person who has, in a sense—

[two brief bursts of feedback hum]

changed the face of folk music to the large American public because he has brought to it a point of view of a poet. Ladies and gentlemen, the person that's going to come up now—

[Yarrow pauses a long time, drawing it out; a few hoots at the pause from the audience]

has a limited amount of time—

[very loud booing and yelling, shouts of "No, no, no"]

his name is Bob [pause] Dylan.

[enthusiastic and sustained cheering and applause from the audience that had watched the electric band set up and which was now watching Dylan plug in his own electric guitar] [a minute or so of noises of things being moved around, levels checked, voices talking about where to set things. No hoots, jeers, calls, or yells from the audience. (Minutes (0:00–7.32 on the tape)]

DYLAN AND GROUP: "Maggie's Farm"

[applause; retuning, a voice asks, "Ready? a little more tuning, Dylan says "Okay." (7:32–8:25)]

DYLAN AND GROUP: "Rolling Stone," (8:25–14:19)

[applause, returning, murmur of musician's voice (14:19–15:03)]

DYLAN AND GROUP: "It Takes a Lot to Laugh, It Takes a Train to Cry," (15:03–18:26)

[applause, musicians' voices: "Let's go, man, that's all." Sounds of movement, which I take to be Dylan and the band moving off the stage, followed by audience yelling "No, no, no." (18:26–18:44)]

YARROW: Bobby was—

[booing]

Yes, he will do another tune, I'm sure. We'll call him back. Would you like Bobby to sing another song? I don't know where he is.

[huge applause, appreciative yelling. "Yes, yes, yes!"] Listen, it's the fault of the— he was told that he could only do a certain period of time.

[Audience yells.]

Bobby, can you do another song, please? He's going to get his axe.[1]

[Audience chants: "We want Dylan. We want Dylan."]

He's coming.

[Audience continues chanting: "We want Dylan. We want Dylan."]

He's going to get an acoustic guitar.

[Audience continues chanting at the same level: "We want Dylan. We want Dylan."]

Bobby's coming out now. Yes, I understand, that's okay. We want Bobby, and we do. The time problem has meant that he could only do these few songs. He'll be out as soon as he gets his acoustic guitar.

[Audience continues chanting: "We want Dylan. We want Dylan." Then it bursts into enthusiastic applause. (18:44–20:26)]

[bit of microphone hum, harmonica testing; Dylan says, "Peter, get another guitar, man." Tunes guitar. Dylan says, "You got another one?" A bit more tuning, mumbled conversation, occasional sounds from the audience. Dylan says, "Please, man, get me a guitar." (20:52–22:42)]

DYLAN: "It's All Over Now, Baby Blue" (22:42–27:37)

[applause 27:37–28:32; someone in the audience yells "Tambourine, Bobby." Someone else yells, "Tambourine Man." Dylan says, "Okay, I'll do this." Tunes, fusses. "All right, I'll do this one. Does anybody have an E harmonica? An E harmonica, anybody? Just throw them all up. Thank you very much. Thank you. Okay. Thank you very much." (29:13)]

DYLAN: "Mister Tambourine Man," (29:13–35:29)

[applause; Dylan says, "Thank you very much." Audience yells, "More, more." 35:29–35:40]

YARROW: Bob Dylan, ladies and gentlemen. Thank you, Bob. Thank you. The poet, Bob Dylan. Thank you, Bob.

[audience continues applauding through this.]

One, two. One, two. Thank you, Bob. Ladies and gentlemen, the next group that's coming up—

[audience: "No! Bob!" Boos. Rhythmic clapping.]

is the group from which all this music started. You know the tradition of blues in our country originally came from the African tradition and the African tradition—

[boos and rhythmic clapping continue]

Ladies and gentlemen, Bob can't come back. The African tradition, when it was brought over originally, was brought over into the deep South, and the music became, to a large extent—

[Boos and yells continue.]

Ladies and gentlemen, please be considerate of Bobby. He can't come back. Please don't make it more difficult than it is. (35:40–37:04)

What the Tape Tells

That is the transcript of the tape made on stage at Newport, Rhode Island, on the night of July 25, 1965. Three things stand out:

1. You can hear a lot of individual things yelled by the audience and the general responses of the audience.
2. All the booing you can hear from the stage is in response to things Peter Yarrow said, not to things Bob Dylan did. ("I had no idea why anybody was booing," Dylan told Jeff Rosen in 2000. "But I don't think anybody was there having a negative response to those songs, though. Whatever it was about, it wasn't anything about what they were hearing." He was right again.)
3. It was Peter Yarrow who first started drawing attention to what kind of guitar Dylan was using. He twice said that he was coming back with an acoustic guitar, and he stressed the word "acoustic" each time. I remember wondering at the time why Peter was making such a big deal of what instrument Dylan was going to use.

I've heard people say that Dylan himself gave proof of how upset he was at the boos when he came back to do those encores with that acoustic guitar rather than two more electric songs with the Butterfield group. Nonsense. Dylan and the blues band did three songs together because that was all the songs they'd prepared to perform together. They hadn't prepared more because they'd been told beforehand that they'd have time for only three songs.

Pete Seeger's Axe

And what about Pete Seeger's axe and rage—the story Greil Marcus tells in great detail at the beginning of *Invisible Republic* and that Maria Muldaur and Paul Nelson recount in Martin Scorsese's "No Direction Home?"

Pete Seeger, more than any other of the Newport directors, had a personal connection with Bob Dylan: it was he who, three years earlier, had convinced the great Columbia A and R man John Hammond, famous for his work with jazz and blues musicians, to produce Dylan's first album, the eponymous *Bob Dylan*. If anyone was responsible for Bob Dylan's presence on the Newport stage that night, it was Pete Seeger.

In an interview for "No Direction Home," Seeger gave his version of what had really happened in the Newport wings when Bob Dylan went electric:

"You could not understand the words, and I was frantic. I said 'Get that distortion out.' It was so raspy. You could not understand a word, and I ran over to the sound system. 'Get that distortion out.'

" 'No, this is the way they want to have it.'

" 'Goddam it, it's terrible, you can't understand it. If I had an axe I'd chop the mike cable right now.' "

So Pete Seeger was, indeed, upset, but not at what Dylan was playing or how he was playing it. Pete was upset that the audience wasn't getting to hear Dylan's performance with the clarity he thought that performance deserved.

When Legend Becomes Fact

Bob Dylan's Newport concert wasn't disrupted by booing, but the story quickly went out that it had. Subsequently, reality overtook fiction. Several of Dylan's concerts, in New York's Forest Hills two months later and London's Albert Hall the following year, were marked by boos from the audience during the electric segments.

Were those boos from people who were really outraged and affronted at Dylan's shift from the folksy acoustic guitar to electric guitar and rock backup, or were they from people who read of or heard the legend of Newport 1965 and thought that was the way they were supposed to behave to be cool? After all, Dylan's first all-electric album, *Highway 61 Revisited*, had been released less than two months after the Newport performance. It was a huge hit; one song on that album, "Just Like a Rolling Stone," was a hit single. By the fall of 1965, America had embraced rock. Not only was Elvis Presley cranking out his three or four albums a year, but the British invasion was in full swing. Both the Beatles and the Rolling Stones had hugely successful U.S. tours in 1964. *Beatles '65* was released on December 15, 1964, and went gold before the month was out. By the time of Dylan's Forest Hills and Albert Hall concerts, rock was hot, and everybody knew Dylan had gone electric. So why go to a concert if you knew beforehand that you were going to be unhappy and your ears were going to hurt? Maybe to have a good time, screaming and yelling, the way kids do.

Al Kooper told Scorsese's interviewer that the Forest Hills audience was happy and appreciative during the first (acoustic) half, but booed during the second (electric) half, save for when Dylan and the group performed "Just Like a Rolling Stone." For that, "They stopped booing and sang along, and when we finished they started booing again."

When I first listened to the stage recording of the 1965 performance, I wondered if that short period of public rage wasn't just one more passing fad, which grew out of distorted stories that came out of a performance that most of the audience thought was pretty damned good, even if the sound mix was, as Pete Seeger said, muddy and overmodulated. After all, kids love fads connected with musicians: hair grew longer after the Beatles started hitting the charts, and white kids started wearing baseball caps backwards and oversize pants after the custom of some black musicians.

I still think all that was in play But I wonder if there may have been something more substantial at work in the aftermath of the 1965 Newport performance.

If, as so many cultural critics insist, that musical event, indeed, represented a pivotal point in twentieth-century-American-popular culture, if it symbolized the moment during which the sentimental sweetness and light of Newport gave way to the mud and drugs of Woodstock and violence of Altamont, if it was a moment when the idealism of the civil rights movement was transforming into the rage and bitterness of the antiwar movement, then that moment needed to be marked by something more than "Oh yeah, that was the year Dylan went electric at Newport." The moment needed a story that would show that something had happened during the course of that specific performance. Whatever was happening was overtly demonstrated in the performance or in the audience's reaction to the performance. It was an event best phrased by Dylan himself in the chorus to "Ballad of a Thin Man," a song first recorded on the 1965 *Highway 62 Revisited*: "Because something is happening here/But you don't know what it is,/Do you, Mister Jones?"

The legend of Newport 1965 took a great musical moment and wrapped it in a narrative of rage, confusion, and change. So what if it didn't really happen that way, in that time, at that place? It would all happen later, in other times, other places.

"Reality may be too complex for oral tradition," wrote Jorge Luis Borges in his essay "Forms of a Legend." "Legends recreate it in a way that is only accidentally false and permits it to travel through the world from mouth to mouth."[2] Stories are the way we domesticate the world's disorder. Facts are incidental.

11 Silver Bullets

Billy's Gun

In late August 1972, my son Michael, then ten years old, and I were in a junk store near Fort Sumner, New Mexico. The owner pointed to an old pistol in a locked glass case. He said it had once belonged to Billy the Kid, whose grave was nearby. I said that if Billy had owned half the guns people said he owned, he couldn't have climbed onto a horse. "Don't know about that," the man said, "but I do know that Billy owned that gun."

Michael stared at the pistol. Clearly, he believed it was Billy's, and he was seriously disappointed. "It doesn't have a front sight, and it's rusty, and it looks like a cap gun," he said. The man told Michael that hardly anybody in those days owned the kind of fancy pistols you saw on television; Michael looked at the man as if he were deranged.

Back in the car and once again heading east along US 60 toward Clovis, he was silent a long time. Then he told me that if the pistol in the glass case was the real thing he preferred what he saw on television.

I started to explain what was wrong with his attitude. I said that he couldn't ignore facts just because he liked fictions better. Then I stopped talking because we both knew I agreed with him: it wasn't for reality that Michael or I or anyone else watched western films, or most other films either. It was the stories that hooked us; facts were incidental. Facts were outside, something else entirely.

Billy

Say "Billy the Kid" and everybody knows whom you're talking about, or believes he knows. The most common line on him is that his real name was William Bonney, that he died at twenty-one, a notch on his pistol grip for every man he'd killed.

But some people insist his name was really Henry Antrim, that he didn't mutilate his pistol grip because he could remember the body count. It wasn't twenty-one anyway, and neither was he.

Who cares what they know or say? The notched gun is easy to visualize, twenty-one dead men coupled with twenty-one years of life has a nice symmetry, and William Bonney works better than Henry Antrim. With Billy the Kid, as with most heroes of folklore and legend, we prefer the better, not the more factual, story.

Billy figures as the central character in scores of films and novels. The films include *The Outlaw*, Howard Hughes's 1943 homage to Jane Russell's breasts (starring Jack Beutel as Billy, Thomas Mitchell as Pat Garrett, Walter Huston as Doc Holliday, and Jane Russell's breasts as themselves); Arthur Penn's 1958 *The Left-Handed Gun* (starring Paul Newman as a moody and introspective Actor's Studio Billy who, out of guilt and depression, tricks Garrett into killing him when he pretends to draw a pistol from a holster everyone but Garrett knows is empty), Sam Peckinpah's 1973 *Pat Garrett and Billy the Kid* (starring James Coburn and Kris Kristofferson as the cynical and doomed eponymous heroes, with a song track by Bob Dylan), and William Beaudine's 1966 *Billy the Kid vs. Dracula* (1966, with Chuck Courtney as Billy and John Carradine as the vampire).

One of the best known books about Billy the Kid is by the man who shot him down, Pat F. Garrett's *The Authentic Life of Billy the Kid, the Noted Desperado of the Southwest, Whose Deeds of Daring and Blood Made Him a Terror in New Mexico, Arizona and Northern Mexico* (1882). Two novels are N. Scott Momaday's *The Ancient Child* (1989) and Larry McMurtry's *Anything for Billy* (1988).

Michael Ondaatje's *Collected Works of Billy the Kid* (1974) is a book that defies category. It is polyphonic and transgeneric: there are poems, ostensible newspaper stories, and interior monologues by Billy, Sallie Chisum, Garrett, and the author. Ondaatje's book also includes photographs, sort of. The top two-thirds of the first page is an empty frame. The text below it begins, "I send you a picture of Billy made with the Perry shutter as quick as it can be worked...." The text continues in specific detail about the sender's photographic experiments and darkroom techniques, all in the service of an empty frame, which perhaps translates as: "I'm sending you an image, but you have to figure out what it looks like." *Collected Works* is a field in which word and image and you meet or merge. The near figure in the second photograph seems to be a bearded army officer in silhouette standing next to a litter of bones. Beyond him is someone who might be a soldier, also in silhouette. Between them, sitting on the ground, a man is painting what looks like a grave marker: "7 CAV." The Seventh Cavalry was Custer's outfit, massacred at Little Big Horn. What does that have to do with Billy the Kid? Perhaps nothing, other than it, too, was legend that trumped fact.

The book's final photo has no caption, nor is it alluded to or identified anywhere in the text. The image—small, the size of a large postage stamp—is in the lower right corner of the book's last recto; the verso after it is blank. The photo shows a young boy, perhaps seven or eight, wearing a cowboy suit, around his waist a holster with a toy pistol, and on his head a broad-brimmed hat. The boy is the young Michael Ondaatje, years before he emigrated to Canada from Ceylon.

The identity of the boy in the photograph is perhaps of far less importance than what the boy wears. For much of the mid-twentieth century, parents in various parts of the world bought their young male children costumes that were based on someone's idea of the outfits worn by nineteenth-century-American gunslingers. The children were sufficiently fascinated with the stories to want to act out their own versions of them, and their parents were sufficiently enamored of those roles and stories to be willing to pay for those cowboy suits, toy guns, and broad-brimmed hats.

Silver Bullets

My parents were among them. My cowboy suit differed from Ondaatje's in that it came with two cap pistols and a black mask. My cousin Marvin Ort and I, along with our pals Alan Hyber, Danny Rich, Teddy Tuchman, and Jackie Newfield, all five or six years old, regularly dressed up (to the extent our individual cowboy suits permitted) and enacted cowboy stories. We also enacted pilots-fighting-the-Japs-in-the-Pacific stories, but most of the time we were cowboys. We lived on Vernon Avenue in Brooklyn's Bedford-Stuyvesant section, a street then occupied almost entirely by Jewish and Italian working-class families. We made up some of our stories, but mostly we adapted them from radio programs. I don't remember where we got our war stories, but our primary western source was the "The Lone Ranger" radio program that aired Monday, Wednesday, and Friday evenings out of Mutual Broadcasting System's WXYZ in Detroit. Locally, it was on New York's WJZ. The smallest among us—not I, happily—had to play Tonto, the Indian, who had only three possible lines: "Yes, kemo sabe," "Do you have a plan, kemo sabe," and "Ugh." Tonto got to help but never to initiate anything.

Like James Bond and Billy the Kid, The Lone Ranger was and remains more famous than any of the actors who played him. He is so famous that, decades after the several radio and television series in which he was the eponymous hero, his name survives as a global metaphor:

> "Di's Little Lone Ranger Flies Like an Heir with the Greatest of Ease" (headline of an April 1985 *People* article on Prince William)

"Jackson and the Pols: Will Jackson Be the Lone Ranger?" (headline of a 1984 *The New Republic* article on Jesse Jackson). The article includes this line: "But black politicians' principal objection to Jackson is that he may assume the role of a political Lone Ranger, riding into San Francisco in August to single-handedly save the day." "Oliver North: A Lone Ranger or Just a Good Soldier?" (*Time*, January 5, 1987) includes the sentence, "No one is yet certain whether North is a cause or an effect, a Lone Ranger who rode out of control or a good soldier who followed orders from above."[1]

"The Lone Ranger" (*Time*, March 25, 1996, on presidential candidate Bob Dole). "Lone Ranger" (*Time*, December 13, 1999, on presidential candidate John McCain).

"A Lot of Entrepreneurs Are Lone Rangers" (Singapore *Business Times*, March 19, 2003).

"Lone Ranger in Iraq" (San Jose *Mercury News*, April 8, 2003) Tony Blair . . . "definitely isn't happy playing Tonto to Bush's Lone Ranger" (Glascow *Herald*, May 18, 2004).

"In 1972, 47-year-old Rehnquist became an associate justice on a decidedly liberal Supreme Court. Among the first cases he heard, Roe versus Wade. He voted against legalized abortion. He voted against affirmative action. As the court's perennial soul dissenter, he developed a nickname, the Lone Ranger (Paula Zahn on a CNN appearance on June 18, 2005).

"What's all this nonsense about Friar Tuck being cut from the cast of characters of the upcoming new Robin Hood series on BBC TV? Sherwood without the tonsured lardball would be like Lone Ranger country without Tonto (Nottingham *Evening Post*, April 6, 2006).

"When we were both Lone Rangers in a way. . . ." Ronald A. Heifetz, speaking to a group of potential donors about the time when, six years earlier, he and newsman David Gergen were starting Harvard's Center for Public Leadership (May 11, 2006).

Only a few real or fictional characters are so deeply embedded in popular culture that their names can be used with no explanation to characterize the behavior or condition of so many different people engaged in so many different activities in so many different places. The Lone Ranger is up there with Rambo, Hillary, Dirty Harry, and Marilyn.

The 2,956 episodes of the radio show ran from 1933 to 1955. There were two fifteen-episode film serials, both of them edited down to feature films. The television series began September 15, 1949, with an episode titled "Enter the Lone Ranger," and continued through June 6, 1957. It concluded with the 221st episode, "Outlaws in Greasepaint," in which the masked man and Tonto help arrest DeWitt and Lavinia Faversham, two members of a defunct Shakespearean repertory company who turned to robbing Wells Fargo Offices. A cartoon series—thirty-minute programs with three episodes per show—began September 10, 1966, and ran through January 6, 1968. In 1981, Lone Ranger cartoons appeared as part of the *Tarzan/Lone Ranger/Zorro Adventure Hour*, with two Lone Ranger episodes per show. With the huge demand for product resulting from 300-channel cable and inexpensive TV dishes, some of the old TV episodes have begun reappearing.

In nearly every episode, the Lone Ranger came upon ordinary people in distress, being abused, being ill-served by a system in disarray, or confronted by bullies. All the Lone Ranger radio and TV programs were built around a small number of regular themes (e.g., local law enforcement is ineffective or a deputy is corrupt; innocent folks are pursued by malefactors or are charged with crimes they didn't commit; innocent people have fortunes they don't know about that the bad guys try to steal). This formulaic approach is one reason we kids could enact and adapt the stories easily to our yards and streets and alleys.

In order to operate without being noticed (that mask was a dead giveaway), the Lone Ranger would adopt disguises: there was the Lone Ranger already disguised, disguised as Pancho the Mexican, an Eastern dude, a professor with a medicine wagon, a miner, a

Swede, an old Soldier, and Othello. (Yes, Othello. That was in episode 221, with the crooked Shakespearians.)

Tonto would say, "Do you have a plan, kemo sabe?" The Lone Ranger would invariably respond, "Yes, I do." Either he'd tell it to Tonto then and there, or it would be enacted over the next several minutes. Sometimes it was a way to trick the bad guy into revealing his misdeed. Sometimes it was merely physical—being in the right place to catch the crooks. Sometimes it was one of those fabulous disguises.

Week after week, the masked man never once said "No" when the Indian asked if he had a plan. "Do you have a plan" translates as "Do you know what to do next?" When you're five or six or seven, you never know what to do next. You don't even know what to do now. I don't know what adults got out of those programs—adults comprised as much of the audience as kids did—but I know I loved the plans and disguises and the fact that the plans and disguises worked. It meant you could always hide if you wanted or needed to, and that there were ways to deal with things you didn't think you could handle.

We listened to the stories on radio, but we saw what we heard. Ondaatje knew exactly what he was doing when he left that opening frame of *The Collected Works of Billy the Kid* empty: we kids were trained in filling empty visual frames. (We did have help in the visualizing: comics and illustrated books, a board game, snow globes, bubblegum cards, a first aid kit, ViewMaster cards, clicker and cap guns, and costumes. You can go on eBay and see them all, all of them selling for lots of money.)

Restoring the Centers

The series was set about 1875 or so, but the themes, like the themes of all successful historical fiction, were contemporary. The Lone Ranger came to birth at the nadir of the Depression, a time when all the institutions seemed in the process of betraying ordinary folks, and he matured in an America full of real bad guys.

In 1932, the year Detroit radio station WXYZ owner George W. Trendle and writer Fran Stryker were midwifing the Lone Ranger,

America was coming out of a decade of gangsterdom engendered by Prohibition. My late friend George Beto—a Lutheran minister, prison director, and criminal justice professor—was fond of saying that the most significant social error in his lifetime had been the Eighteenth Amendment. Prohibition, he said, for the first time made it acceptable for otherwise law-abiding citizens to seek out and have regular congress with professional criminals. The result was a measure of criminality and public corruption previously unknown, and still with us.

Nineteen-thirty-two was the year of the Lindbergh kidnapping. It was the year of the Bonus Army in the capitol. FDR was elected, and the next year the Twenty-First Amendment repealed Prohibition but didn't get rid of the gangsters. They found other things to do with the techniques they had developed and connections they had made and politicians they had bought. Two of the big movies of those transitional two years were *Little Caesar* (1930) with Edward G. Robinson ("Mother of Mercy, is this the end of Rico?") and *The Public Enemy* (1931) with Jimmy Cagney (who, with an unforgettable sneer, grinds half a grapefruit into an astonished Mae Clarke's face).

Prohibition, as Andrew Bergman notes in *We're in the Money: Depression America and Its Films* (1971), gave us the legendary murderous bootleggers (Al Capone, Dutch Schultz, Legs Diamond); the Depression gave us the legendary murderous bank robbers (Dillinger, Bonnie and Clyde, Pretty Boy Floyd, Creepy Alvin Karpis, and Machine Gun Kelly). The bootleggers drove big cars around town, shooting one another to pieces; the bank robbers drove big cars across state lines, escaping the jurisdiction of local police, thereby providing the rationale for what became our first armed national police force—the Federal Bureau of Investigation.

The center seemed not to hold. The system was in disarray, and the agencies that were supposed to protect us became more and more corrupt or impotent. It was a time for heroes. Enter the masked man with the never-ending supply of silver bullets.

He owed nothing to anybody, and his only close friend was Tonto, a tribeless Indian in a white world, another outsider. The

Lone Ranger had one living relative, his nephew Dan (who would be the father of the next century's crime fighter, also crafted by Trendle and Stryker, The Green Hornet, who would have his own exotic companion, a faithful Japanese sidekick named "Kato." The format was exactly the same, only the costumes and mode of transportation were altered).

Furthermore, the Lone Ranger is nearly nonviolent: he has gorgeous guns and bullets but never kills anybody; he shoots the bad guy in the hand, or he shoots the gun out of his hand. He doesn't hang around for a "thank you." He's the archetypal hero who comes upon the scene when needed, solves the problem, and then goes away.

The Lone Ranger was restricted to no place and was based nowhere. The chorus of Woody Guthrie's "Pastures of Plenty" could have been written about him: "I come with the dust and I'm gone with the wind." He found and defeated evil in desert, mountain, ranchland, open plains, mining country, and town. His territory was delineated by where evil flourished and good was shorthanded, not by any map.

In the world of the Lone Ranger (as in the world of Green Hornet, Batman, Superman, Dick Tracy, Wonder Woman, and all the others) evil is never defeated for long, but it is defeated for now, in this place, on this day. The battle continues episode after episode, year after year. The Cavendish gang—the villains who ambushed a posse of six Texas Rangers and killed them all but the one nursed back to health by Tonto and who became the Lone Ranger—were always breaking out of jail. You could lock evil back up, but it always got loose again. That was its nature, just as it was the hero's nature to meet it one more time. The story was of transient containment, not of triumph.

"Where You Get That 'We,' White Man?"

There was a joke a few decades back: The Lone Ranger and Tonto are surrounded by hordes of hostile Indians. The Lone Ranger says, "Well, we're really in trouble this time." Tonto says, "Where you get that 'we,' white man?"

The joke marks the pivot time: the Lone Ranger and Tonto were still around, but they were starting to become embarrassing. In the 1930s, 1940s, and 1950s, you could have mass media narratives in which a smart Indian gave up all home life, all association with family, friends and tribe, to become the devoted sidekick of a white man who got all the credit for righting the world's wrongs. But in 1969, real Indians occupied Alcatraz Island in San Francisco Bay to protest centuries of mistreatment and betrayal. A few years later there would be the bloody siege of the Pine Ridge Reservation in South Dakota. White-Indian relations were no longer a joke. By the late 1960s, people would ask what was wrong with that Indian. How come he talked funny: "Me go" and "Him come" and "Ugh"? Indeed, how come most of those guys never had any girlfriends? The comedian Lenny Bruce would quip, "Mandrake and Lothar, Daddy Warbucks and the Asp, Green Hornet and Kato, Lone Ranger and Tonto—all those couples." Once their sexuality became a topic for nightclub jokesters, their days were numbered. The only places left for them were high-camp and late-night cable TV.

The Lone Ranger was a hero for a time when you didn't have to explain why you needed to do good other than that you wanted to. You could have a relationship like the Lone Ranger and Tonto's with hardly anyone wondering who was doing what for or to whom. You could tell stories about the West with no nod to the real history and condition of the West. It was a time when you could wear eccentric clothes and not be thought campy or cartoonish.

Where the West Was

Before the American West was explored, European painters imagined it as a new Golden Land, full of spectacular landscapes and wonderful animals. Some of America's most important nineteenth- and early twentieth-century artists focused on the West and the people who inhabited it: George Catlin, Frederick Remington, Charles Russell.

In print, dime westerns were best sellers in the nineteenth century. You can still find their equivalent—Louis Lamour's novels, for example—in any large airport newsstand right next to the section of romance paperbacks. Cormac McCarthy began writing novels set in Tennessee, but he now lives in Laredo and writes novels set in Texas and Mexico: *All the Pretty Horses*, *The Crossing*, *Blood Meridian*. Larry McMurtry's best-selling novel *Lonesome Dove* was also an Emmy-winning TV miniseries. The image of the manly westerner is so powerful that it continues to be used by Marlboro to peddle cigarettes—no longer permissible on billboards or television—but a frequent image still in magazines and bars.

One of the first narrative films—and what is often cited as the first film with real editing—was a Western: *The Great Train Robbery*, ten minutes long and made in Fort Lee, New Jersey, in 1903. More than 7000 westerns have followed. In the early 1950s nearly 25 percent of American film production was westerns. There were hundreds of western serials back in the days when going to the movies on Saturday afternoons meant two features, up to fifteen cartoons, Movietone News, coming attractions (it would be years before anyone outside the film industry called them "trailers"), and episodes of one or more serials. Dozens of television series were set in the imaginative nineteenth century American West. One of them—*Gunsmoke*—ran for two full decades (1955–1975). Clint Eastwood's first important role was Rowdy Yates in *Rawhide*, a series about a cattle drive that was always en route but never seemed to get anywhere. Sergio Leone saw those programs and hired Eastwood for the trilogy that rejuvenated the theatrical western and made Eastwood an international star: *A Fistful of Dollars* (*Per un pugno di dolleri*, 1964), *For a Few Dollars More* (*Per qualchi dollari in più*, 1965), and *The Good, the Bad, and the Ugly* (*Il Buono, il brutto, il cattivo*, 1966). *Gunsmoke*, *Bonanza*, and *Rawhide* still appear on cable.

The action of most films advertised or characterized as "westerns" is situated in the American Southwest, but they are also set in Florida, Alaska, California, Washington, and the Adirondacks. Some westerns are about cowboys, but others are about farmers, sheepherders, migrants, miners, pimps and whores. Some were about war and some about love. Some are about whites, some about blacks, some about Mexicans, some about Indians; some are about relations between these groups. Some are about the vastness of Western space. Some are up close, like classical drama; some are broad, like classical epic. In some the battles are enormous, and in others the battles are intimate. The American West is a great canvas upon which myriads of stories are told. It is a very large real place, and it is and remains a much larger imaginative space.

The Global West

Peter Fonda tells about being on location in Peru with Dennis Hopper in 1971, filming *The Last Movie*. A horse fell off a cliff, landed on a ledge, and broke its back. It was screaming in pain, so one of the stunt men climbed down and shot it with the chrome-plated .44 revolver Peter carried with him everywhere in those days. The gun had originally belonged to the famous western actor Tom Mix and had been given to Peter by his father, Henry.

Within a few hours two helicopters of heavily armed police arrived and lined up the entire film crew. The officer in charge demanded the gun. They were in a remote town, a full day's drive from the nearest city, and there were no telephones. Somehow the police official had found out about the gun and had arrived with his troops to get it and to arrest its owner. Real pistols were illegal there for anyone but police and military, Peter said. Except for "Old Tom," all the guns used by the film crew were made of rubber.

At first Peter insisted there was no gun, but when it was clear that they were all going to be taken away and the production shut down, he got it out of his bag and gave it to the officer. Now only he and Hopper were to be taken away. Peter told the policeman to be careful with the gun, that it was valuable; it had belonged to Tom Mix.

The policeman froze, looked at the gun, and then asked Hopper, "Is true, *jefe*? The gun of Tom Mix?" Hopper said it was indeed true; it was the gun of Tom Mix. The policeman, Peter said, walked along the two rows of his men, all of whom still had automatic weapons pointing at the film crew, holding the pistol in the palms of his two outstretched hands as if it were religious object, saying again and again, "The gun of Tom Mix. The gun of Tom Mix. The gun of Tom Mix." Then he gave the gun back to Peter, herded his men into the helicopters, and they all flew away.

Tom Mix hadn't made a film since 1935 and had been dead since 1940. Yet the iconic power of Tom Mix as western hero and the real gun he had held in those fictive silent and sound films were powerful enough to turn a serious criminal incident into a sacred moment.

A Grand Time

The world of Tom Mix, the Lone Ranger, and all the other filmic gunfighters was a time and place when the world was grand, when the pistols and gestures were beautiful (as Michael insisted when we left that Fort Sumner junk store), and issues unambiguous.

Hollywood producers justify graphic violence in recent films in the name of realism, but in the case of the gunfighter western, earlier films were probably more realistic than most of what came later. The quick and simple gunfight in the 1923 *Virginian* was closer to reality than any gunfight in any film directed by Sergio Leone or Howard Hawks. The first men to play cowboys in westerns made in California were cowboys who had driven herds of cattle to California. Silent era actors Tim McCoy, who had been a real western marshal, and Tom Mix, who had been a real Texas Ranger, played western marshals and Texas Rangers in their films.

Few real-life cowboys or sheriffs or badmen had the time or skill or money to be the superb marksmen they so often were in films. Putting a bullet where you want it to go is like putting a tennis or golf ball where you want it to go: accuracy requires diligent and regular practice. One may practice the day long with a tennis or golf ball for little cost, but revolver cartridges were and are expensive. Few men trying to get by in the nineteenth-century American West would have shot up a month's pay putting holes in targets, but I remember only one film—*Warlock* (1959)—in which the hero discussed the great cost of the ammunition he consumed in his daily practice.

The splendid Buntline Special and Navy Colt pistols, so common in film, were rare in reality. Few men had use for them: gunfights beyond a few paces were avoided or negotiated with rifles or shotguns. Only an ill-prepared fool would put all his trust in a weapon as inaccurate as a pistol, and ill-prepared fools did not have great life expectancies in the West, real or fictive.

Shots in the back, common enough in reality, appeared in the films only when they were of special narrative moment, as in Henry King's *The Gunfighter* (1950). In that film, an ambitious punk named Hunt Bromley shoots famed gunfighter Jimmy Ringo in the back. The sheriff is about to arrest Bromley, but the dying Ringo insists he went for his gun first. The sheriff says everybody knows that isn't true; Bromley insists he doesn't need any favors. Ringo tells Bromley he's not doing him any favors: he's sentencing him to a life in which he will never be free of ambitious homicidal punks like Bromley himself.

In a 1973 episode of the television series *Gunsmoke*, a farmer pressed into a Dodge City posse inadvertently shoots in the back the killer being pursued. The entire town turns against him, and the town children even slaughter his young daughter's cat. Marshall Matt Dillon, the protagonist of the series, finally ends the abominations, but he is uncomfortable about his interference. Not even Matt Dillon can abandon the rules of propriety in the film's version of the great American West.

Only villains and noncombatants ignore the rules, and only women are excused from them. Marshall Will Kane's Quaker wife in *High Noon* (1952) shoots a villain in the back when his guns are unloaded. A few minutes later she distracts another badman about to have a gun duel with her wounded husband, enabling Kane to kill him. Ordinarily, a gunfight won by improper means is a spoiled triumph. "I remember when I first killed a man," says the gunfighter marshal in *Warlock* (played by Henry Fonda). "It was clear and had to be done, though I went home afterwards and puked my insides out. I remember how clear it was. Afterwards, nothing was ever clear again, except one thing: that's to hold strictly to the rules; it's only the rules that matter, hold on to them like you were walking on eggs. So you know yourself you've played it as fair and as best you could."

Was this real life in the real West? No more than the Lone Ranger's silver bullets had to do with anything that ever existed anytime or anywhere. In the world of the storied heroes, the rules are clear, the consequences are absolute, and guns do not rust.

Tradition

Writing in 1954, critic Robert Warshow famously said that the western is "an art form for connoisseurs, where the spectator derives his pleasure from the appreciation of minor variations within the working out of a pre-established order."[2] Warshow was writing about gunfighter westerns in particular, those in which the action is resolved by a gun battle between two opponents. The gunfight was an early theme: like the chase and the cattle drive, it was easy to depict on screen and didn't require much explanation for the audience to understand what was going on.

But it changed over time. In the second film version of *The Virginian*, made in 1923, the gunfight toward which the entire film has been heading is over in two or three seconds and is viewed from a wide angle more than a hundred yards away. The only way we know it happened is one of the two men in the scene falls down. The gunfight in Sergio Leone's *Once Upon a Time in the West* (1969) is exquisitely choreographed and scored, and takes four minutes, an eternity in screen time. At some points a single eye fills the entire screen. The fight is between a mysterious harmonica-playing wanderer played by Charles Bronson and an unmediated malefactor played by Henry Fonda (ten minutes into the film, he murders a father and three children preparing for a wedding reception). At the end of this ballet, Bronson whips out his pistol, fans the hammer, and Fonda's character falls to the ground, a bullet in his heart.

In real life, that bullet had as much chance of hitting a crow flying overhead. Fanning—a swift slap on the hammer with the heel

of one's free hand to cock the pistol and advance the cylinder—
came into films sometime in the 1920s when a director said to actor
Tim McCoy that he needed something new and different in his
gunfight scene. Either McCoy or the director came up with the idea
of fanning the hammer. McCoy told me he'd never heard of anyone
in a real life gunfight fanning a pistol; fanning makes it nearly
impossible to control the vertical position of the muzzle, which
means the pistol is nearly impossible to aim. Nonetheless, fanning
quickly became a film standard. Reality was not at issue.

All art is in some measure about other art. Like other artists,
filmmakers are aware of the workers and work they follow. In 1961,
the great Japanese director Akira Kurosawa, a fan of western films,
made *Yojimbo*, which is about a samurai who comes to a small town
where two gangs are warring. He hires out to both of them
and, by the time he leaves, nearly everyone in both gangs is dead.
Three years later, the Italian director Sergio Leone plagiarized the
plot for *A Fistful of Dollars*. In 1995 Walter Hill used Kurosawa's
plot, with full acknowledgement, for *Last Man Standing* with Bruce
Willis.

Schlock filmmeister Roger Corman used the plot to make a
sword-fighting movie starring David Carradine, *The Warrior and
the Sorceress* (1984). It differed from the others in two primary
regards: the location was a mythical planet with two suns, and the
leading lady plays the entire film naked from the hips up. In his
autobiography, Carradine says he called Corman to say he liked the
script but was worried about the similarity to *Yojimbo*.

Roger said, "Yes, it is rather like *Yojimbo*.
I said, "It's not like *Yojimbo*. It IS *Yojimbo*."
Roger said, "Let me tell you a story. When *Fist Full of
Dollars* opened in Tokyo, Kurosawa's friends called him up
and said, 'You must see this picture.' Kurosawa replied, 'Yes, I
understand it's rather like *Yojimbo*.' His friends corrected
him, 'No, it's not like *Yojimbo*, it IS *Yojimbo*. You have to sue
these people.' 'I can't sue them,' he responded. 'Why not?'
'Because,' Kurosawa confessed, '*Yojimbo* IS Dashiell Ham-

mett's *Red Harvest.*' " (Carradine, *Boston and Tokyo: Journey,*
1995, 539)

The repeated transformation of the basic story is exactly what
happens to tales in oral tradition when they move from place to
place. The core narrative remains fairly constant, but the details are
changed to fit the new context.

Individual Combat and Master Status

The American heroic western took shape in a new space and
received its most powerful dissemination in a new medium, but the
action is old. Fran Stryker and George W. Trendle invented the
Lone Ranger, but not the imaginative world he inhabited. Nor did
the authors of the nineteenth-century dime novels and the producers of the late twentieth-century filmic bloodbaths. I quoted
Robert Warshow's statement that the western was "an art form for
connoisseurs." Warshow thought that the order was one that had
been defined in the western film tradition itself. He didn't look far
enough. The gunfighter western is a recent avatar of a much older
narrative order.

The great epics—*Odyssey, Iliad, Aeneid, Beowulf,* and many
others—deal with the same concerns: power, law, peace, order,
death, chaos. As with these older narratives, the western film with
the gunfight as central dramatic device is always predicated on a
sense of unendurable disorder hovering just outside whatever
boundaries are established or assumed: outside town, outside the
ranch, beyond the range—forces which may, from no internal prov-
ocation but quite on their frivolous and gratuitous own, come in and
ravage everything.

The action is always one of restoring equilibrium: the beast
Grendel violates the peace of Hrothgar's castle in *Beowulf,* the
suitors violate the security of Odysseus's home in *Odyssey,* Paris
violates the rules of visitation in *Iliad.* The film *Warlock* begins with
the senseless murder of an unarmed barber. The action that begins
Clint Eastwood's 1976 western, *The Outlaw Josey Wales,* is the brutal

slaughter of a farmer's wife and child by a gang of wandering thugs;
no reason is ever offered for that violence.

Such is the enemy—the random and sudden violence that ru-
dely shatters the boundaries of normal life—for those mythic and
legendary heroes of the epics, and for those gunfighter heroes of the
film's recreation of the American West

The mainspring of the western is individual or single combat,
which is grounded in the notion that physical performance can be
equated with virtue, and that through a single well-done act, a person may achieve all the status he might want or need. Killing the
fastest gun in the West immediately makes the killer the new fastest
gun in the West. No need for intermediate steps, no slow ascen-
dance through the ranks. The win immediately engenders a radical
change in status, and the opportunity is there for anyone who encounters the present titleholder on the street, at a bar, or in the alley.

Real life isn't like that. With rare exceptions, the slow progress
that leads to success is boring. Usually it is meaningless except in
retrospect, it needs the stretched-out dimension of time past to have
any apparent meaning at all, and it needs a decent social nexus and
even some luck to occur. That is the process of success for most
people, though it surely isn't the way most people would prefer,
which is why folk and popular literature and films are filled by narratives documenting a faster kind and style of certification. (It's also
why state lotteries—lousy investments by any standard—have done
so well: "Hey, you never know," say the lottery ads in New York.)

We hear in folktales of the magic wish heard and fulfilled, the
dreadful beast properly slain, the king's beautiful daughter won and
married. In the folktales all kings' daughters are beautiful, and the
marriages mean that the poor country boys get to move from farm
to castle, from amorphous rural space to the center of power. In
westerns, we see the quiet cowboy enduring insult and outrage for
just so long. Then he lets go with the fastest forearm reflexes in local
memory, and the badman is outdrawn and blown away.

We can go back for examples at least four thousand years—to
the great Babylonian creation myth, the *Enuma Elish*, in which the
young god Marduk kills Tiamat, the great and malevolent mother,

in one of the goriest homicides in folk literature. Tiamat had created evil beings to destroy her own children, so the gods hired Marduk as their marshal to go against her in battle. He takes the contract, but demands authority to commence creation anew, to rebuild the world his own way. The elder gods are desperate and drunk, so they quickly agree to his terms. Marduk and Tiamat assemble spectacular armies, but they meet in single combat to decide the fate of the world.

Marduk first immobilizes Tiamat with his net, and then orders Imhullu, the wind, to blow in her mouth so forcefully her belly bloats; he shoots an arrow through the belly to the womb, and then kills her with his sword. In a grim parody of parturition, he uses her split cadaver to form the universe we know. Even the masters of slice-and-dice teenage slasher movies would blanch filming this encounter.

After Tiamat is dead, nobody knows quite what to do with Marduk. He got rid of the beast, he restored order, but how does one live with a character so powerful? The problem of what to do with the successful hero after he's done his job appears regularly in myth and legend and in western films.

The Babylonians solved the problem by making Marduk abstract. They affixed to him all the powers of all the fifty gods in their pantheon, then had him assign his day-to-day powers to some local officials who would be his earthly representatives—the priests of Babylon. Marduk was kicked upstairs and out of town.

Heroic success invokes alienating stigma. When Beowulf defeats Grendel, the poet tells us there is no man more worthy of kingship. Not only has he destroyed the most pressing evil and is, therefore, considered capable of managing the general good; also they have no idea what else to do with so capable a person when there was no combat in progress. Either elevate him to a form of kingship or run him out of town—those are the two alternatives. In similar fashion, the outside hero who comes in to save the town in the gunfighter films nearly always leaves at the end. It happens in *Warlock, My Darling Clementine* (1946), *Death of a Gunfighter* (1969), and scores of other westerns. It happens in every radio, television, and film episode of the Lone Ranger. Even when the savior is the insider who has heroically risen to the occasion, he is sufficiently changed so he no longer fits his old role once he has excised the community's infection. Owen Wister's Virginian begins as just a ranch hand, rises to foreman, and then, after lynching his best friend and killing his enemy Trampas in a gun duel, he gets the girl and, in the novel, becomes a wealthy industrialist.

America's Last Romance

Star Wars writer and director George Lucas told a *Rolling Stone* reporter in 1977, "One of the significant things that occurred to me is I saw the western die. We hardly knew what happened, one day we turned around and there weren't any westerns anymore."[3] Lucas wasn't at all right. Westerns continue to be made, though far fewer of them than in decades past. Kevin Costner's *Dances with Wolves* (1990) won an Academy Award for best picture, as did Clint Eastwood's *Unforgiven* (1992). *Lonesome Dove* (1989) won an Emmy. Mel Gibson starred in a film version of TV's *Maverick* (1994), and Kevin Costner starred as *Wyatt Earp* (1994). Sharon Stone played a gal gunfighter in Sam Raimi's *The Quick and the Dead* (1995). Jeff Bridges starred in Walter Hill's *Wild Bill* the same year. Hill, who directed *The Long Riders* (1980), directed Bruce Willis in *Last Man Standing* (1995). The following year Jim Jarmusch directed what might be the first hallucinatory Western: *Dead Man,* starring Johnny Depp as William Blake and Gary Farmer as an Indian named Nobody. In spring 2004, HBO followed its immensely popular *Sopranos* with the western series *Deadwood*, set primarily in a mining town's whorehouse and hardware store. The filmic mud was fabulous; how much it had to do with the real west was anyone's guess.

The real West was only incidental to the action going on in all those westerns anyway. It may have been, as I've suggested, just a local backdrop against which a far more basic action could be played out, just as were the undifferentiated universe of the Enuma Elish for the final battle between Marduk and Tiamat and the black sky for the final battle between Luke Skywalker and Darth Vader.

We can understand why young Michael looked with such loathing at the ostensible gun of Billy the Kid, why the Peruvian policeman viewed with such reverence the gun of Tom Mix, and why Michael Ondaatje and millions of other kids wore those cowboy suits. The scholars are still mining and parsing this material, but every one of us kids understood perfectly well what those symbols and stories were about all along, and we still do.

12 The Deceptive Anarchy of *Let Us Now Praise Famous Men*

The key problem every storyteller must solve—whether it be someone telling a story at a family gathering, a novelist, a filmmaker, a lawyer in summation, or any other narrator—is finding the correct voice for the narrative. The matter of voice and the matter of story are not separable: the story exists in the voice in which it is told; without that voice you have only someone talking about a story, not someone performing or telling one. It is perhaps the most important and the least understood aspect of the storyteller's art. What would *The Sound and the Fury* or *Frankenstein* or *Moby-Dick* or *Huckleberry Finn* or *Catcher in the Rye* be if they had been written in third-person omniscient? What would the biblical Exodus, *War and Peace*, *Ulysses*, *The Sun Also Rises* and *Gone With the Wind* be if the narrative voice had been first person?

One of the best and most important books about 1930s America is James Agee's and Walker Evans's *Let Us Now Praise Famous Men*. It took a generation for the book to be recognized as the masterpiece it is. It is a book like Ralph Ellison's *Invisible Man* or Flaubert's *Madame Bovary* or Basho's *Narrow Road to the Interior*, books that in voice and vision so perfectly captured and defined the spirit of their subject and mode of depicting them that neither their authors nor their competitors were ever able to transcend them.

Let Us Now Praise Famous Men is special in that category in that it not only tells a story, but also argues the impossibility of telling the story it is in fact telling. One of the authors (Evans) attempts no words whatever, and the other (Agee) constantly tests, challenges, and faults his own capacity to use words adequately, as well as the capacity of words to represent the real. The book has two narratives: one the verbal and photographic story of the Alabama farmers Agee and Evans visited, the other Agee's verbal story of himself and Evans trying to make a story out of the stuff they found.

The Stammerer

Let Us Now Praise Famous Men, originally published in 1941, was long out of print when I was a senior at Rutgers in the spring of 1960. People talked of it as if it were the Grail: brilliant, redemptive, universally inaccessible. James Agee's text was said to be as visionary as Blake's, and Walker Evans's photographs were the ultimate visualization of the rural southeast at the heart of the Great Depression. The college library did not own a copy; I knew no one who had read it, let alone owned it. When the second edition was published that year, I bought it immediately.

I got as far as Agee's third or fourth insult to the reader, which is about the third or fourth page of the text proper, and assigned it to one of those piles of books to be read when there was a lot of time to spare. Usually, that means books I never look at again. For some reason, a year or two later, I did return to it, and that time I read it transfixed. The book was the same; I can't tell you what had changed in me between the two readings. I remember only that this time I began reading it late at night; when I finished, it was long after the morning light had overwhelmed the reading lamp by my chair.

It is a difficult and in some ways an intimidating book. Agee is offensive in the early pages, and deliberately so, but I'm certain that the last thing in the world he wanted was to be opaque. I now think he's rather like a stammerer, trying to get it out faster than he's able.

He was exquisitely sensitive to the problem confronted by every serious writer about the real: the printed word is serial, with one word following another, as does every sentence and paragraph and page and chapter. But the world of human experience is multivalent: in the same instant, we are fully capable of experiencing all five senses and a range of passions as well. He was trying to sing a multivalent song in a serial world. Little wonder he got surly and crazy from time to time.

Doing It

Work on the book began in 1936, a time of extraordinary literary energy and experimentation. It was the year of Margaret Mitchell's *Gone with the Wind*—but it was also the year of Djuna Barnes's *Nightwood*. It was the year of Faulkner's masterpiece, *Absalom, Absalom!* one of a series of novels which explored radically different modes of narrative and voice: *The Sound and the Fury* (1929), *As I Lay Dying* (1930), *Sanctuary* (1931), and *Light in August* (1932). Hart Crane's epic *The Bridge* had been published in 1930, with photographs by Evans, who was Crane's friend. *Ulysses,* in which James Joyce utilized a wide variety of narrative modalities, had been street legal in the United States for three years, eleven years after its publication in Europe. Both Agee and Evans early on owned copies of the 1922 European edition.

James Agee was working as a staff writer for *Fortune Magazine,* when, in June 1936, the magazine's managing editor assigned him a piece on tenant farmers and agreed to let him have Walker Evans as photographer. Evans was then documenting the Depression for the federal government's Resettlement Administration (RA). Roy Stryker, who headed the photographic section of the RA, agreed to let Evans work on the *Fortune* assignment, so long as the negatives belonged to the government.

The two young men—Agee 26 and Evans 32—went south in search of tenant farmers. After a series of preliminary adventures, a few of which are narrated in the book, they wound up in Hale County, Alabama, where they spent a month or so with three families named Burroughs, Tengle, and Fields (in the book Agee calls them Ricketts, Woods, and Gudger). Evans later said that he and Agee had little to do with one another while they were deep in the work, and there is no reason to doubt him. Evans took photographs, mostly with an 8″ × 10″ view camera. He also used a Leica 35 mm camera and maybe a 4″ × 5″ view camera as well. Agee filled notebooks with impressions, dialogue, and descriptions of what he saw.

I don't suppose you could have two more different collaborators: Agee couldn't work without making himself part of the subject; Evans couldn't work without getting his self out of the frame. Agee insisted on what Evans hid: the presence of the first person singular. Evans obscured the first person singular like his master Flaubert; Agee imposed it like his master Walt Whitman. A student at the University of Michigan in 1971 asked Evans to describe what makes a good photograph. He responded, "Detachment, lack of sentimentality, originality." Agee would insist on the last, he'd pretend to believe in the second, and he wouldn't even pay lip service to the first. He was no more capable of detachment than he was of unaided flight.

Agee delivered to *Fortune* a manuscript ten times longer than anything the magazine could possibly use. After a year, the editors gave up trying to edit it and released it. So far as I know, no copy of that manuscript exists, and I don't know anyone who has seen it. Neither do I know which photographs Evans sent with it. In 1938 a friend got Harper and Brothers to offer a book contract. Agee delivered the manuscript in the summer of 1939. They asked for some changes, Agee refused, and the deal collapsed.

The next year another friend hooked him up with Houghton Mifflin, which had only one condition: that the text not include any words for the publication of which you could be arrested in Massachusetts. This cost Agee about eight words, nearly all of which could be inferred anyway. He agreed to the condition and *Let Us Now Praise Famous Men* was published in August 1941.

There could hardly have been a worse time. Two years earlier John Steinbeck's *Grapes of Wrath* had cornered the poor farmer market. The Depression was over, and the war effort was underway.

Slightly over three months after *Let Us Now Praise Famous Men* was published, the Japanese bombed Pearl Harbor, and the 1930s were over. The book sold a few hundred copies and was finally remaindered and went out of print in 1948.

Evans became a book reviewer for *Time*, then a staff photographer and later associate editor of *Fortune*. He stayed with them until 1965 when he became a member of the Yale faculty. He died in 1975.

Agee wrote articles for magazines, film reviews for *Time*, better film reviews for *The Nation*, several film scripts (the best known of which is *The African Queen*, for which John Huston wrote the end because Agee was in the hospital getting over a coronary). And he wrote fiction. He drank too much, smoked too much, did everything too much except take care of himself. He was only forty-five when he died of a heart attack in a New York City taxicab in 1955. "In the end," wrote his friend John Hersey in an introduction to the 1988 reprinting, "he jumped to his death by indirection; he was defenestrated from the upper stories of his life, as if in slow motion, by alcohol, nicotine, insomnia, overwork, misused sex, searing guilt, and—above all, we can guess—by his anger and want and despair at finding that with all his wild talent he had never been able to write the whole of the universe down on the head of a pin."[1]

His novel *A Death in the Family* was published in 1957; it won the 1958 Pulitzer Prize. At the time, not one of his other books was in print, but within two years they all were. The 1960 edition of *Let Us Now Praise Famous Men* was immensely popular. The psychiatrist Robert Coles tells of black and white civil rights workers in the south in the early 1960s carrying the book as if it were a bible or talisman. My late friend Charles Haynie, who was one of those civil rights workers, said to me, "We grew up in a world where it wasn't all right for men to be emotional about things. Women could, but we didn't know how. Agee taught us it was okay to feel. All those feelings of his about intruding in people's lives, it was important for us to know that it was okay to have those feelings. We went into people's houses when we did voter registration. That book taught us how to go into someone's house."

Ducks Aren't Supposed to Fly

As soon as you open the book, you know there's something wrong. There's no title page, no words at all: just a blank page followed in the first edition by thirty-one photographs arranged in three groups. The photographs have no captions or locating information of any kind.

Books have an order of access, just as do movie theaters, churches, and concert halls. In the movie theater, as I noted in chapter 3, we obtain and hand over our tickets. We pass through a lobby and then perhaps a corridor. We sit in an auditorium, often next to people we do not know and whom we never look directly in the face. The lights dim and we sit in the dark with those strangers whose faces we do not know. There may be trailers, messages, or other preliminary pieces. Then the film itself begins in the darkened hall. By the time we see the first scene, we are psychically a long distance from the street, and we've traversed that distance by a process that is fully familiar to us, which is why we're comfortable sitting in the dark with those strangers, and we are able to enter the narrative world of the film almost immediately.

In a nonfiction book we look at the cover, then open the book to a blank page, which is followed by a half-title page, which is followed by a full title page, which is backed by copyright information, which is followed by a dedication page, which is followed by a contents page, which is followed by a foreword and/or introduction, which is followed by the book itself. That's the way books are made. Our familiarity with that structure is what lets us know where we are in them and how to read the words before us.

Agee was perfectly aware of this structure. In an early design for the book, there was to be a table of contents, a list of persons and places, then book 1, which would be photographs, book 2, which would be text, and finally a section of notes and appendices. Sometime between that design and submission of the final version, Agee and Evans decided to be far more radical. *Let Us Now Praise Famous Men* begins with the images, which appear before all words—before the title, before the copyright, before the table of contents.

Agee and Evans agreed on that positioning of the pictures, but it's an arrangement that has Evans's fingerprints all over it. He loved good writing. He often said that the most important influences on him were Flaubert and Baudelaire, and his closest friends were writers, but he never liked to let words get too close to his pictures. When he was hired to provide illustrations for Carlton Beals's *The Crime of Cuba* in 1933, he insisted that his photographs be printed as a group at the end of the book without captions. In the book version of his 1938 Museum of Modern Art show, *American Photographs*, he arranged the pictures in two groups, and at the end of each group, he provided a list of sparse identifying lines: "Sidewalk in Vicksburg, Mississippi, 1936"; "Main Street of County Seat, Alabama, 1936"; "Lunch Wagon Detail, New York, 1931"; "Roadside Gas Sign, 1939"; "Faces, Pennsylvania Town, 1936"; and "Main Street Faces, 1935." He placed the introduction by his good friend Lincoln Kirstein after the pictures, not before them.

The photographs in *Let Us Now Praise Famous Men* are followed by some very eccentric front matter: a table of contents that consists of only six words on four lines ("Contents/Book One/ Preliminaries/Book Two) that doesn't tell you Book One is already over. Unattributed quotations from *King Lear* and Karl Marx. A page from a child's geography book. A list of characters and places, nearly all of them made up. A "design" for Book Two, which isn't a table of contents but, once you know the book, really does tell you how the thing is structured. Next we get prose; prose poems; poems; Whitmanesque catalogues; sequences of lines, of voices heard, and overheard; the Sermon on the Mount without introduction; newspaper articles; and Blake's proverbs of Heaven and Hell. Some of the poetic prose is so dense you cannot read it without pause, and often it is followed by descriptive prose about living space, education, work, and food so precise and specific the lines fairly snap.

Some critics write about *Let Us Now Praise Famous Men* as a book out of control, a book that is nearly great but missed it for this or that reason, a book that suffers from excess. One wrote: "When one first reads *Famous Men*, many passages may strike one as pretentious, mannered, precious, pompous, pontifical, smug, self-righteous, self-indulgent, willfully obscure, doctrinaire, self-congratulatory, soph-omoric, belligerent; even Agee's self-abnegation, self-loathing, and modesty may offend."[2]

Yes, but. When I was in graduate school in the 1960s, I had to read several essays that dealt with the dramatic failure of *Hamlet*. One was by T. S. Eliot. The essay tells us why the play is a failure. The essay is, as were all of Eliot's essays, erudite, brilliantly written, and well reasoned.

The only problem, as you've perhaps thought already, is that it's wrong. *Hamlet* works very well indeed. It works better than nearly any other play in the English language. Every time I see it I am again astonished at what a good play it is. *Hamlet* is like that old canard about *le canard*: according to all rational principles of engi-neering, it should not be able to fly. But fly it does. Look up and you will see it.

Likewise *Let Us Now Praise Famous Men*. What's wrong with that list of things? "Wrong" with it is this: The book works. That group of thirty-one uncaptioned images fires the imagination. Those pages of lunatic structure and mad prose make, after a while, extraordi-nary sense. The funhouse lines turn out to be vertical and horizontal after all. The sentences turn out to have a sublime lucidity.

Some parts don't make sense until the second time around. You don't know that the three parenthetical "On the Porch" sections are really the frame and rationale for the book until you reach the very last page. But so what? Several of the key images in the Benjy sec-tion of *The Sound and the Fury*, which comes first, make no sense until you read the Dilsey section, which comes last. The final half-sentence of *Finnegan's Wake* is the first part of the half-sentence with which the novel begins, which you cannot know until you get to the very end and remember the very beginning.

Agee and Agee

The director Henry King said in a 1976 conference on western films that he chose to use black and white for his 1950 film *The Gunfighter* even though color film was available because "it was a film with one idea: a man who wants to quit but doesn't know how." Color, King said, would have complicated the film's exploration of that idea. "Because color is a character, you see."

Every element in a work of art is, in that sense, one of the characters. The frame is part of the picture; the concert hall is part of the symphony. And the "I" of the narrator trying to be direct and honest with us is as much a construct as any character made up out of his or her freakiest imaginative convulsions. The only difference is that "I" looks more like someone we think we know than the character from the freaky convulsion.

"Je est un autre," wrote the twenty-one-year-old Arthur Rimbaud. "I is an other." The James Agee who wallows, complains, wails, rails, traces, and retraces his eye and his sensibility and his ability to report anything with any measure of truth in *Let Us Now Praise Famous Men* comes out of the James Agee who made notes in a fine small hand, the one who reworked those notes again and again, but he is not the same entity; he doesn't exist in the same universe. He is a creature existing only on paper. What Agee says of the relationship between his writing and a real person applies equally to him:

> In a novel, a house or person has his meaning, his existence, entirely through the writer. Here, a house or a person has only the most limited of his meaning through me: his true meaning is much huger. It is that he *exists*, in actual being, as you do and as I do, and as no character of the imagination can possibly exist. His great weight, mystery, and dignity are in this fact. As for me, I can tell you of him only what I saw, only so accurately as in my terms I know how: and this in turn has its chief stature not in any ability of mine but in the fact that I too exist, not as a work of fiction, but as a human being. Because of his immeasurable weight in actual existence, and because of mine, every word I tell of him has inevitably a kind of immediacy, a kind of meaning, not at all necessarily "superior" to that of imagination, but of a kind so different that a

work of the imagination (however intensely it may draw on "life") can at best only faintly imitate the least of it.[3]

So instead of looking at Agee as a writer fumbling to get wherever he's going, let's look at Agee the writer placing between himself and ourselves a character named James Agee who is wrestling with problems of representation and truth, who obsesses with questions about what can be known and what can be said. *Let Us Now Praise Famous Men* is a documentary twice over, first the documentary of what two young men saw in the American southeast in the summer of 1936, and second the documentary of the struggle to translate that adventure into a work that could be printed on paper, that would be comprehensible to others. Instead of Agee as self-indulgent writer lacking control, what if Agee was in exquisite control the entire time, was using his written self exactly as he was using the quotations from the Bible or Blake, the survey from *Partisan Review* he quotes and attacks, the eccentric structure? Perhaps, when reading *Let Us Now Praise Famous Men*, we should think of Borges's line about Walt Whitman: "The mere happy vagabond proposed by the verses of *Leaves of Grass* would have been incapable of writing them."[4]

Agee is not disingenuous; he's direct. But *Let Us Now Praise Famous Men* isn't just a book *about*; it's also a book *of*. Just as telling you the subject of a poem tells you only the least important fact about that poem, a statement about the plot of this book tells you nothing useful. This book is no more and no less about cotton tenant-farming than *Moby-Dick* is about whaling, which is to say *Let Us Now Praise Famous Men* could not exist without cotton tenant-farming, and you'll learn about cotton tenant-farming reading it. But you probably won't learn the most useful things. And what you'll miss entirely is precisely the experience of what matters.

It was a book by two men who believed in reality and the possibility, however difficult, of documenting some portion of it. One might mistake Agee for the first postmodern writer, the man who more than any other of his time questioned our ability to know, let alone to say. But unlike the postmodernist, he, like Evans, believed in the real and in our ability to know it and to tell one another about it. He proved that by insisting that Evans was not his illustrator but rather his full collaborator.

The real is what *Let Us Now Praise Famous Men* is about: real things in real gardens, a real photographer and a real writer trying to make real sense of it, trying to find a way to give some appreciation of the human and physical complexity to strangers miles and years away.

The key difference between documentary and fictive art is this: in documentary the referent is always essential whereas in fiction it's merely occasional. In documentary—however good or bad a job—there's something out there that is. Those photographs by Walker Evans standing before any words in *Let Us Now Praise Famous Men* are Agee's insistence to us of his belief in the profundity of the real.

He can't explore the consciousness of the people he and Evans met in rural Alabama, nor does he really try. He explores the surface of their world and what he can see of the depths of his own world, not by showing you himself but by helping you to see through his eyes. We must understand, therefore, the limitations of those eyes, that mind, that sensibility. He uses the first person not to tell us what to see, but how to see. It is as if he is saying, "You think you are standing here and seeing this? Well, you're not, because you are this and this and this. You and I, in this together." Perhaps no American writer other than Allen Ginsberg has been so close to Walt Whitman in this regard. "I would do just as badly to simplify or eliminate myself from this picture as to simplify or invent character, places or atmospheres," Agee writes. "A chain of truths did actually weave itself and run through: it is their texture that I want to represent, not betray, nor pretty up into art."[5]

Agee set a deliberately offensive rhythm to the first edition, one that played on our sense of what a book is, how a book is made, on our notion of the order of things. He wanted to make sure that by the time we got to his text proper we were thinking about what goes on in a book, what kinds of things are told to us, what kind of trust is possible, what kind of truth can be told and heard.

Cracking the Structure

The structure of *Let Us Now Praise Famous Men* is grounded in the relationship between the words and the pictures. "The photographs," Agee tells us, "are not illustrative. They, and the text, are coequal, mutually independent, and fully collaborative."[6] He means it. He insisted that the publisher not distribute bound galleys without the photographs because reviewers would be incapable of understanding what the book was about if they received only the words. The deceptive clarity of those thirty-one photographs is the anchor in reality that permits him to fly. He doesn't tell you what the photographs are about until you're more than halfway into the book, but he doesn't have to because they're there all the time. You've already seen them. You have a vision of the reality he's writing his way toward.

The relation of the words and pictures changed radically in the 1960 edition. Agee's part was the same, but Evans's wasn't. Evans doubled the number of photographs and recropped most of the photographs he kept. In going from thirty-one photographs in the 1941 edition to sixty-two in the 1960, Evans didn't just expand the number of images of the area Agee had written about. He moved outside it: several of the photographs weren't from rural Alabama, some weren't from Alabama at all, and some had been taken before Evans worked for the Resettlement Administration. More important, he wrote an essay, which appeared between the dedication page and Agee's preface, and that cracked the structure of the book.

In the first edition, Evans was silent, and the pictures were only of things that Agee wrote about. In the second edition, Evans had a voice about the dead Agee, and he had images of places Agee hadn't gone to, just as Agee had written about explorations inside himself no one but he could have gone to.

Why did Evans insert those alien photographs into this book about a very specific place? I can only speculate. I've never been able to find anything Evans said about it. One possibility is that Evans decided that the book really wasn't about that very specific place, but rather was about a larger slice of human experience. Therefore, the expansion was legitimate.

Another is more personal: perhaps he realized that this book was where his mark was being made, and he had to become more of a presence in it than he had in the first edition. Walker Evans is one of the best-known twentieth-century American photographers now, but he wasn't in 1960. His only major published work then was *American Photographs*, the book based on his 1938 solo show at the Museum of Modern Art. "Until 1960," William Stott writes, "his reputation was limited, esoteric. In that year *U.S. Camera* observed that some of the best photographers America ever had worked for Roy Stryker on the FSA, named seven of them, and omitted Evans."[7]

Let Us Now Praise Famous Men is not one book—it is two books. When you look at the version available now, try to subtract those excellent later essays by Evans and Hersey that follow the photographs and title page and precede Agee's prose. Or imaginatively shift them to the back of the text as they'd be positioned in a French edition. Then you'll have an idea of the book that Evans and Agee really made, one in which the very structure is part of the story.

The Real Thing

Agee and Evans would do further work after *Let Us Now Praise Famous Men*, but neither would again do anything as interesting or as important. Agee would thereafter write movie reviews and movie scripts and in *The Morning Watch* and *A Death in the Family* fictional versions of his own experiences as a boy. Many credit him with inventing film criticism, for being one of the first people to treat film the same way people treated books and paintings. But he would never rise to this level of complexity; he would never again write a book that defied the definitions of genre.

Evans would take more photographs, mostly suites for *Fortune*. But the Resettlement Administration work (1935–1937) was his greatest period, and this would be his last major project in that period. The literary critic Alfred Kazin wrote of him:

Yet Evans's deepest work comes out of the thirties, a time of 'ruin.' Some ages are more conducive to great work than others. The thirties were an age of documentation unlike ever before in American history. The Depression was like the Civil War, a crisis affecting the whole county. . . . A purely aesthetic and technical study of Evans's career cannot account for the wondrous fact that he found himself in the thirties, and the thirties in him.[8]

Neither can an aesthetic and technical study of the career of either man account for the fact that each found in the other what he needed to create a masterpiece. As Agee's good friend Robert Fitzgerald (the great translator of Homer and Virgil) wrote, "It is a classic, and perhaps the only classic of the whole period, of the whole attempted *genre*. Photographs and text alike are bitten out by the very juices of the men who made them, and at the same time they have the piteous monumentality of the things and souls represented. Between them Agee and Evans made sure that George and Annie Mae Gudger are as immortal as Priam and Hecuba, and a lot closer to home."[9]

Let Us Now Praise Famous Men ends with the third of the "On the Porch" sections. In none of the three does Agee tell us whose porch it is or where that porch might be found; we can only assume it is in Hale County and that it belongs to one of the three tenant families. Agee's assault on our concept of the structure of a book that began with the placement of Evans's photos and the table of contents that told us nothing in the opening pages continues to the very end. "On the Porch: 3" appears after Agee has written that the book is over; it appears after the notes and after the appendices.

What Agee assumes to be two foxes have been calling, singing, to one another in the darkness. Agee and his companion—unnamed, but we take it to be Evans—listen to the music of the night. When it ends, they begin to talk about the work they had each done that day, but their words are transcended by the ineffable beauty of the moment and the lingering memory of the music. The final paragraph is the whole book writ small:

> Our talk drained rather quickly off into silence and we lay thinking, analyzing, remembering, in the human and artist's sense praying, chiefly over matters of the present and of that immediate past which was a part of the present; and each of these matters had in that time the extreme clearness, and edge, and honor, which I shall now try to give you; until at length we too fell asleep.[10]

13 Words to Kill By

Myth and Talk

Violence is the name we give to things that disrupt or negate or dissolve or abrogate order. One way we contend with violence is on its own terms, with more violence: you hit me, I hit you; the evil land baron brings in a hired gun dressed in black, the farmer brings in Shane dressed in fringed buckskin; unknown malefactors attack the World Trade Center and the Pentagon, and the United States invades Afghanistan, whose government seemed to have something to do with that attack, and Iraq, whose government did not have anything to do with that attack. It's not rational; if it were rational, it wouldn't be part of the cycle of violence. Eventually, through attenuation or exhaustion or will, that escalating cycle stops. In the Icelandic *Njalsaga*, Kari and Flossi, the two surviving antagonists, after separate pilgrimages to Rome, abandon their rage and spend a winter together telling and listening to stories. When the bloodletting is over, we still must find meaning in what was done and what was experienced or suffered. The instrument at that point isn't the gun; it's language.

Stories, as I've suggested throughout this book, are our primary device for understanding, remembering, organizing, and naming experience—for making sense of the world. Not just myth, which addresses major and spectacular things like the origin of the world and why we have volcanoes and death and nightfall, but ordinary narratives like the opening statements by opposing attorneys in court and a doctor's fusion of apparently random and discrete symptoms into a diagnosis of a disease that has a specific life history, one that finds a place or explanation for everything the patient and tests have thus far said or demonstrated.

Stories aren't just retrospective: they rationalize, compartmentalize, and organize the past, but they also license the future. Our narratives provide the charter for moral decisions, define the permissible and impermissible, the good and the bad. Once other people are embedded in preexisting narrative roles, who they are as individuals matters less than how that role is narratively situated. They are characters, not persons.

With stories we know our world and where we are in it and where everyone else is in it. Narrative is not just something we have; it is also (and perhaps more importantly) something we do. Warren Bennis told me he thought the best psychoanalysts helped one establish a viable narrative for one's life. "For cures, go to a psychopharmacologist," Warren said. "Analysis, when it works, helps you get things to make sense." It gives you a story you can live with.

Context is what often determines whether a particular action is or isn't violent. Lovers may in the course of sexual passion bite their partners or draw blood with fingernails and not only may it be exquisite in the moment for both, but tonight's minor wounds may be tomorrow's delightful reminders. But if you or I do either of those things to someone we don't know awfully well. . . .

Distinguish rough stuff from violence. What goes on during the plays of a professional football game is rough stuff, not violence. The ball is snapped and certain people are permitted to hit other people in certain ways, all of them carefully prescribed. It may be brutal, it may injure, but it's ordered and limited and logical. You hit the wrong man and your entire team loses territory, sometimes, as in the case of downfield pass interference, a great deal of it. Most penalties in football are for excess or impetuousness, both of which are seen as minor failures. The game permits both anger and spontaneity; penalties are part of the game, not external to it. Punishments for going outside the game are major. Tackle the pass receiver after he's stepped outside the sidelines and the whistle has blown, or tackle the referee at any time, and you're in serious trouble: you're out of the game, perhaps out of a job.

One of the jobs of such sports as boxing and competition karate is domesticating behaviors that would otherwise be violent by subjecting them to rules and regulations. In the funeral games for Patroclus in book 23 of *The Iliad*, the Argives engage in all the violent arts they've used to slaughter Trojans in the preceding books, but no one dies, no one is seriously hurt, and the encounters all end with prizes and gifts rather than death.

Rough stuff makes perfect sense to everyone involved; it's often consensual. Violence doesn't make sense and it ignores consent.

Playing by the Rules

A psychiatrist friend who works with victims of violent crime told me that the victims often try to discover what they did wrong that led to their victimization. "Taking on some of the blame sometimes seems preferable to confronting the randomness of it," she said. A narrative that makes sense helps make the violence that happened bearable.

Those who do violence also need language, narrative, to make their actions permissible. They need it to keep themselves distinct from the people they do violence to.

Except for a few lunatics, every killer I've ever met has had what he or she thought was a good reason why killing was necessary or useful or insignificant. The lunatics didn't feel they had to provide reasons that made sense in our terms, or they weren't even aware that the events had taken place, which is why they were found to be lunatics. Indeed, that's how we define lunatics.

Governments and individuals offer the same kinds of reasons for killing. The principal, and sometimes only, difference in killing by the state and its agents and killing by everyone else is that the claim to necessity or legality of state killing is usually made before the act, individuals make their claims after they've finished doing it. Just before commencing its long-planned invasion of Iraq, the George W. Bush administration mounted an elaborate campaign arguing that its forthcoming violence was not only just, but necessary. In speech after speech, members of the administration gave now-discredited descriptions of Saddam Hussein's chemical and nuclear programs and ties to the September 11 terrorists. Perhaps the most famous performance in that campaign was Secretary of State Colin Powell's PowerPoint presentation at the United Nations on February 5, 2003.

"I suspect," said civil rights attorney William M. Kunstler in 1969, "that better men than the world has known and more of them have gone to their deaths though the legal systems than through all the illegalities in the history of man. Millions of people executed by the Third Reich—legal. Sacco and Vanzetti—legal. The Haymarket defendants—legal. The hundreds of rape trials throughout the south where black men were condemned to death—all legal. Jesus—legal. Socrates—legal."[1] There is an important distinction between homicide, which is the act of killing a person, and murder. Murder is a subset, a special case of homicide: it is voluntary, considered, and unjustified. The operative word is "unjustified." Many kinds of voluntary and considered killing are rewarded: a soldier killing the enemy in war, a policeman killing a robber pointing a gun at a potential victim. Other kinds may not be rewarded, but are permitted: a homeowner killing an armed intruder in the night, a woman killing a rapist.

Killing is always located in narrative, defined by context. Scapegoats are useful or necessary only when the members of a community have a responsibility or culpability they want to lay off; neither the blissful nor the eminently powerful have need of scapegoats. The state of the German economy in the fourteen years after World

War I was a factor in the ease with which Hitler took power and with the kind of power Hitler took. The rate of lynching in the American South, a crime perpetrated almost entirely by the white lower class against the black lower class, correlates in a perfect inverse ratio with contractions and expansions in the business cycle. As jobs for whites and the price of cotton went down, the number of lynchings went up.

There are rules that define the categories of violence and let us know when the behaviors are legitimate or illegitimate, and the rules are precise. The Nazis carefully defined what was *lebensunwerten Leben*—"life unworthy of life"—and who was, therefore killable without guilt. Our hospitals have specific rules when the prosthetic devices that replace lung and heart and kidney may be turned off, specific dates before which a fetus is nonhuman and after which it is a person.

Until the 1970s, a male Texan could shoot his wife if he caught her in bed with a lover, but he could not shoot his wife if the lover left before the husband got his gun loaded. If the wife caught her husband having sex with someone else, she was limited to calling a lawyer. The legislation specifically privileged the husband.

Extra steps may be taken to ensure that the victim is killed correctly. The Roman historian Tacitus said that in the Emperor Tiberius's time strangling was the preferred method of execution, but it was considered impious to strangle female virgins. Were female virgins, therefore, exempt from execution by strangulation? Of course not. The executioners raped the women who were virgins, or those they preferred to think were virgins, and then they strangled them.

This notion that proper killing requires that you kill the right thing in the right way at the right time and in the right place applies equally to our killing of animals and our killing of people. It is all right to kill rats and roaches and other vermin but it is not all right to kill neighborhood cats and dogs and robins. It is all right to shoot a duck in flight but bad sportsmanship to shoot a duck floating on a pond. Killing Bambi's dad one step inside a game preserve or one hour before or after the season opens or closes is a criminal act. One may shoot an intruder who sticks his head through the frame of one's bedroom window; one may not shoot him if he is on the lawn, unless he is pointing and about to fire at your house what you have good reason to believe is a loaded and functioning weapon. In war, one may shoot an approaching enemy soldier who keeps his hands behind his back, one may not shoot him if his hands are on or above his head. Prison officials must execute someone the courts have said is to be executed, but if that same condemned person attempts suicide or falls ill minutes before the execution, those same prison officials must use all means at their disposal to save that condemned person's life, then the execution is put on hold until he or she is healthy enough to appreciate what's going on.

In each of these situations something makes it all right, something distances the actor or legitimizes the killing. With animals and with people, there's no problem with killing—the difficulty has to do with when and where and under what auspices the killing takes place.

Killable Others

A New York social worker once pointed out to me a young thug who had taken to climbing to the roof of his New York tenement with a full garbage can; he would throw the can off the roof and attempt to hit people walking on the street with it. "How can you do such a thing?" the social worker asked him. "It's okay," the young man said, "I only do it to people who ain't from the block." Diane Christian interviewed a young woman who, at the instruction of her boyfriend, had shot a hitchhiker to death. Diane asked her why she had done it. "Charley said I had to waste that hitchhiker to prove I was a real woman." "But what about the hitchhiker?" "Him? Oh, he was a nothing." According to Tom Segev, Rudolf Höss, commandant of Auschwitz, told his brother-in-law that the concentration camp prisoners "are not like you and me. They are different. They look different. They do not behave like human beings. They have numbers on their arms. They are here in order to die."[2] A former member of Japan's Unit 731, the World War II military group that killed hundreds of thousands of people directly and conducted horrible medical experiments on thousands more, told a Wiesenthal Center interviewer that the victims of the experiments "were logs to me.... They were already dead. So now they die a second time. We just executed a death sentence."[3]

People who ain't from the block, people who are a nothing, people on whose arms the murderers had tattooed numbers, logs: all of them are people defined as outside the moral code and, therefore, outside the scheme of social accountability. The person killed is not like us.

The Nazis defined those they would kill as other than human and then developed a vocabulary that called what they were doing something other than killing. Raoul Hilberg examined thousands of Nazi documents and didn't encounter the word "killing" until he came to a document having to do with dogs. Nazis were, by no means, unique in using euphemisms to describe those they intended to kill or the killing itself; members of any organization that kills on a regular basis employ similar devices.

American gangsters are reported to use such terms as "ice," "clip," "hit," "waste," "do," "off," "pop"; rarely do they say "kill." When U.S. military officers in Vietnam spoke of "pacifying," "sanitizing," and "sterilizing" areas, they meant killing all hostile or suspected hostile Vietnamese in the area and moving everyone else out, thereby emptying them of human life. American bombers engaged in "protective reaction strikes" (destroying areas before they became dangerous) and "surgical strikes" (presumably destroying only what had previously been defined as malign or malignant. The same term was used by the Reagan administration spokesman who announced an air attack on Muhammar Qaddafi's living quarters). People in Vietnam weren't killed; they were "zapped," "greased," "wasted," or "wrecked" —unless they were infantry lieutenants killed by their own troops, in which case they were "fragged." In 1995, CNN broadcast a film of Rwandan government officials handing out rifles to villagers and, according to the reporter, telling them to go "clean up." In the former Yugoslavia, Serbs spent a decade engaged in "ethnic cleansing." Michael Ignatieff, analyzing the Serb atrocities in Kosovo, wrote in the Sunday *New York Times*, "Racial contempt provided the moral license for the men in ski-masks who raped women, executed children, herded men into cattle barns and shot them all, afterwards burning the corpses" (June 20, 1999).

The euphemisms don't license the killings; they're just a way of representing them. The license comes from a model of human relationship that excludes some persons from the community protected by law or custom. The Nazis' medical model franchised all their killing operations. At the center were the doctors, who had the highest rate of professional membership in both the Nazi party and the SS. A Nazi doctor asked by Robert Jay Lifton how he reconciled his work in the death camps with his Hippocratic Oath responded, "Of course I am a doctor and I want to preserve life. And out of respect for human life, I would remove a gangrenous appendix from a diseased body. The Jew is the gangrenous appendix in the body of mankind." The Nazi doctors, wrote Lifton,

> did not literally believe these euphemisms. Even a well-de-
> veloped Auschwitz self was aware that Jews were not being
> resettled but killed, and that the "Final Solution" meant
> killing all of them. But at the same time the language used
> gave Nazi doctors a discourse in which killing was no longer
> killing; and need not be experienced, or even perceived, as
> killing. As they lived increasingly within that language—and
> they used it with each other—Nazi doctors became imagi-
> natively bound to a psychic realm of derealization, disavowal,
> and nonfeeling.[4]

The Nazis perhaps perfected the device of othering those who were to be killed, but they had no monopoly on its use. The U.S. Army platoon commanded by Lieutenant William Calley shot or bayoneted to death approximately 370 men, women, and children in the Vietnamese village of My Lai on March 16, 1968. Many of the men were very old, many of the children were infants, and many of the women were raped after their children were killed in front of them.

The problem of My Lai for the military wasn't that all those civilians were slaughtered; rather it was that there was no demonstrable justification for the killings, and the outside world found out about them. The army produced a small number of military trials, none of which resulted in serious punishment for anyone. A U.S. senator from Louisiana said the Vietnamese slain in My Lai "got just what they deserved," and a South Carolina senator wondered if soldiers who made "a mistake in judgment" were going to be tried as murderers.

A "mistake in judgment." What was the big deal about the killings? After all, far more noncombatant men, women, and children were killed by bombs dropped from B-52s ten miles downwind by the time their bombs reached the ground. Killing was never an issue in Vietnam or any other war; killing is what one does in war. Take out the killing and we're back to diplomacy. The only problem in killing is when you get caught in flagrant violation of the rules, getting caught without a story.

Getting caught without a story is what happened in the 2003–2004 Abu Ghraib prisoner abuse scandals. The problem wasn't that some of the prisoners tortured in the American military prison in Iraq died, but rather that photographs of grinning soldiers posing over the bodies of the abused and murdered Iraqi prisoners got out on the Web. How to explain it? Certainly not as a direct consequence of Bush administration policy—which investigative reporter Seymour Hersh argued it, in fact, was ("The Grey Zone," *New Yorker*, May 24, 2004)—but rather as the aberrant behavior of a small number of bad soldiers. The tortures, humiliations and killings, the government insisted, were the responsibility of a few lower-level soldiers who broke the rules. Court martials followed, and a few of the soldiers in the photographs went to jail. End of story.

Under ordinary circumstances, the soldier sets his sights on "gooks," "chinks," "krauts," "slopes," "insurgents," "hajis"—all things, none of them people. The soldier wears a special uniform when he kills. (The rules of war permit immediate execution of a captured enemy soldier only when he poses as a civilian or wears the wrong uniform, when he takes his proper uniform off.) He is identified by rank and serial number; he is fungible, a replaceable part. When he gets to go home, he is not a killer taking a break, but rather himself, the civilian, guiltless and out of it. He gets discharged;

he takes off the uniform and with it goes all responsibility. Or so they say.

Capital Punishment

The most considered killing of all, the killing subject to more levels of accountable review than any other, is killing by the state resulting from a criminal prosecution. The three important changes in capital punishment in America since the invention of the modern prison at the end of the nineteenth century are:

1. It is predicated more on the mind of the murderer than the fact of the crime; society rids itself not of the person who did that thing, but the person who did it for this or that reason.
2. Execution, like all punishment, has become private. Not secret, just private. In the eighteenth century, the sentence of execution was read, and the audience, assembled to watch it, was told that it resulted from a trial to which none of them had access. In the twentieth century, the trial and announcement of sentence are public, and the resulting imprisonment or execution is concealed. There are witnesses to the state execution, but they are selected and approved. The execution is not televised, though the trial may be and so may be interviews with all participants—including the condemned and his or her soon-to-be-survivors, as well as survivors of the victims, and the various officials involved in the process. Invariably, at least one of the officials interviewed informs the public how well or badly the condemned accepted the administration of death. The process, which exists almost as an official embarrassment, is perhaps best described in the final section of Truman Capote's *In Cold Blood,* 1965.
3. Finally, the physical pain has been confined to a brief moment. "The guillotine," wrote Michel Foucault, "takes life almost without touching the body, just as prison deprives of liberty or a fine reduces wealth. It is intended to

apply the law not so much to a real body capable of feeling pain as to a juridical subject, the possessor, among other rights, of the right to exist." Execution, he said, "no longer bears the specific mark of the crime or the social status of the criminal; a death that lasts only a moment—no torture must be added to it in advance, no further actions performed upon the corpse; an execution that affects life rather than the body."[5] In 2006 several scheduled U.S. executions were delayed while appellate courts satisfied themselves that the condemned would not suffer physical pain during the killing process.

"To execute." If you've ever inherited money, you've probably thought about that verb a great deal. The executor executes the will, and you get a check or the house or the silver set. That is, the executor carried out the orders expressed in the will.

In criminal matters "execute" means carrying out the sentence, which, until the invention of the prison, was primarily upon the body. Whipping or maiming were execution, as was beheading. With the invention of the prison, the only legitimate bodily punishment preserved in most western countries was death.

The way the word "execute" is used now reminds me of Pete McKenzie and Jack Henry Abbott, and how both found perfection in the passive voice. When we talk about "executing a will," we mean carrying out the terms of a will. But when we talk about capital punishment, we don't say, "Execute the sentence"; we say, "Execute Jack," and "Jack was executed." The equivalent in inheritance terms would be saying, "Aunt Betsy's beloved Weimaraner was executed" when what is meant is that the dog was handed over to Cousin Shirley, who truly loves it and who is now giving it a fine home and lots of treats. "Executed" is the most passive of passive expressions for killing. The terse narrative phrase, "He was executed at 12:01 A.M." means "we killed him at 12:01 A.M." When we say, "he was executed" what drops out of the sentence is the "we" who killed him. A legal execution is slow and deliberate; it is dramaturgic; and no one is responsible for the death that is its product.

- The *jury* decides only the facts of the case—is the person in the dock the person who did it? If the person did do the killing, is it the kind of killing that gets a death sentence or the kind of killing that gets a prison term?
- The *judge* imposes the sentence required or permitted by law.
- The *appellate court* considers aberrations by the prosecution and the trial judge (and, if it finds that they cheated, the process is nullified).
- The *warden* carries out an order from his superiors (which he must ignore if it is technically improper in any regard).
- The *prison guards* who strap the condemned into the death chair are merely intermediaries following orders.
- The *executioner* is the agent of the state, angry at no one. (In *A Man for All Seasons,* Sir Thomas Moore gives the executioner a coin and tells him he bears him no ill will for Moore knows he is just a man doing his job).
- The *priest* comforts the condemned and puts the Fifth Commandment on hold and, thereby, certifies that the event is morally as well as legally valid.
- The *witnesses* swear the execution was carried out in a proper manner and did in fact occur.
- The *doctor* first makes sure that the condemned is healthy enough to be executed and then makes sure that the death was rendered successfully.

No one, anywhere in the process, has simply *chosen* to kill that man or that woman at that point in time. And the dead man there on the gurney—he was, well, he was executed.

The Necessity of Lunatics

My original intention was to exclude psychotic murderers from this discussion. Psychotic murderers are clutter; they make no sense; they're outside the scheme. They can't tell a straight story. I wanted to write about people who are rational enough to know when they're being profoundly violent, people who can explain it from beginning to end, people who get the story right.

Now I think those psychotic murderers are essential because their apparent irrationality or arationality lets us hold as responsible all the others. They're like pass interference in football, icing[6]and fistfights in professional hockey—at once part and not part of the game. Our definitions of legitimate and illegitimate homicide are precise only because we have a precise definition for homicide that makes no sense at all, either to us or to the killer.

Many killers change their moral minds later. The passion killers usually do it before the body is cold, which is why so many of them call the police to turn themselves in. I've wondered if at least part of post-Vietnam stress syndrome results from that—not the sentimentalized stuff of men now reacting to the brutality they saw then, but rather men now trying to take or avoid responsibility for a moral structure they once espoused but no longer find tenable.

Our courts deal with insane killers in two ways. If there is doubt as to their sanity at the time of the killing but they are judged mad now, the trial is put on hold indefinitely. If they're never found to be sane, there will be no trial. If doctors at some point decide they've regained their sanity, then the trial can proceed, providing all witnesses haven't died off in the interim. If, on the other hand, they are found to have been insane at the time of the event, then no crime occurred. Someone was killed, but there was no murder because a condition of murder is intent. In our system of justice, you cannot murder by accident. You may kill by accident, but in law that is not murder, unless the killing takes place while you are deliberately committing another felony.

In order to keep their murders moral, the Nazis found it necessary to reaffirm continually that irrational murders did exist; the important thing was to keep the killings of the cripples, Gypsies, prisoners of war, Jews, and others defined as *lebensunwerten Leben* from becoming moral transgressions also. That was accomplished in two ways: first, as I said earlier, by having an extensive vocabulary and medical model that named killing in various ways but never used the words "kill" or "murder," and second, by developing the concept of "excess."

"Excesses," Raul Hilberg writes, were violent acts prosecuted criminally because they were immoral; they were immoral because they were done for the wrong reasons. In practice, any killing that was not seen as an "excess," was proper and in the line of duty. "Excess" was very much like the notion of insanity in our criminal trials: what mattered was not one's conduct, but one's reasons for such conduct.[7] In 1939, for example, the Supreme Party Court considered the cases of thirty men charged with excesses. None of the twenty-six defendants who had killed Jews in a pogrom was punished because the court found "no 'ignoble' motives," but four men who had raped women were thrown out of the party and were, wrote Raoul Hilberg, "handed over to the courts. Moral crimes could not be justified by the pogrom. In these cases the men had used the riot only as a pretext for their actions." Hilberg cites "an advisory opinion by a judge on Himmler's Personal Staff, Obersturmbannführer Bender. Bender dealt with procedure to be followed in the case of unauthorized killings of Jews by SS personnel. He concluded that if purely political motives prompted the killing, if the act was an expression of idealism, no punishment was necessary unless the maintenance of order required disciplinary action or prosecution. However, if selfish, sadistic, or sexual motives were found, punishment was to be imposed for murder or manslaughter, in accordance with the facts."[8]

For the Nazis, the concept of excesses established a continuum of behaviors: it asserted some killing was all right and some was not, some killing behavior was moral and some killing behavior was not moral. Those who killed for the wrong reasons were not like us; they were criminals. Those who killed for the right reasons are very much like us; they are good citizens. Rational good citizens. Heroes of the Reich.

Killing by soldiers in war is excused because it is for the good of the state; killing by police at home is excused because it is good for the community; killing by madmen is excused because they cannot know the implications of their actions. Excused or legitimate killing and inexcusable and illegitimate killing exist in balance, each defining and justifying the other. The same was true in the biblical world. The page following the enunciation of the Ten Commandments outlines in exquisite detail the conditions under which capital punishment shall be required. In theory and in practice, the rule has always been, Thou shalt not kill—unless thou'st got a fairly good reason.

"Myth," the literary philosopher René Girard said in a 1973 seminar I attended, "does not want to face the fact that violence is meaningless. That is my definition of myth." In his classic study *La Violence et le sacré* (1972), Girard looked at ways we use narrative and ritual to provide order to events that are unbearably disorderly. Jack Henry Abbott and Pete McKenzie used diction to manage for themselves actions that ordinary logic couldn't manage satisfactorily. All three of them, one highly educated and the other two autodidactic, went to words, to stories, to verbal art, as a way of coming to terms with things that, in fact, transcended the power of words.

Perhaps the key way humans differ from other animals is in our ability to use language to create and articulate abstract concepts. All discussions of meaning require the ability to engage in abstract thought and talk. The very same capability we use to abstract behavior and ascribe meaning to behavior with language licenses and enables all but the most irrational administration of death.

The great French sociologist Emile Durkheim argued that society needs the criminal because only in knowing where the outsider preys can we know where the insider resides. The perimeter of the circle at once defines two places: here and everywhere else, inside and outside, order and chaos, the city and the desert. Definitions of society are not made in the center; they are made, however nebulously or imperfectly, on the far side of the border. The outsider and insider need one another to know where each is.

The inexplicable and technically guiltless conduct of the psychotic killer fixes all other killings. Psychotics are those who kill and who are not of us, not like us; they don't have a story that makes any sense at all. Their presence at the edge of the scheme is critical in the geometry of who can kill whom and under what situations and who is guilty and who is not guilty and who is excused from the question of guilt in the first place.

The psychotics mark one endpoint in a locus of death that includes the murderer, whose narrative explanation makes sense but is socially unacceptable; those who kill inadvertently and out of fear (householders protecting their families); the morally legitimized person whose explanation is imposed from without (the soldier, the policeman, the executioner) and goes all the way to those who are not violent. The same line marks the boundaries of society, the corridors of power, the heart of legitimacy, the good and the evil. The line is terminated on one side by the perfectly mad and on the other by the perfectly innocent. Between the two is the world of responsible action and moral culpability—the world of power and powerlessness, the world of executioners and victims, the world that you and I inhabit.

III The Story Is True

BRESSON'S MOVIES

A movie of Robert
Bresson's showed a yacht,
at evening on the Seine,
all its lights on, watched

by two young, seemingly
poor people, on a bridge adjacent,
the classic boy and girl
of the story, any one

one cares to tell. So
years pass, of course, but
I identified with the young,
embittered Frenchman,

knew his almost complacent
anguish and the distance
he felt from his girl.
Yet another film

of Bresson's has the
aging Lancelot with his
awkward armor standing
in a woods, of small trees,

dazed, bleeding, both he
and his horse are,
trying to get back to
the castle, itself of

no great size. It
moved me, that
life was after all
like that. You are

in love. You stand
in the woods, with
a horse, bleeding.
The story is true.

—ROBERT CREELEY

14 The Storyteller I Looked for Every Time I Looked for Storytellers

The Storyteller takes what he tells from experience—his own or that reported by others. And he in turn makes it the experience of those who are listening to his tale.

WALTER BENJAMIN, "The Storyteller"

A nd then there are those killers of men whose violence leaves not a corpse behind, who tell everything they know and are finally guilty of nothing at all. How can they get away with it? Let me tell you about one of them, a man I call Jim Bennett because there is no point telling you his real name.

Lydia's Call

My friend Lydia Fish called one fine autumn day and asked, "Are you still working on that book about oral histories from the Vietnam War?" I told her that I'd left the project for a while to do other things and that I'd never gotten back to it. "Well," Lydia said, "I've got someone who wants to meet you. When you meet him, you may find yourself back in it again."

Not likely, I told her, not likely at all. I was deep in the editing of a film, a job that would consume most of my nonteaching time for the next several months. There were other projects and speaking commitments, too.

There were more compelling reasons, but I didn't tell Lydia what they were. I'd begun the research for the oral history book in

1976. I thought it would be useful to record how veterans were remembering the war and what they had to say about coming home. I knew well enough how the past is rewritten constantly by memory and that the further you are from an event, the further you can be from any accurate redaction of it. The stories would change over time, as is the way of stories in active tradition. The project properly should have begun six, seven, or eight years earlier, but back then I had been too deeply involved in antiwar activities to have thought of or been able to do anything like it. The politics of which-side-are-you-on were pretty much over by the mid-seventies.[1] Former war-resisters had realized that the vets weren't the guys who had kept the war going, and many of the vets had tired of defending a war that made sense in no terms other than sunk costs. It was hard to write off the antiwar movement as subversive and the vets as right-wing militaristic thugs when war hero John Kerry and paraplegic Vietnam vet Ron Kovic (in speeches and in his book *Born on the Fourth of July*) were, by their own witness, contradicting those stereotypes.

Even so, I thought we'd be at least as long coming to terms with the emotional residue of that war as we would the economic burdens it imposed on us and our children. So the interviews seemed like a useful thing to do.

They were more conversations than interviews, but there was a small group of questions I asked in the course of nearly every one, each of which produced long and involved answers. One was, "What did you do in Vietnam?" Most men would answer, "What do you mean by *do*?" to which I'd shrug or say, "I don't know. Whatever you think it means." And then they'd take some meaning of "do" and hang a bunch of narratives on it. Another question was, "What happened when you came home?" To which several said, "What happened in what regard?" to which I'd also shrug or say "I don't know," and that would occasion another narrative or string of narratives.

Lydia was teaching a class that semester called "The Vietnam Experience." She had asked me to talk to her students, nearly all of whom were Vietnam vets, about the antiwar movement at home.

She said I would find the visit interesting and that I needn't prepare a formal talk. The class had a pattern of a lot of vigorous give and take. She and I had been friends a long time, so I said okay, but I expected a lot of flak.

The flak didn't materialize. Maybe it was that the war was, by then, long enough in the past or because Lydia had told them I had been in the marines or because some of the men in the class knew I'd run for Congress in 1968 as an antiwar candidate.

In the course of the discussion, one of them said something like, "In World War II and in Korea, people went over as a unit and stayed together as a unit and came back as a unit. And the going and coming took a long time. With us, we went alone, stayed a year, and came home alone."

"If you made it through the year," someone else said.

A third man said, "You got to understand the feeling you get when you're in Nam one day and the next day you're in San Francisco airport getting spat on by an old lady."

"That happened to you?"

"A buddy of mine."

This anecdote had turned up more frequently than any other in my interviews. The first few times I heard it, I had marveled at the rudeness of the old lady and the stupidity of the hippie. I mean, you'd have to be crazy to spit on a guy you assume is only hours back from shooting at people in the jungle. I'd ask, "What did you do when that happened?" and invariably I got a vague answer. I began pushing: "A hippie spat on you?" The answers were like those that came up in Lydia's class: "Well, not me, exactly. A good buddy of mine. It happened to him."

So I asked Lydia's students: "How many people in this room had a buddy that was spat upon by an old lady or a hippie or something like that?"

Maybe a third of the hands went up.

"How many people in this room were spat upon themselves?"

No hands went up.

"Don't you think that's odd—that one out of three people in this room has a pal that happened to but it didn't happen to anybody here? I mean, if you guys are at all representative, and I'm sure you are, then it happened to a large percentage of men coming home through San Francisco. So how come it didn't happen to any of you?"

"It happened to some guys we know," someone said.

"Yeah," someone else said.

"What's your point?" someone else said.

I told them that my point was that stories aren't just facts, they are also strategies. When people told them to one another, when they were hanging out, it was okay to just listen and come back with your own. But when we talked about them in a classroom or other analytical situation, we ought to be looking behind the narration for the reasons a particular story has a particular power.

While I was talking to them, I understood for the first time what the story was really about: in addition to the personal experience narratives that each man used to manage his own past, there were also a group of shared narratives that were taken on as if they were personal experiences. The lie was that it happened to the teller; the truth, too hard to articulate, was that the stories were a way of containing a desperate need. Earlier in this book, I quoted Jorge Luis Borges: "Reality may be too complex for oral tradition. Legends recreate it in a way that is only accidentally false and permits it to travel through the world from mouth to mouth."

After the class, several of the veterans invited me to join them at the campus bar. We closed the place, drinking beer and telling stories. Later, I interviewed some men from the class. They were similar to the other interviews I'd done.

I started wondering if some kinds of narratives in my interviews were as common as they seemed or if something I was doing was eliciting those kinds of narratives rather than others. I wondered if I was finding real patterns or if I was finding what I wanted to find. So I prepared a list of what had developed as my basic outline questions and asked several friends in various parts of the country to do a few interviews using those questions as starting points. Some were done by men, some by women; some were done by Vietnam vets, some by people who had never been on a military base; some were done by people who thought the war an evil America had imposed on the world, some were done by people who thought the war had been a noble enterprise. Though they were different in detail, the contours of these interviews were similar to mine, so I thought I was on the right track.

Then Diane and I got to know a couple whose only son had been killed in Vietnam one week before he'd been due to come home. The Department of Defense told the father his son had been killed by enemy fire. When the body was shipped home, the local undertaker telephoned the house and said, "There ain't no holes in Billy's body." It took the father a year to learn that the son had been struck in the chest by a piece of metal from his own artillery shell and had died of a heart attack. The father wanted us to do a book about what happened to his son and the family's experience during the year the Department of Defense avoided telling them the truth.

We told him that the book already existed, C. D. B. Bryan's *Friendly Fire* (1976), and it was a very good book.

"This is different," the father said.

"What's different is it happened to you," I told him.

"Just read the letters," he said.

I did. I read all the letters the boy had written to his parents and all the letters he'd written to his girlfriend. Some were interesting, some were poignant in light of what happened, and most were the kind of letters a kid far from home writes the people who are grounding him in the world. They reminded me of letters I had written home when I'd been in the marines twenty-five years earlier. I told the man I couldn't do his book for him.

And I realized I couldn't do mine either. I just hadn't earned it; I was doing fieldwork on autopilot. I abandoned the project. I didn't even transcribe most of the tapes. They're in a box somewhere; I could probably find it if I looked.

That's how I reconstruct it now, but my motives maybe weren't all that pure at the time. A good deal of material about Vietnam vets had begun to appear publicly, and perhaps I thought that by the time I got through with all I had to do, the subject would be used up, stale, old news. Even my working title—"Coming Home"— had appeared as the title of a successful movie starring Jane Fonda and John Voight. The Vietnam War experience had become trendy: racist fantasy films by Chuck Norris—the one-time sparring partner of martial arts movie star Bruce Lee—were making megabucks around the world (the U.S. government couldn't get the POWs out or even convince itself that there were POWS; Norris's characters did both). The Vietnam War was on network TV as sentimental background for popular private eye programs like *Magnum, P.I.* and *Simon and Simon.*

That's why the tapes were packed in boxes. Someday, maybe, I'd get back to them. Or they'd have some archival value. But that would be another time, another person.

Jim Bennett

That's where things were when Lydia called. "It's a student," Lydia said, "he's read your books, and he wants to meet you. He was in Special Forces in Vietnam, then he came back to the States for OCS [officer candidate school] and he came across your stuff while he was in OCS in Texas. Then he went back to Vietnam in Special Forces as an officer. He made captain, was discharged with disability; he's got several major decorations. Now he's a student here getting a degree, and he's helping me on my research project. He's a terrific guy. And he told me that one of the reasons he came here was he hoped to meet you."

I'm no more capable of resisting a line like that than anyone. "Oh," I said, "in that case, set something up."

"Don't have to," she said. "He's coming to the screening of *Death Row* at the college Friday." *Death Row* was a film Diane and I had made several years earlier about men waiting to be executed in Texas.

Lydia found us in the lobby after the screening. With her was a thin, wiry man in his thirties. He introduced himself: "Hi, I'm Jim Bennett, and I've been wanting to meet you for a long time. When I was in the special army program at University of Texas, one of the teachers assigned us *A Thief's Primer*, and I thought it was a fantastic book. You really got into that guy's world. I'd like to do something like that someday with some of the people I know." He said that when Lydia had assigned the book in her fieldwork course earlier in the term, he'd been delighted at the coincidence. Then when he'd learned that Lydia was a friend of mine, he'd asked her to arrange an introduction. He'd been through a great deal, he said, and he hoped to be able to write about it someday. He wondered if—he knew I was a very busy man, and said I shouldn't be at all embarrassed if I had to say no—I'd be willing to talk to him some time about doing fieldwork, about interviewing, about going from fieldwork to printed documents.

"I was working on some Vietnam vet interviews," I said, "but it wasn't right. Maybe you can do the book I bailed out of."

"Maybe," he said, "and that's what I'd like to talk to you about. How about it?"

This was a perfect delight: What better way to free myself of those unutilized interviews than to help someone with far more right to the subject than I?

Over the next month we met three or four times. Jim came to dinner, and we talked deep into the night. Mostly it was war stories. Some of the stories were like stories I'd heard in my interviews, some were entirely new to me, and some reminded me of Korean War stories I'd heard thirty years earlier. We got in deep really fast because, I think, it was like the conversation was already in progress when we joined it for the first time.

Jim telephoned early one morning. "How'd you like to meet Westmoreland?" There was, he said, a luncheon with the general before his talk at the state college later in the week. About thirty people would be going, and he had reserved tickets for us.

I'd just read Westmoreland's autobiography, *A Soldier Reports*. He was still blaming civilians back home for the failure of the American war he had directed in Vietnam. He hadn't understood then why he was losing, and he couldn't admit now why he had lost. His only triumph was in a slander suit against CBS. During the

years of his command, our troop commitment expanded geomet-
rically, frequently on the basis of promises by him that if he were
given only this or that many more young bodies, he'd take care of
the commies in no time.

"You still there?" Jim said.

I told him I had been thinking about something. I said some vile
things about Westmoreland.

"If you feel that strongly," Jim said, "then you certainly should
come. See who you're so angry at." I couldn't argue that, so I said
we'd meet him down at the Waterfront Hilton.

Westmoreland, dressed in a conservative blue suit, was a good
deal smaller than I'd expected. Most of the army publicity photos of
him must have been taken from fairly low angles. He talked briefly
about the grand mission they'd all been part of over there and said
how much he respected and thanked them every one and how
much he missed the boys who didn't make it back. There was great
applause and communal feelings. The rest of the luncheon was
pleasant enough, though it reminded me of the scene in *Night of the
Generals* when the homicidal Nazi general played by Peter O'Toole
is to address the surviving former members of his SS battalion. I
guess there's timelessness to such events, and interchangeability of
the participants.

Jim got close to Westmoreland and introduced himself. He
reminded the general of the time Westmoreland had come to a line
outfit to visit the troops and Jim had been there. "I was just a
lieutenant then," Jim said. He told the general what his nickname
had been. Westmoreland brightened, said he remembered, and
shook Jim's hand enthusiastically. Jim introduced us. Westmoreland shook our hands enthusiastically. Then he moved on, shaking
other hands, happy with people who understood him. "Great guy,"
Jim said, "and he's got a great memory. He remembers everybody."
Later he told us that everyone in Nam had a nickname. "That made
it easier for everyone else when someone got killed, and it made it
easier coming home because it was easier separating yourself from
what you did over there. At least for some guys. It was good for me
that way."

Jim called to say he had something that would interest me. "You use a Nikon, right?" I said I did. "I got a night scope that fits on a Nikon lens," he said. You can take pictures in match light from a thousand feet. You can read lips in starlight. The CIA developed it. You can fit it on a movie camera, too. Fantastic. We used them in Nam for nighttime sniping. But you can use it for anything. Look around at the other cars in the drive-in, for instance."

"I don't go to drive-ins."

"With this lens, it might be interesting going to drive-ins." He had two of them, he said, and he'd let me have one for as long as I wished.

He didn't have the scope when he came over for dinner a few days later. He'd meant to bring it, he said, but he'd forgotten. He wanted to tell me about a project he'd been thinking about for some time but had thus far hesitated to mention.

"Go ahead," I said. "What is it?"

"No," he said, "I don't want to impose."

"Don't be silly," I said.

"Well, it's about your project about guys coming home."

"My ex-project."

"I know. You told me. But I think you ought to do it. But not as a book. Do it as a movie, a documentary. There's lots of guys I can introduce you to, some of them living in the bush, some of them who wouldn't ever talk to anyone else, and you can do a film about what it was like for them coming back then and what it's like for them now. Not just guys: there's some nurses you ought to meet. See, for a lot of us, it's not over. It won't ever be over. And people don't know that. These are *interesting* guys. Interesting to me, anyway." I nodded and shrugged: of course they'd be interesting to me as well. "But we'd have to travel to where some of them are, and you probably don't have time for that."

The more reasons he gave for difficulty, the more interested I became. By the end of that visit, I was making notes about possible funding sources. We'd interview and follow with our camera vets in New York, Texas, Montana, California, and New Mexico. Some of Jim's people had jobs and families; some lived like jungle rats. The location work would take months, and editing would be a monstrous job, but, we agreed, it would be worth it.

The matter of credits came up. Jim said he didn't care about credits; he just wanted to do the job. Diane and I said he had to be either director or producer. His contacts, after all, would make the film possible, and his expertise on the post-Vietnam experience would provide the perspective. I think we wound up with Diane and me as producers and Jim as director. We would apply for the grants jointly, with the three of us as project directors: he, the expert on war; we, the experts on documentary film.

The next time he came over, we talked about funding possibilities for the film. He again didn't have the scope with him. Though I was lusting for the thing, I didn't say anything about it. I didn't want Jim to think that I was interested in him only for what he could give me, like information and nifty devices. That is, I didn't want him to know what was pretty much the truth: without the war information and without the devices, we didn't have much to talk about, and we sure wouldn't have been pals. (Every fieldwork relationship has that measure of opportunism to it, I think, but the important thing is making sure that it's at least reasonably reciprocal.) We talked about the film. Diane had talked to someone at the National Endowment for the Humanities to see if there was a possibility it might fit one of their funding programs. Jim said he thought we could get money from some corporations that had highly placed vets in management, like Federal Express, whose president was a Vietnam vet. "I can get the names and addresses of those people," Jim said. "No problem at all."

We made preliminary budget notes: film, processing, travel, equipment, and salaries, one of which would be for Jim for a year. I asked how much he wanted. He said a number—I no longer remember what it was—but I do remember that it was far too low. I doubled it. "Oh," he said, "do you really think that's a reasonable amount?"

"Sure," I said.

"Well," he said, "all right then. I guess it's okay."

After he left, Diane said, "I don't think he was satisfied with the salary we put him in there for." I reminded her that it was double what he'd suggested. "Yes," she said, "but I had a feeling he was just being modest or something, that he knew perfectly well he was asking for too little, that he expected us to kick it up. And I don't think we went as far as he wanted."

"Maybe you're right. I'll increase it another 50 percent. How's that?"

"Fine with me," she said. "But you should check with Jim."

I did. I called him the next day, said Diane and I had been going over the budget and we'd decided his salary was still too low for someone of his expertise and experience, especially given his centrality to the project. "So well boost it another 50 percent."

"Fifty percent more on what I proposed or on what you proposed?"

"On what we proposed."

"Good," he said, "that is okay."

He had been trained, he said, in the whole panoply of infantry weapons, but he had specialized in those that were silent, especially the crossbow. He was known everywhere among the Green Berets, he said, as the expert with the crossbow. He was also, he said, an expert in the use of nitroglycerine. I'd never heard of military people using nitro. When I'd been in the marines, we'd had plastique, and I'd received a little training in its use. I knew that there were stronger versions of plastique around during Vietnam. "Why nitro?" I asked him. "Why not plastique?"

"Because plastique has to be made in a factory, and you need to fuse it somehow. Nitro, if you don't have it, you can make it. They taught us how to make it. Just like with the crossbow: they taught us how to make that, too. So if you're caught out somewhere, you're not defenseless. You can do 'em anywhere," he said.

One time he'd been on an assassination mission in enemy territory with his crossbow, and after the kill he'd been separated from the others in his unit and then wounded. He holed up for several days until he could make his way back. His wound became infected.

He treated the infection using a folk remedy he'd learned from a Buddhist monk: he got maggots from a dead animal and put them into his wound. He had no anesthetic. "Maggots are nature's way of keeping the world clean," he said with terrific equanimity. Diane asked if it didn't hurt terribly. Jim shrugged. The shrug said, these are the kinds of things warriors like us endure.

He told us in great detail about the respect everyone had for the monks. "You could be in a terrific firefight," he said, "and a line of those saffron monks would come out of the bush and walk across the clearing and go into the bush on the other side. The whole time they were there, all the firing stopped. On both sides. Nobody said anything. It was just what everybody did. And then when they were gone, the firing started up again like nothing had happened."

"Why did the Communists stop shooting?" Diane asked.

"Because the monks were holy men. Doesn't have anything to do with Communism or anything else."

Jim told us he was involved in the CIA's Phoenix Project— assassination of village officials with supposed VC connections. "Not just the officials," Jim said. "Their wives and children and goats and chickens. Everything died." He didn't like talking about that phase of his experience, he said. Maybe another time. He told us that since he was attached to the CIA for that part of his tour, his work was so secret that false military records were made as cover and for deniability later. Even his DD214, his official discharge document, covered up his real assignments. "You look at it," he said, "and you wouldn't know I was in Nam or that I was wounded twice or anything. The only way you can see my real records is if you got top secret clearance, and even that might not do it."

It was the secret nature of his assignments during his second tour in Vietnam, he said, that was the cause of his problems with the Veterans Administration. He had been trying to get disability payments for the lung disorder resulting from the time he'd been doused with Agent Orange while he'd been on recon. "Those pilots couldn't have known we were that far north," he said. His gripe wasn't with them. The pilots were just doing their job, and a dangerous one it was; his gripe was with the VA, which wouldn't give him disability. They disallowed his claims because their version of his records didn't show him in Vietnam at all; they just showed him in Germany, which was his cover story. He said he was trying to get the people who control such things to declassify his records so he could get what was coming to him. He felt it was really rotten that after all that had happened to him, he had to fight so hard to get his benefits.

Jim fell off a roof. I visited him in the hospital a few times. He told me war stories, talked about his job as a sheriff's deputy, told me again about how he had come across one of my books while he'd been in the special officer's training program at the University of Texas. He said his lung problems and improper healing of some old wounds weren't making getting over the fall any easier. Then we talked more about the project.

Jim got out of the hospital, and I visited him at home. Several guys from the local vets' organization were there. They told stories about people at school, not much about the war. One of the guys said, "Say, Jim, you through with my medals? My wife, she's after me to get them back."

"Oh, sure," Jim said.

Someone else said, "If you're doing that, I'd like my CIB, if you're done with it."

"No problem," Jim said. He got out of the chair with obvious difficulty and limped into the bedroom. He came out with several framed medals. I couldn't see them all, but I made out a Silver Star, Bronze Star, Purple Heart. And he held an unmounted Combat Infantryman's Badge.

The guy with the medals left, and the others went into the kitchen for more beer. While they were gone, I asked Jim, "How come you had their medals?"

"Oh, mine got lost in one of those moves and Alice [his girl-friend] and some other people wanted to see what they looked like."

One of those moves. I had no idea what moves he was talking about, but it seemed a minor point so I didn't pursue it.

I looked around to see if I could spot the night scopes, but they weren't anywhere in sight. This didn't seem an appropriate time to ask, and Jim never raised the issue.

Bud Johns, a friend in San Francisco, called to say hello. That was the night things with Bennett began to unravel. Bud told us what was going on with him, and we told him what was going on with us. We had one of those conversations you have with distant pals once or twice a year to keep the lines open so when you do manage a visit there isn't an inordinate amount of catching up to do. We told him about Jim.

"He sounds fantastic," Bud said.

"He is," I said.

"So why do you believe him?"

"What do you mean? Why shouldn't we believe him?"

"I don't know," But said, "but you might at least give it some thought, and it doesn't sound like you've done that yet."

While Diane chatted with Bud, I began going over what I'd said to him thus far. I'd told him at least a half-dozen terrific Jim Bennett stories. There weren't many people about whom I could repeat so many stories so easily—and that's what Bud responded to. It's what I, at that moment and for the first time, began thinking about critically. Everything Jim told us was spectacular. So many great stories. And there he was, just waiting to meet me. I had been so pleased that he'd been waiting to meet me that I never considered the silliness of the desire: why should a guy between combat tours going through OCS in Texas want to meet a professor in Buffalo? Sure, it was a possibility, but it wasn't likely. Though each of those other stories was a possibility, in contiguity they weren't likely. Not close to likely.

Before joining Levi Strauss, Bud had been a newspaper reporter for many years. When Diane put me back on the phone, I told him that he'd ruined my evening and his old journalistic cynicism was coming out. "Maybe," he said, "but I wouldn't call it 'cynicism.' 'Caution' is what I'd call it. I always preferred finding out a story was wrong before it got printed than afterwards." He gave me an avuncular lecture on checking the facts, especially the ones that are so good they're almost too good to be true. I asked if that were more newsman's savvy. "No," he said, "I got that from a Dashiell Hammett story."

I hung up the phone and said to Diane, "Bud's a cynical bastard."

"I know," she said.

"I think he may be right."

"I know," she said.

We began going over the coincidences in Jim's various stories and also the things that didn't get delivered, like the night scope—which I was now convinced had never existed—the records that couldn't be found or were so secret they couldn't be shown, and the medals that had been lost "in one of those moves." We talked about how he was capable of telling stories deep into the night but always managed to find a reason why that night wasn't a proper one to do any tape recording. I said that I thought it weird that someone's military records were so secret that he'd have difficulty getting medical attention from the VA.

"It's worse than weird," Diane said.

It was the nitro, and the Langvei story, that brought him down.

Jim told about the time his Special Forces camp in Langvei had been overrun by tanks and fried with napalm. The Americans hadn't known the VC had tanks or napalm, he said, so they weren't ready for either. Nearly everyone was killed. The survivors barely made it to the marine base at Khe Sanh, which at that time was in the middle of a major assault.

Something was vaguely familiar about the story, and I said so. "Sure," Jim said, "anyone who was in Special Forces knows about it." I wasn't in Special Forces, so Jim's explanation didn't satisfy me. Later, I recounted the conversation to Lydia. Lydia said, "It's not just Special Forces vets who know the story. Anyone who's read Michael Herr's *Dispatches* knows it. Herr tells it really well."

A Special Forces vet heard Jim tell the story several times, and after a while something in the narration didn't ring right to him. He called the Special Forces Association (SFA) in Washington. "The guy there said only a dozen guys came out of that battle, and he knew the names of every one of them and Jim Bennett wasn't one of the names." That wasn't all: SFA had no listing for anyone named Jim Bennett ever having served in Special Forces at any rank. Someone else asked a colonel pal, now based in the Pentagon, to look into the matter of Bennett's service. The colonel checked the names of all men above the rank of warrant officer who had served in Southeast Asia; he found no record of anyone named James or Jim Bennett with our Jim Bennett's middle initial. What if Bennett had been doing top-secret work, our friend asked the colonel, would his records be hidden from you now? This, the colonel said, is the one place the records would not be hidden. "This is where we do the hiding."

I wasn't present for the nitro fiasco, but Lydia was. Jim was going on about his nitro expertise, and some guy he didn't know, who was sitting on the edge of the group and apparently hardly paying attention at all, looked at the ground and said in a flat voice, "You're full of shit, Bennett."

"What are you talking about, man?"

"I said you're full of shit. There wasn't any nitro in Nam."

"Damn right there was. And lots of it too."

"No. No, there wasn't. There wasn't any at all. Nitro is unstable over 85 degrees, and in Nam it didn't hardly ever go under 85 degrees. You take nitro off the ice, and it blows up. No way you could take it into the bush 'less you took a truckload of ice, too. So that's why you're full of shit. I don't think you ever were in Nam."

Later, Lydia told me that some of the men in the veteran's group had figured Jim for a phony several months before it all unraveled. One had seen some official records that said Jim had spent his entire overseas time in Germany and that he'd left the military under a cloud. Lydia had asked one of the group's leaders why they didn't say anything. "He was doing such a good job calling campus attention to veterans' problems," the vet said, "that we thought we'd wait a while."

About that time, I ran into a vet who had been in my classes some years ago, a fellow who was still around the fringes of the university trying to get a degree. He was less crazy than when I'd known him, but he was still a spooky guy. I asked him if he had known Bennett. "Sure," he said. I asked if he'd known that Bennett was a phony, "Sure," he said. He'd been a Green Beret himself, and he'd been at one or two of the places Jim said he'd been, so he knew Jim was making it up.

"Why didn't you ever blow the whistle on him?"

"Wasn't doing me any harm. And he told such great stories. I loved listening to him tell those goddamned stories. I mean, I was there, and I couldn't tell stories like that guy."

Substitute Lives

I've told you about a project that didn't happen, about how my own desire for a project with meaning let me ignore meaningful facts already in my field of view, how it took the intuitive remark of a transcontinental journalist pal in the course of a casual telephone call to turn on the light.

I'd felt like a fool, but at least I'd learned something: it's not enough just to think about how you can execute your project; you've also got to think about your investment in the project and evaluate how that investment may be ordering the way you're looking at the world. Faustus went all the way, but we're making deals with our devils too. I don't know if we ever really win, but I do know that if we're not aware of the compromises, the negotiations, the battle to achieve some vision that goes beyond our own interests, we're sure to lose. Or betray.

I was still running on emotion. I was still thinking about it all in terms of myself, how I'd been deceived because I'd been complicit in the enacted narrative. It wasn't until I sat down to write what you're reading now that the second realization hit, and it, too, was about a failed inquiry. The first resulted from Jim's scam and my willingness to be complicit in it; the second resulted from my willingness to let it end there.

Because the end of that project that didn't happen was really and already the middle of another one that did, an inquiry for which I already had a good deal of data: not the story of the heroes, but the others, those who are so desperate to acquire the reality of another they gather up and process more folklore than any folklorist ever could or would, more adventures than any adventurer could or might, more stories than any storyteller might draw from any single real life. Had Jim's stories been only true, I would have been involved in a project of obvious interest; had I been objective enough to look at the story Jim and I were both enacting, I would have been led to something that dealt not with stories told but with the telling of stories, a study not in texts but in the deep and usually private needs that make texts necessary and useful.

Busy Men Who Weren't There

Jim Bennett wasn't unique, and I wasn't the only person who should have known better. Since I encountered him, I have learned of numerous men who went to extraordinary lengths to convince people they had seen combat in war, and who were even more successful at their deceptions than he.

- Pulitzer Prize-winning historian Joseph Ellis told his Mount Holyoke students and then—when he became a famous writer—reporters, stories about his exploits as an airborne platoon leader in Vietnam, which he never was.
- Jeffrey "Mad Dog" Beck, a broker with Drexel Burnam Lambert, told, like Jim, spellbinding tales about his adventures as a Special Forces platoon leader in Vietnam. He had a scar on his wrist from, he said, enemy rifle fire. He said his hand had been saved by his thick wristwatch. He had a Silver Star, two Bronze Stars, and four Purple Hearts. Beck became friends with and consultant to director Oliver Stone. Actor-director Michael Douglas planned a movie based on his life. But none of Beck's stories was true: he had never been in Vietnam; he never had any

connection with the army other than a stint in the reserves. Like Jim Bennett, Beck claimed the discrepancies between his stories and his official records resulted from his having been an intelligence agent.

- In 1989 a Salt Lake City resident named Robert Fife committed suicide at the age of forty-six and left behind a 449-page manuscript that detailed his experiences as a POW in Vietnam. He had been seeing a therapist who had been treating him for post-traumatic stress syndrome related to his time as a prisoner of war. He told of flying 130 combat missions, being taken prisoner, and escaping from the prison camp. He claimed to have received the Navy Cross. After Fife's suicide, his wife, attempting to have his name included on Utah's Vietnam War memorial, learned that it was all a sham. Fife had been in the military for only eight months after his September 1965 enlistment. He had been given a medical discharge because a childhood injury to bones in his right foot had never healed property, and the only decoration he received was the Defense Service Award, which had been given to everyone in U.S. uniform from 1950 to 1954, 1961 to 1974, and 1991 to 1995.

- Toronto Blue Jays' baseball team manager Tim Johnson was famous for his stories about being a marine in Vietnam. During his years as a baseball player (1973–1979), he told about his Vietnam experiences, including one particularly gruesome tale about shooting a young girl. When he became a manager, he frequently told the stories to his players—to inspire them, he said. But Johnson had never been a combat marine, had never killed anyone, and had never served anywhere in Southeast Asia. During his military service he'd been a stateside mortar instructor. Once the truth surfaced, Blue Jays morale plummeted, and in March 1999 the owners fired Johnson.

This chapter is about appropriating and incorporating other people's narratives of experience, a process not unique to the Vietnam

War; Vietnam is just one recent major occasion of it. The Korean War, for example, has the mass murderer Edward Daily, who never killed anybody.

Ed Daily was a Korean War hero: Silver Star, Distinguished Service Cross, and more. He was promoted to first lieutenant on the battlefield, had been taken prisoner and escaped captivity, and rescued buddies in trouble. He wrote three books about his unit, the Seventh Cavalry Regiment (best known, to most of us, for having been wiped out at Little Big Horn when it was commanded by George Armstrong Custer) and was instrumental in organizing its veterans group. He was a key informant in the 1999 Associated Press Pulitzer Prize-winning story about the July 26, 1950, massacre of Korean civilians under a railroad trestle near the hamlet of No Gun Ri by Seventh Cavalry soldiers. Of all the people AP eventually interviewed for that story, Daily was the only one who had direct knowledge that the killings were carried out on direct orders from higher up. He was quoted at length by other newspapers; he appeared on network television news shows. He spoke eloquently about the pain he still felt over the young children he slaughtered that day. "Mr. Daily was," wrote Michael Moss in the *New York Times* ("The Story behind a Soldier's Story, May 31, 2000), "without question, a linchpin in efforts to preserve and honor the memory of the Seventh Cavalry and served as its president in the early 1990s. In 1993, he attended a peace ceremony in South Dakota with members of the Lakota Sioux tribe to help make amends for the 1890 massacre at Wounded Knee by the Seventh Cavalry."

A fabulous guy. A fabulous story, which is all it was: a story.

Edward Daily had seen no combat in Korea or anywhere else. "In fact," wrote Moss, "military records show, Mr. Daily served as a clerk and mechanic in the lusterless Twenty-Seventh Ordnance Maintenance Company, only joining the Seventh Cavalry for a few weeks the following year—eight months after the No Gun Ri massacre is said to have occurred." Not only were the documents for his decorations forgeries, but so was everything he showed to real veterans of the Seventh Cavalry, reporters, and anyone else who would listen to his exploits. "There are two versions of the regiment's Christmas-dinner roster," wrote Moss, "one with Mr. Daily's name typed at the bottom of the list— slightly crooked at that. A group photo of the regiment he showed to friends is also suspect: Mr. Daily's head, marked with an arrow and the word 'me,' appears to be superimposed on another man."

Daily brought this to a level Jim Bennett, "Mad Dog" Beck, Robert Fife, and Tim Johnson never reached. He didn't merely weave stories he'd heard told by others into his own personal narrative, he also wove himself into the stories they told about themselves. He was a real-life Zelig, a Forrest Gump. He'd meet people at conventions, he'd talk to them on the phone, and Daily would remind them of the time something had happened involving both of them. The event had, indeed, happened, and the person Daily was talking to had, indeed, been there. He managed—in Moss's wonderful phrase—"to airbrush himself into their fragile memories of the Korean war." Some of the people he tried it with didn't buy the extra man in the narrative, even though the event in question had happened fifty years earlier—but enough people did buy it, people who allowed him to have spent years as war buddy, military hero, and, at the end, penitent mass murderer.

Why We Fall in Love with Our Con Men

A con man I once knew told me that "It takes two people to run a con. Somebody like me and somebody who wants it to happen. I'm the realist; he's the dreamer."

Jim Bennett, Jeffrey Beck, Robert J. Fife, Tim Johnson, Edward Daily, and others like them, may have been dreamers when it came to their careers in war, but when it came to managing most of the people with whom they came into contact, they were the realists. They created the pasts they preferred to their own, and they got a number of highly educated and experienced people acting in terms of their creations.

I think one reason I wasn't critical earlier of Jim's stories and self-critical of my own motives in listening to them was that Jim fit perfectly the kind of narrator I wanted to hear at that time. His stories were rich in detail and visual in imagination; as he talked, I knew his stories would work well on a printed page.

I'm not the only writer who did that. A famous instance of that kind of shared narrative reality is *New Yorker* writer Joe Mitchell's long relationship with bohemian hustler/genius Joe Gould, documented in Stanley Tucci's film *Joe Gould's Secret* (2000). Gould convinced Mitchell he had thousands of pages written for "An Oral history of Our Time," a work he said was eleven times longer than the Bible and still growing. Mitchell did a long *New Yorker* profile of Gould in 1942, "Professor Seagull," so titled because of Gould's claimed ability to have mastered the language of seagulls. In time, Mitchell realized there was no manuscript, that Gould was simply telling Mitchell what he thought Mitchell wanted to hear. Gould had told his story to other people, but he told it to no one in such depth and to such length as to Joe Mitchell, who heard the words and, in the instant, saw them on the future page. (Remember Marco Polo's line in Calvino's *Invisible Cities*: "It is not the voice that commands the story... it is the ear.") The relationship disintegrated as Mitchell's belief in the never-quite-seen manuscript (Gould's version of Jim Bennett's night scope) went south. Gould died in 1957. Five years later Mitchell published in *The New Yorker* "Joe Gould's Secret," the story of the chimerical manuscript. The story was as much about Mitchell as it was about Gould. Joe Mitchell showed up at his *New Yorker* office every day for the next thirty-two years, but he never published another word. His story and Joe Gould's were so interwoven that after his obituary for the narrative relationship, he was written into silence.

The political content of Jim's Bennett's stories allowed me to be involved in a political rapprochement I don't think I sought, but which I welcomed when it appeared. We could do something about the vileness of the Vietnam War without, at the same time, disparaging the sacrifice of the people who, for whatever reason, suffered there. It gave me a chance to do something with all those earlier interviews, that uncompleted, unresolved inquiry occupying boxes of tapes, piles of transcription folders. And probably, at a deeper and more personal level, the conversations and rapport with Jim (whose military years were almost exactly halfway between the time of our relationship and my own military years) provided a middle-aged professor a secondhand but, nonetheless, welcome connection to his own distant and romanticized youth.

If I had designed the perfect storyteller for this project, the storyteller I would have designed would have been Jim Bennett. Jim sensed my need, and he gave me what I wanted. He was able to do that because (like Joe Mitchell's Joe Gould) —for reasons very much his own—he already had cast and directed himself in the role he had long readied himself to play. In addition to all the other mistakes I made in our discussions about the project was who was going to occupy what role: Jim was director, all right. He was also producer and one of the principal actors. I was another actor and also part of the audience.

But why did he bother? What were his reasons for this elaborate deception?

I don't believe you can ever fully know someone else's motives; you only know for sure what they do. Jim was a terrific collector and processor of stories. He listened to people, he read, and then he began to tell. He was like those Serbian narrators described by Albert Lord in his classic study of oral performance, *The Singer of Tales* (1960), who would listen to master performers, learn their story outlines and formulaic phrases, and eventually become performers themselves. If he had a way of telling the story in the third person, he would have been a writer of documentary books or a novelist.

But because he had no venue for such narrative, he was, instead, pathologic. His need wasn't to find a good story in someone else's life, rather it was to find a good story for his own. Since his own experience didn't provide that story, he set about expropriating the narratives of other people. Instead of becoming a successful social scientist or reporter or novelist, he became a fraud. He was brilliant at creating venues in which he could recite his stories. He was self-creative, not self-destructive, as evidenced by the protective devices he tried to set up, such as the story about his top-secret dossier and his avoidance of being tape-recorded. My friend Lydia, who had become deeply involved with Jim in a long-term research project, provided one kind of listener and offered one set of opportunities; I provided another. Working with the two of us, Jim accumulated power: he was a central coordinator of Lydia's research project, and he was going to be director of our film. He became a big shot in one of the local veterans' organizations. The stories got some of the war heroes—one of whom he had fervently wished to be—to accept him as one of their own; they also got influential academics to steer resources his way. None of these things would have happened to an enlisted man doing menial kitchen work in Europe.

But what a curious narrative he devised! Jim designed a minefield, then shredded his map of it and clomped straight across toward the other side. I suspect he knew he had to blow himself up, that he'd be caught, and that he'd be thrust into the real world and branded as a phony, a liar, a sicko. He was dealing with gullible but not stupid people: the eventual arithmetic was inevitable. Jim wasn't stupid either; it took real intelligence to absorb and retell all those extended narratives, to manipulate so many of us in so complex a scenario. He could have backed off, but he kept pushing on.

Here's my guess on Jim's real payoff: once he got found out, Jim Bennett became what he wanted to be more than anything else—a Vietnam War casualty. It didn't happen to him in Southeast Asia, but it came out of that war anyway. He created a wound that really was his own, a scar the authenticity of which none of us can or would deny. I'm telling you about it right now. His Vietnam story was a lie, but the pathology revealed and the shame created by that lie are real. Jim Bennett may not be one of the honorably wounded, but he's one of the wounded, nonetheless. That's as close as he could get, and close as you can get is sometimes good enough. Once he was exposed, there was no longer any dissonance between his imaginary and his real worlds, between his private and public selves, so he could, perhaps for the first time, relax perfectly.

For many, if not most or even all of us, there is a murky area at the edge of experience that can be used to tune our narratives and enhance our understanding of real life moments. It's the place where it's okay to talk about getting spat on in the San Francisco airport by the hippie, where it's efficient to collapse what happened to you one year into what happened another, where it's comfortable to be cooler or smarter or more alert than anyone outside of movies and memory ever is. Jim Bennett went to the far side of that area, to a place where the narratives became a substitute for real life rather than a way of understanding it. Jim Bennett ran into a no-man's land of the imagination and couldn't come back until we caught him there. When it happened, I thought we were finding him out; now I think we were a rescue party.

That's what I think. I don't know what Jim thought, because after things fell apart, we never spoke to one another again. Neither of us thought we had anything more to say to the other.

That was another error. We had lots more to talk about, and should have.

I've told you Jim Bennett's story, and maybe what I've said here adequately describes Robert J. Fife and others like them; but it still doesn't explain any of them. Many, perhaps most, of us would like to have fair claim to pasts more glorious or romantic or heroic or interesting than the ones we happen to have accumulated. That is one of the key pleasures of literature and narrative film: we can, for a while and usually without risk, immerse ourselves in other people's stories; we can *identify*. When the process of occupying another person's narrative takes place on a stage, we call it acting; when it takes place in real life, we call it impersonation—literally, inhabiting someone else's person. We know beforehand that the stage actor is impersonating, and that is why we applaud the job when it is done well. We only know afterwards about the real-life impersonator, and that is why we react to it with anger, despair, or sadness.

In his 1999 biography of Ronald Reagan, *Dutch*, Edmund Morris created a fictional character who was himself, providing information about Reagan's youth, years before the real-life Edmund Morris was born. But the book made clear what Morris was doing, and he insisted he did it to help him animate his narrative, not because he was trying to insinuate himself into someone else's life. Maybe. Maybe not. I think in some measure we all, each and every one of us, continually recreate ourselves. Accidents of fate or whims of the moment in the distant past become, with the fulfillment of the present, meaningful, and we see those accidents and whims in structures that, if they ever existed at all, were invisible to us at the time.

We understand human affairs in terms of narrative, and the narrative of our lives is protean, forever subject to new depths or breadths of understanding, new configurations and alignments of parts that previously seemed carved in stone. That is perhaps the primary reason our personal experience stories—the stories we tell about ourselves over and over again—change over time. As our sense of contexts changes, so changes our sense of what mattered, what was big and what was little, which words were essential and which words were not.

"The story of our life is not our life," warns novelist John Barth, "it is our story." He is, of course, right. The only problem is, except for this moment—the one we're in right now—everything about our life except our story is over. The story is alive every single moment we're thinking or telling it. True or not, our experience or someone else's, the story is real.

15 Farinata's Silence

Warren called from California, gloomy and grim. He'd just finished dinner with an old friend, a man in his nineties, who had always been vigorous, optimistic, involved in projects, dapper, full of stories. Now there were food stains on the Turnbull and Asher shirt, and the projects, optimism, and vigor were gone. "All he's got are those stories," Warren said. "His life now is composed of those stories in the past. Without those stories. . . ."

And I thought: That's what death is. Death is the place where there is no future, no story being spun out in imagination. Because the stories we weave aren't just the stories in the past, but the imagined stories of what's going to happen next: what I'm going to do on Thursday, next spring, the dinner I'll have with Josephine Kand, and the sex I may or may not have after this movie is over. In our stories the relentless arrow of time is always reversible; anything can be revisited, reimagined.

I am writing these final pages on a splendid spring day in 2006. Our old friend Penelope Creeley is visiting. The school her daughter attended just received an eight-seat rowing shell named for Pen's late husband Robert. For the past several days, we've been telling one Bob story after another. Late last night Pen told about the days she'd spent with Bob's sister Helen while Helen was dying. Helen was a tough New Englander, and she'd had a tough life: she worked hard, a daughter was killed in an auto accident, her husband turned out to have a second family halfway across the country, the man she became involved with after she discovered her husband's perfidy (who she said was the love of her life) was killed in an accident. And now she was in a hospital room in Maine, waiting for the end. "Let's rewrite your life," Pen said, "let's do the story the right way." Helen brightened and for the next two hours they told one another the other story of Helen's life. Pen sat there and Helen lay there and jointly they told the Novel of Helen. Shortly after that Helen slipped into a coma and died.

Death is the end of all potential, all possibility, all alternatives. We tell our stories not just to rehearse the past but also to condition the present and, thereby, to prepare the future. What is the compelling charm, after all, of those utterly stupid horoscopes so many of us secretly read in the paper if not the irresistible pleasure of imagining a future rich in possible narratives? All stories require time; beginning, middle, and end can no more occupy the same temporal space than can two corporeal objects in the physical world. Death abolishes the dimension of time.

The horror of death isn't only that we won't get to know and do new things. It's also that everything we know, all those stories that in combination make us the unique beings we are, will disappear forever. The dying Roy Batty, the replicant leader in Ridley Scott's 1982 dystopian film *Blade Runner,* says, "I've seen things you people wouldn't believe.... All those moments will be lost in time, like tears in rain. Time to die."

It's easy enough to imagine being ourselves in another body. We do it when we look at old photographs of people who have our name only they're younger, or when we imagine ourselves as a specific movie actor or political figure or other sexy or powerful creature or person. But how many of us can imagine our body—at whatever age—occupied by another mind and that creature still being us? That's the stuff of a horror movie: *Invasion of the Body Snatchers.*

What is consciousness without memory, without stories? What is hope without the possibility of a future? Hell, perfect hell.

Which brings me to Farinata degli Uberti, the Florentine Ghibelline leader who died in 1264 and who was condemned for heresy in 1283. Dante the character finds him in the tombs of the heretics in the Sixth Circle of Hell, which Dante the poet describes in Canto X of *Inferno*.

Farinata tells the fictive Dante that the condemned can see the past and the future, but the only present of which they are aware is the present of their punishment. The punishment of the condemned will be perfected on the Day of Judgment because on that day time ends, so there will be no more past and no more future, only this moment, this pain, forever. For Farinata, and for everyone else in all the Circles of Hell, the only consciousness will be the never-ending present of their punishment. Every soul in Dante's hell exists with pain and without hope. Beginning on the Day of Judgment, however, they will also exist without narrative, which both the fictive and the corporeal Dante think is even worse.

But for those of us this side of death's barrier, there is Stéphane Mallarmé's fourteen-line poem "Don du poème" (Gift of the Poem). At the first breaking of dawn, the poet brings to his wife the poem he created in agony during the long night. He tells her that only by the grace of her nurturance can the poem, the "child of the Idumean night," take breath, live.

All those storytellers: Jim Bennett, O. J. and his lawyers and prosecutors, George Beto, Bill Kunstler, Chuck Schumer, Warren Bennis, Howard Lippes, Stephen Spender, Homer, Dashiell Hammett, William Faulkner, Jessica Jackson, Rachel Jackson, Mary Shelley, Pete McKenzie, Peter Fonda, James Agee, Pen Creeley and Bob's sister Helen, Larry Beahan the movie-makers, the novelists, the spin-meisters, the dream-weavers, you and me. All our stories. Told again and again, cast and recast, molded perfectly for this moment, this very moment, this audience, this very audience.

No story exists out there by itself. Every story takes life from two of us: the teller and the listener, writer and reader, actor and watcher, voice and ear and eye. Each is a necessary participant in the creation of the space in which the utterance takes life, in which all our utterances take life.

So this is the good part: all our stories are coauthored, and as long as we keep telling them and seeing or hearing or reading them, we are never really alone.

Notes

Chapter 1: Telling Stories

1. 1978; Pinter also wrote the script for the 1983 film version, directed by David Hugh Jones.
2. 93(4):308.
3. There are important scholars who have adopted very different vocabularies for engaging some of the issues and behaviors I am addressing here: M. Bakhtin, *The Dialogic Imagination: Four Essays*, trans. Michael Holquist and Caryl Emerson, Austin: University of Texas Press, 1981; Mieke Bal, *Narratology: Introduction to the Theory of Narrative*, 2nd ed., Toronto: University of Toronto Press, 1997; Gérard Genette, *Narrative Discourse: An Essay in Method*, trans. Jane E. Lewin, Ithaca: Cornell University Press, 1980; Gérard Genette, *Narrative Discourse Revisited*, trans. Jane E. Lewin, Ithaca: Cornell University Press, 1988; and Wallace Martin, *Recent Theories of Narrative*, Cornell University Press, Ithaca, 1986. These vocabularies are useful for what they are doing, but I am doing something else. I am writing about narratives that exist in plain language, and I think to discuss them in plain language is both possible and useful. If you catch me in any jargon, send me an email at bjackson@buffalo.edu., and I will try to fix it in the second edition.
4. John Barth, *On With the Story: Stories* (New York: Back Bay Books, 1997), 30.
5. Primo Levi, *The Monkey's Wrench*, trans. William Weaver (New York: Penguin Classics, 1987, 35.

6. In *The Complete Poetry and Prose of William Blake*, ed. David V. Erdman with a commentary by Harold Bloom (Norwell, MA: Anchor, 1997), 259.
7. BuffaloFilmSeminars.com.

Chapter 2: The Fate of Stories

1. Levi, op. cit., 35.
2. Italo Calvino, *Invisible Cities*, trans. William Weaver (San Diego and New York: Harvest Books, 1978), 133.
3. David Tereshchuk, "Lives: An Unreliable Witness." *New York Times Magazine*, January 28, 2001, 66.
4. Quoted by Matthew L. Wald, "For Air Crash Detectives, Seeing Isn't Believing," *The New York Times Week in Review*, June 23, 2002.
5. The University at Buffalo had a few years before organized itself into seven faculties—Arts and Letters, Social Science and Administration, Engineering, Health Sciences, and so forth—each headed by a provost, who performed pretty much as deans do everywhere else. Over the next three years Warren became vice-president for academic affairs and then executive vice-president as well, a combination of functions that pretty much describes the role of provost in modern universities. So when Warren was provost of Social Sciences and Administration at Buffalo he was really a dean, but when he stopped being the provost he really became a provost though that title hadn't yet come into currency.
6. Christopher Marlowe, *The Jew of Malta*, ed. T. W. Clark (New York: Hill and Wang), 1966, 71.
7. Calvino, op. cit., 80.

Chapter 3: The True Story of Why Stephen Spender Quit the Spanish Civil War

1. Stephen Spender, *World within World* (Berkeley and Los Angeles: University of California Press, 1951), viii.

Chapter 4: The Stories People Tell

1. *Good Morning America*, December 21, 2000.
2. Walter V. Robinson, "Professor's Past in Doubt. Discrepancies Surface in Claim of Vietnam Duty," *Boston Globe*, June 18, 2001.

Chapter 7: Commanding the Story

1. Primo Levi, *The Monkey's Wrench*, 34.
2. Dashiell Hammett, *The Maltese Falcon* (New York: Vintage, 1989), 61.

3. Ibid.
4. Ibid., 64.
5. Ibid.
6. Ibid.
7. Ibid., 65.
8. Calvino, op. cit.,

Chapter 8: Stories That Don't Make Sense

1. Roald Hoffman, "Storied Theory," *American Scientist*, 93(4)(July-August 2005), 308.
2. Albert Einstein, "Über einen die Erzeugung und Verwandlung des Lichtes betreffenden heuristischen Gesichtpunkt." *Annalen der Physik* (series IV) 17:132–148.
3. Sam Schager, *The Trial Lawyer's Art* (Philadelphia: Temple University Press), 1999, 11.

Chapter 9: The Real O. J. Story

1. Quoted by C.A. Patrides, *Milton and the Christian Tradition* (Oxford: Clarendon Press, 1966), 103–104.

Chapter 10: Bob Dylan and the Legend of Newport 1965

1. Greil Marcus, *Invisible Republic: Bob Dylan's Basement Tapes* (New York: Owl Books [Henry Holt &Co.], 1998, 12. "Axe" was then pseudo-hip for "guitar."
2. Jorge Luis Borges, "Forms of a Legend," in *Other Inquisitions, 193–1952*, trans. Ruth L. C. Sims (Austin: University of Texas Press, 1995), 149.

Chapter 11: Silver Bullets

1. *The New Republic* article is by Barbara Reynolds; the *Time* article on Oliver North is by Richard Stengel.
2. Robert Warshow, "Movie Chronicle: The Westerner," in *The Immediate Experience* (New York: Anchor Books, 1964), 66.
3. Paul Scanlon, The Force Behind Star Wars, http://www.rollingstone.com/news/story/7330268/the_force_behind_star_wars.

Chapter 12: The Deceptive Anarchy of *Let Us Now Praise Famous Men*

1. John Hersey, "Introduction," in *Let Us Now Praise Famous Men,* ed. James Agee and Walker Evans (Boston: Houghton-Mifflin, 1988), xxxv.

2. David Madden, "The Test of a First-rate Intelligence: Agee and the Cruel Radiance of What Is," in *James Agee: Reconsiderations*, ed. Michael A. Lofaro (Knoxville: University of Tennessee Press, 1992), 34.
3. James Agee, *Let Us Now Praise Famous Men*, 12.
4. Jorge Luis Borges, *Other Inquisitions: 1932–1952*, trans. Ruth L. Simms (Austin: University of Texas, 1975), 68.
5. Agee, op. cit., 240.
6. Agee, op. cit., xlvii.
7. William Stott, *Documentary Expression and Thirties America* (New York: Oxford University Press, 1973), 268.
8. Alfred Kazin, "Ours is a Visual Period," Double-Take 3(2) (Spring 1997), 31–25.
9. Robert Fitzgerald, "A Memoir," in *Remembering James Agee*, eds. David Madden and Jeffrey J. Folks (Athens and London: University of Georgia Press, 1997), 14.
10. Agee, op. cit., 470–471.

Chapter 13: Words to Kill By

1. Personal communication.
2. Tom Segev, *Soldiers of Evil: The Commandants of the Nazi Concentration Camps*, trans. Haim Watzman (New York: McGraw Hill, 1987), 211.
3. Howard W. French, "Japanese Veteran Testifies in War Atrocity Lawsuit," *New York* Times, 21 December 2000. http:/select.nytimes.com/search/restricted/article?res=F10911F8355D0C728EDDAB0994D8404482
4. Robert Jay Lifton: *The Nazi Doctors: Medical Killing and the Psychology of Genocide* (New York, Basic Books, 2000), 16, 445.
5. Michel Foucault, *Discipline & Punish: The Birth of the Prison*, trans. Alan Sheridan, (New York: Pantheon, 1997),12, 13.
6. A term in professional hockey for a certain kind of illegal shot.
7. Raul Hilberg, *The Destruction of the European Jews* (Chicago: Quadrangle Books), 648.
8. ibid. 28, 648.

Chapter 14: The Storyteller I Looked for Every Time I Looked for Storytellers

1. The "Swift Boat Veterans for Truth" vs. John Kerry dustup during the 2004 presidential election wasn't evidence that this war at home was still on; it was, rather, a manufactured affair, successful sucker-bait for the mainstream press, which is why it evaporated as soon as the election was over.

Index